Continuing Presences

Continuing Presences

Virginia Woolf's Use of Literary Allusion

Beverly Ann Schlack

The Pennsylvania State University Press
University Park and London

The author gratefully acknowledges permission granted by the Henry W. and Albert A. Berg Collection of the New York Public Library, Astor, Lenox, and Tilden Foundation, and Professor Quentin Bell, to quote from the manuscript and typescript drafts of the five novels examined in this study.

I am also indebted to Professors Joanne Trautmann and Anna S. Benjamin for their encouraging praise, careful readings of the manuscript, and valuable suggestions for improvement.

Library of Congress Cataloging in Publication Data

Schlack, Beverly Ann.
   Continuing presences.

   Includes bibliography and index.
   1. Woolf, Virginia Stephen, 1882–1941—Technique.
2. Woolf, Virginia Stephen, 1882–1941—Knowledge—
Literature. 3. Allusions. I. Title.
PR6045.072Z8745   823'.9'12   78-68163
ISBN 0-271-00208-5

Designed by Glenn Ruby

Printed in the United States of America

For My Parents—

this verbal token
of an affection
too deep for words

Contents

Preface

In *A Room of One's Own* Virginia Woolf eloquently declared: "Great poets do not die; they are continuing presences." The persistent allusiveness of her fiction furnishes ample demonstration of that humanistic conviction. Her use of literary allusion is at once idiosyncratic and ideally suited to many of her preoccupations: the immanence of the past in the present moment; that universality which transcends purely personal truths; the permanence within change and the unity within diversity; the symbiotic interplay of life and literature; the search for a remedy for the modern sense of discontinuity and fragmentation. Moreover, allusions are a particularly appropriate device for an author as indirect, inferential, and ambiguous as Woolf. They can reveal authorial values without requiring the sort of overt narrative commentary that Woolf disliked in traditional novels. They are a more complex, multisignificant strategy than other forms of metaphor and analogy. And they possess those qualities of simultaneity and density which Woolf thought inherent in our experience of reality.

Allusiveness is a discriminating and demanding technique. Wide acquaintance with literature is only the basic requirement. It must be accompanied by the ability to make an inspired selection from the copious materials at hand. While it can be endlessly debated how often particular examples of Virginia Woolf's allusiveness deserve to be called inspired, there can be no doubt that she had at her command the necessary knowledge of world literature. That knowledge spanned thousands of years, from Greek tragedies to contemporary novels, and cut across the boundaries of genre, style, and language. She was the introspective youngest daughter of that distinguished man of letters, Sir Leslie Stephen, born into an atmosphere saturated in literary culture; her very arrival was celebrated in verse by her poet-godfather, James Russell Lowell. Her cloistered way of life, which was both necessitated and reinforced by her delicately balanced health, allowed her unsupervised access to her father's vast, eclectic library. Very early in life she became an omnivorous reader, acquiring an especially detailed knowledge of English authors, great and obscure. Her father read aloud from Scott's

Preface

Waverley novels, *Treasure Island, Tom Brown's School Days, Vanity Fair,* Shakespeare, Milton, Austen, Wordsworth, Tennyson, and Matthew Arnold, to name but a few. With such pervasive and sustained exposure to world literature, it would have been noteworthy if Virginia Woolf had *failed* to exploit that profound familiarity in her own writing.

While her book reviews, essays, diary, letters, short stories, biographies, feminist tracts, and novels abound in literary allusions, critical silence on this stylistic phenomenon has been the rule rather than the exception.[1] This neglect has meant that allusions are almost never interpreted, although sometimes they are fleetingly identified. Yet such mechanical notation—for example, a critic of *The Waves* will note that Bernard imitates Byron—never addresses itself to the issue of why Byron, not one of several hundred other other poets, was invoked, and what that particular invocation adds to Bernard's characterization or to the theme of the work. In place of an interpretive analysis of allusions, critics have substituted comments on Woolf's reading, compared her to other writers, indulged in influence hunting, or ascribed multiple indebtednesses, derivations, and borrowings. This is an indirect but still unsatisfactory acknowledgment of Woolf's persistent allusiveness, and as so many of the critics do not scruple to differentiate between influence and reference (where that is possible), the result is a fatal blurring of the distinction between *influence upon* and *allusion to.*

Total silence on the part of critics with regard to Woolf's allusions probably reflects their assumption of the inherent triviality of the technique. Several of them seem to have decided, against the nagging quantitative evidence, that the many allusions which pepper Woolf's pages are qualitatively unimportant. They may recognize the importance of literature *to* Virginia Woolf, but they treat literary allusions *in* her works as superficial embroidery and are generally impatient with the whole procedure of invoking the literature of the past. In short, her habit has gone either unremarked or unadmired.

But Virginia Woolf's recurrent allusiveness is not to be dismissed as the extraneous, highbrow ornamentation of an elitist style. It is neither ostentatious, obtrusive, nor futile; it is a genuinely functional technique, which contributes to characterization, setting, structure, theme, and such plot action as may exist. The most brilliantly successful of her allusions—like the *Comus* allusion in *The Voyage Out*, the *Cymbeline* quotation in *Mrs. Dalloway,* or the Percival allusion in *The Waves*—do most or all of these things at once. Vivid as traffic signs, they direct us to important aspects of textual meaning, and they remind us of our obligations as good readers, for they were not deliberately put there to be deliberately ignored. To slight them is to fail to realize the full work as given, with the personal penalty of impoverished aesthetic enjoyment.

Preface

A statement about human fallibility, however obvious, must be made regarding the accuracy of the information within a study such as this. Anyone who sets out to track down Woolf's allusions is pitting his or her solitary literary knowledge against Woolf's own massive learnedness. I am certain I have overlooked references in my hubristic endeavor. Gone is the doctoral candidate's certainty with which I first embarked upon this heady project, with a passionate dedication to uncovering "everything." That ideal reach was bound to exceed my practical grasp, and I leave for other scholars the modifications and corrections necessitated by this initial one-woman undertaking. Whatever the limitations of my grasp, however, that reach for a comprehensive view of the aesthetic brilliance and profound humanity of Woolf's allusiveness I believe to be a worthy one.

Perhaps a word about the particular novels examined in this study is in order, lest it be charged with arbitrariness. The novels were selected to constitute a cross section of Woolf's work. I began by choosing each of the three singular, unclassifiable novels in the canon: *Jacob's Room*, the first fruit of Woolf's search for her own unique voice; *Orlando*, a comic fantasy-novel masquerading as a biography; and *The Waves*, a lyric drama of the psyche, Woolf's most difficult and profound work. My two remaining choices were meant to be representative of the larger types of fiction Woolf declared herself to have written. From that group of more or less traditional narratives which she called "novels of fact," I selected her first novel, *The Voyage Out*. *Mrs. Dalloway* too is a "first": the first of those "novels of vision"—again the phrase is Woolf's own—which probe deeply the hidden inner life.

However representative or unique, factual or visionary the novel, Woolf's allusiveness persists like a fact of nature. She did not see literature as an unconnected succession of isolated works written by irreconcilable authors who shared no common bonds across time, cultures, and language. She recognized and exploited the literature behind literature. She wrote—and we should read her this way—as if literature were a dense and richly imaginative world of continuing presences, echoing and re-echoing down the corridors of our minds.

one

The Voyage Out

Virginia Woolf's first work of fiction has been the victim of a double neglect: the entire novel and the allusions within it have been ignored and in many cases dismissed. But *The Voyage Out* does deserve attention, for whatever one's estimation of the artistic merit of Woolf's fledgling effort, precisely because it is a *first* effort it reveals more nakedly than subsequent works Woolf's aesthetic strategies and the rudimentary beginnings of her "experimental" techniques. One of those characteristic techniques is of course frequent use of literary allusion.

In *The Voyage Out* no less than in its successors, Woolf's preoccupation with the complexities of personality is readily apparent. For her the external aspects of character are not nearly so interesting or important as the reality of the interior life. Thus, where more traditional novelists build character out of discrete factual units (e.g., the heroine's hair color or the hero's age), Woolf will offer intellectually and psychologically revealing data, such as their taste in literature. This is perfectly appropriate, given that her characters more often than not possess uncommon sensibilities, much culture, and intellectual ability. Thus there is a merging of the worlds of literature and life that some critics and readers find disconcerting, either because it is alien to their own notions of reality or because they are prepared to raise the issue of elitism of form or content. Yet Woolf's use of literary allusion to throw light upon her characters has both a psychological and an aesthetic *raison d'être* missed or discounted by critics who object to the profusion of writers, works, and quotations to be found in her pages. Such critics are not usually inclined to allow that literary allusions have a genuine characterizing function. One, for example, has called them mere "external tags," and condemned as "childishly superficial" Woolf's habit of "making the sort of reading people do stand for the sort of people they are or the stage of development they have reached."[1] In fact, however, Woolf's allusiveness is directly relevant and necessary to her efforts to depict with verisimilitude *her* chosen character types and their life-style.

Even the minor characters in *The Voyage Out*—a contingent of eccentric British tourists staying at the Santa Marina hotel—are drawn with allusive brushstrokes. Their character is often derived *primarily* from their expressed literary preferences. For example, a few allusions invoked in conversation quickly delineate the personality of old Mrs. Flushing, who exclaims, " 'Shakespeare? I hate Shakespeare!' " (268). (Her husband then admires her unorthodox bravado by remarking, " 'I believe you're the only person who dares say that, Alice.' ") Or she will ask Ridley Ambrose whether the *Symposium* is in Latin or Greek, and upon being answered, observe that she would " 'rather break stones in the road' " than learn Greek (199–200). If readers add this to her hatred of Shakespeare, they begin to see in her hearty anti-intellectualism as much unattractive Philistinism as admirable vitality.

Mrs. Flushing's rejection of Shakespeare is counterpointed by Mrs. Thornbury's exchange with the intellectual St. John Hirst, in which she defends the common people as persons who may not have read Hirst's beloved Gibbon, but who nevertheless " 'are the people, I feel, among whom Shakespeare will be born if he is ever born again' " (202). Quickly and efficiently, this suggests Mrs. Thornbury's differences from Mrs. Flushing, especially the largeness of her humanistic sympathies. It also contains within it seeds of that social criticism which can accompany characterizing allusions and expand their significance. Using Shakespeare as her paradigm, Mrs. Thornbury disputes Hirst's insistence upon formal education as the criterion for judging human beings. Shakespeare is a telling refutation of Hirst's class snobbery, which supposes that great writers must be great scholars, or at the very least good Cambridge men.

When the unconventional Evelyn Murgatroyd, another secondary character, tells Rachel that one of her rejected suitors said of her, " 'I'd no heart, and was merely a Siren' " (246), the remark supplements our understanding of her unsuccessful attempts at establishing personal relationships. Like her counterpart in classical mythology, Evelyn has enticed her sailor even unto death; poor distraught Sinclair has threatened to shoot himself if Evelyn will not marry him. There is humor in the discrepancy of the contrast between Evelyn Murgatroyd, an illegitimate child who wants to establish a home for fallen women but cannot adequately arrange her own haphazard life, and those tempting creatures who sang seductively to passing voyagers from a meadow littered with the corpses of their conquests. Despite Evelyn's active aspirations toward intimacy with others,[2] she has "no heart," another similarity to those Siren birds who are inhabited by the souls of the dead.

Then there is Susan Warrington, the recipient of some even more pointed characterization through allusion. She enumerates the trivial details that compromise her uneventful life in her diary: " 'A. M.—talked to Mrs. Eliot . . . Read a chapter of *Miss Appleby's Adventure* to Aunt

E . . . . Mem.: ask about damp *sheets'* " (104–5). Insipid ladies' fiction, read aloud to one's Aunt Emma—it is emblematic of the meaningless boredom of the proper young lady's life. When she hears Reverend Bax read two Psalms that stress vengeance upon one's enemies, Susan listens "with the same kind of mechanical respect with which she heard many of Lear's speeches read aloud" (227). Reverend Bax has just quoted the Old Testament supplicant who makes the bloodthirsty request, "Break their teeth, O God, in their mouth." Woolf's allusive analogy points readers toward the Lear who is the irrational father, who believed himself the victim of filial ingratitude and called down upon his daughter the curse of "sterility," or, failing that, a "child of spleen" (1.4.300–9). The Psalm quotation, deftly placed so as to compare with Lear's distraught revenge-seeking, underscores the larger authorial distaste for organized religion, especially for that strain of vindictive retaliation which underlies the exhortations of prayer.

Miss Allan, another of the minor characters who populates the hotel, is an English teacher whose very existence seems to be a function of her literary endeavors. She exchanges letters with her sister Emily, also a teacher, in which the talk veers toward literature; for example, "Surely Meredith lacks the *human* note one likes in W.W.?" (179). Even Emily's passing reference to Wordsworth has a practical purpose, however; it underscores her sister's preoccupation with that poet. Miss Allan habitually reads Wordsworth's *Prelude*,[3] "partly because she always read the 'Prelude' abroad, and partly because she was engaged in writing a short *Primer of English Literature*—Beowulf to Swinburne—which would have a paragraph on Wordsworth" (103).

For her *Primer*, Miss Allan dissects the living body of literature into the usual periods: " 'Age of Chaucer; Age of Elizabeth; Age of Dryden, . . . I'm glad there aren't many more ages. I'm still in the middle of the eighteenth century. . . . Euphues. The germ of the English novel' " (253).[4] Sometime later she announces that she has nearly finished her *Primer:* " 'That is, omitting Swinburne—Beowulf to Browning—I rather like the two B's myself' " (316). Miss Allan's expansive personality finds a complement in her admiration of those two Bs, one a larger-than-life heroic epic of the conflict between good and evil, the other a poet of optimism and robust vitality. The trials and tribulations of having to say "something different about everybody" (316) in a maximum of seventy thousand words end in triumph, however, and the spinster prevails: Woolf has skillfully linked the making of Miss Allan's generalized but instructive *Primer* to the equally vague but humane and useful personality that created it.

Another interesting and eccentric minor character, Mr. Grice, is the ship steward and poet-philosopher in the rough. He has a conversation with Clarissa Dalloway, who along with her husband Richard makes a brief appearance in this novel, which anticipates her full-scale treatment in *Mrs. Dalloway*. Commenting upon the oceanic treasures Mr. Grice has collected, Clarissa says, " 'They have swum about among bones.' " Mr. Grice replies, " 'You're thinking of Shakespeare,' " and reads, " 'Full fathom five thy father lies' " (54). After he and Clarissa agree that *Henry the Fifth* is their favorite Shakespearean play, Woolf supplies readers with a capsule characterization of Grice, via allusion:

> *Hamlet* was what you might call too introspective for Mr. Grice, the sonnets too passionate; Henry the Fifth was to him the model of an English gentleman. But his favorite reading was Huxley, Herbert Spencer, and Henry George; while Emerson and Thomas Hardy he read for relaxation. (54)

The sort of man who would find *Hamlet* "too introspective" is a man who evades or is incapable of fine or deep thinking, and a man who would find the sonnet sequence "too passionate" may well be inhibited about sexual matters. Grice's three favorite authors are beyond the literary realm. As for the writers he reads "for relaxation," Emerson produced the sort of quotable epigrams Mr. Grice would find "inspirational," while Hardy's somber world view and pessimistic naturalism are not out of keeping with Grice's Darwinian preferences in scientific literature.

Woolf's specificity with regard to Shakespeare's Henry plays is also not without purpose and point. Mr. Grice does not favor the two *Henry IV* plays, which contain that magnificent creation, Falstaff. Nor does he favor one of the three *Henry VI* plays. Grice likes best *Henry V*, in which the King exhorts his soldiers, "Once more unto the breach, dear friends, once more" (3.1.1). If the overstrained patriotism of "God for Harry! England! and Saint George!" (3.1.34) leads the reader to suspect that Woolf is mocking such values, her distaste for smug patriotism is beyond doubt when she (allusively) characterizes the Dalloways' pretentious nationalism.

The Dalloways are taken aboard the *Euphrosyne* after traveling on the Continent, "chiefly with a view to broadening Mr. Dalloway's mind" (39). In Spain they rode mules, "for they wished to understand how the peasants live" (39), as Woolf's merciless sarcasm puts it. Dalloway's wife "inspected the royal stables, . . . photographed Fielding's grave,[5] and let loose a small bird which some ruffian had trapped, 'because one hates to think of anything in a cage where English people lie buried' " (39–40). The allusion to *Tom Jones* hidden within this sentence is discernible only through recognition of two subtle clues: that author's name, given ear-

4

lier, and a minor plot incident from his most famous work. Obscure as it may be, once recognized it offers further evidence of Woolf's critical stance toward Clarissa Dalloway, for as Fielding's Master Blifil explained his action with pieties about a captive bird being an unnatural and un-christian thing, which situation he felt obliged to correct, so too does Clarissa deal in sentimental pieties about desiring no captivity to exist where an Englishman is buried.[6]

If Clarissa's nationalism is ostentatious, her literary culture is super-ficial. When the scholarly William Pepper quotes in Greek from the *Antigone*, Clarissa comments that she would " 'give ten years of my life to know Greek' " (45). But this admirable resolve melts as soon as Ridley Ambrose offers to teach her the Greek alphabet, and the status-seeking aspect of her desire becomes apparent: "She saw herself in her drawing room in Browne Street with a Plato open on her knees—Plato in the original Greek" (46). Ten years of promised devotion to learning are quickly exchanged for the easy wish that "a real scholar . . . could slip Greek into her head with scarcely any trouble" (46).

Discussing Greek with Pepper and Ambrose, Clarissa says " 'I own that I shall never forget the *Antigone*. I saw it at Cambridge years ago, and it's haunted me ever since. Don't you think it's quite the most modern thing you ever saw?' she asked Ridley. 'It seemed to me I'd known twenty Clytemnestras' " (45). There is Clarissa's fashionable su-perficiality again, in that "quite the most modern thing." And there is incisive wit, plus moral judgment, in Clarissa's likening of some twenty of her friends, "Old Lady Ditchling for one" (45), to Clytemnestra, who took a lover and murdered her husband. But more importantly, Clarissa has placed Clytemnestra in *Antigone*. The error could be Woolf's;[7] on the other hand, Clarissa is a character whose shallow and somewhat scatter-brained grasp of literature would give rise to a confusion of one Greek tragedy with another. Deliberate allusive error, with its ironic character-izing function, seems more than likely, for Clarissa goes on to garble yet another allusion:

> "At your age I only liked Shelley. I can remember sobbing over him in the garden.
>
>> He has outsoared the shadow of our night,
>> Envy and calumny and hate and pain—
>
> you remember?
>
>> Can touch him not and torture not again
>> From the contagion of the world's slow stain.
>
> How divine!—and yet what nonsense! . . . I always think it's *living*, not dying that counts. . . . But I don't expect you to agree with me!"

5

She pressed Rachel's shoulder.
"Um—m—m—" she went on quoting—
Unrest which men miscall delight—
"when you're my age you'll see . . . " (58)[8]

In the same conversation Clarissa asks a rather fatuous question about Cowper's *Letters* (" 'Are they nice?' ") and exclaims, " 'I really couldn't exist without the Brontes! Don't you love them?' " (57). As if that were not enough to spotlight the vagaries attendant upon her efforts to understand literature, she then jumps to " 'I'd rather live without them [the Brontës] than without Jane Austen' " (58).

Clarissa gives Rachel a copy of *Persuasion*, which she deems "a little less threadbare than the others" (62). *Persuasion* does indeed have a wider social perspective than Austen's earlier novels; Woolf herself pointed out that its world "is larger, more mysterious, and more romantic." She called Austen's last completed novel "a little *voyage* of discovery" (italics mine). She also noted the "bored" authorial voice and the harshness of the satire, remarking that Austen "has almost ceased to be amused by the vanities of a Sir Walter or the snobbery of a Miss Elliott."[9] But Clarissa Dalloway has *not* ceased to be amused by the wide world of social vanities. We find her (62) reading aloud the opening sentence from *Persuasion*, a sentence that stresses exactly those class-conscious vanities which drew Woolf's critical comment.

As the title of Austen's novel denotes conversion, the shaping of Rachel's reading tastes is one of Clarissa's motives. She leaves *Persuasion* behind as an amulet, with her name and address inscribed on the cover. Her husband Richard supports her preference for Austen with smug nationalistic propriety, informing Rachel that Austen is the greatest woman writer "we possess" (62). She is great, Dalloway continues, because " 'she does not attempt to write like a man. Every other woman does; on that account, I don't read 'em' " (62). Dalloway here promulgates Woolf's own estimation of Austen: "Only Jane Austen did it, and Emily Bronte. . . . They wrote as women write, not as men write."[10] He nevertheless proceeds to fall asleep upon hearing Austen read aloud, exactly as his wife had predicted.

Richard Dalloway's opinions of literature are often self-serving. He is convinced he is more valuable to society than poets. He brags to Rachel that he is prouder of his life of public service than he would be " 'of writing Keats and Shelley into the bargain!' " (65). Rachel is too shy to stand up to Dalloway's pragmatic *hubris*, but he does not go uncontested by the scholarly Ridley Ambrose:

"I don't quite agree, Richard," said Mrs. Dalloway. "Think of Shelley. I feel that there's almost everything one wants in 'Adonais.' "

6

"Read 'Adonais' by all means," Richard conceded. "But whenever I hear of Shelley I repeat to myself the words of Matthew Arnold, 'What a set! What a set!' "

This roused Ridley's attention. "Matthew Arnold? A detestable prig!" he snapped. (44)

These lines accomplish a good deal. First, they expose the inconsistency of Clarissa's opinions: she here finds "everything" in *Adonais;* a short time later she will dismiss it as "divine nonsense" (58). Second, they add another dimension to Richard Dalloway's philistinism, for beneath the mundane practicality of his active political life lurks a fear of nonconformity. His quick recourse to argument by authority (the authority of a solemn Victorian critic at that) is a revealing stroke of characterization. Clearly Shelley's radical and "immoral" life-style threatens conventional men like Dalloway, who proceed to display Arnold's shocked middle-class morality over "irregular relations."[11] Using Arnold as an intellectual prop, Dalloway can justify the kind of thinking that discounts "Keats and Shelley into the bargain." In Arnold's infamous definition of Shelley as "a beautiful *and ineffectual* angel, beating in the void his luminous wings in vain,"[12] Dalloway finds a respectable precedent for his own view that "artists *find* things in a mess, shrug their shoulders, turn aside to their visions—which I grant may be very beautiful—and *leave* things in a mess" (45).

When Ridley Ambrose reacts by calling Arnold "a detestable prig," his epithet underscores the difference of temperament and mental power between them. Ridley's rejection of Arnold is also a rejection of Dalloway, who is in agreement with Arnold's values. This sort of disagreement is part of that larger conflict of active and contemplative natures which Woolf builds into all of her fiction. Here the tension between the scholar (Ridley) and the man of business (Rachel's father, Willoughby Vinrace) is expressed with the help of allusion: "Ridley was bringing out the third volume of Pindar when Willoughby was launching his first ship. They built a new factory the very year the commentary on Aristotle—was it?—appeared at the University Press" (24–25). When Willoughby is "at his documents," Ridley is "at his Greek" (33), and in the scene in which Ridley defends Shelley, Willoughby aligns himself with Dalloway's anti-artist position.

Ridley Ambrose is the ranking member of this novel's quartet of scholarly characters. He is obsessed with his professional reputation and possessed of considerable egotism. His wife finds him " 'the vainest man I know' " (98), and others think he is "what Shelley would have been if

Shelley had lived to fifty-five and grown a beard" (98). This comparison—to the very poet Ridley had defended against Matthew Arnold's priggishness and Richard Dalloway's conformity—hints at a personality based on conflicting traits. Shelley was very much a puzzle of vanity and modesty, egotism and altruism, strength and passivity, and when one critic writes that Ridley is "self-conscious, absent-minded, touchy, scrupulous, with a queer egotism and queerer nobility,"[13] we might be reading a description of Shelley—or even of Sir Leslie Stephen, the father about whom Virginia Woolf was nothing if not ambivalent. Once the Shelley comparison is established, even the ways in which it does *not* hold true contribute to Ridley's characterization (in an ironic, diminishing way). Ambrose is not a creative genius subject to romantic inspiration and lyric intensity, as "some silly woman" (98) romanticized him, but a painstaking scholar persevering at his specialized task.

Ridley has an eccentric habit of reciting verse aloud to himself. He is introduced to readers as he strides along dramatically exclaiming, " 'Lars Porsena of Clusium / By the nine gods he swore' " (10), " 'That the great house of Tarquin / Should suffer no more' " (11). This deftly chosen allusion to Macaulay's "Horatius" reveals Ridley's proclivity for the heroic gesture and underscores his esoteric taste for the exotically unfamiliar, the remote in time and spirit. The lines strike the pose of the conquering hero as they tell their story of "How well Horatius kept the bridge / In the brave days of old" (70.7–8). Ridley obviously identifies with Macaulay's robust, virile imitations of the *Iliad* manner.[14] But an admiration that borders on identification may indicate something of a bully lurking beneath the would-be hero. In Mr. Ramsay of *To the Lighthouse* (who like Ambrose is a fictionalized portrait of Sir Leslie Stephen), the tyrannical aspects are *overtly* rendered. There Ramsay paces about, declaiming lines from Tennyson's *Charge of the Light Brigade* (a poem with the same British-Hero, Manly-Action tone that Ridley's quotation evokes). In this novel there is but one overtly dramatized suggestion of Ridley's tyranny—some passing children call Ridley "Bluebeard!" (10). The likening of Ridley (who possesses even the beard) to a black-hearted villain who systematically murdered his wives is of course exaggerated and ironic. Nevertheless, something quite decisively negative is communicated to the reader by so forceful an image of cruelty and misogyny.[15] If nothing else, we have been subliminally warned not to take the attenuated scholar as altogether mild and harmless.

Much as Miss Allan's sense of self was inextricably wedded to her literary endeavor, Ridley Ambrose's identity is bound to his editing of Pindar. Pindar's odes, like Macaulay's *Lays of Ancient Rome*, are remote from modern experience. Perhaps more revealing of Ridley's character, Pindar's odes are commissioned poetry for victors: heroic, difficult to the point of obscurity, elegant, definitely for the uncommon reader, yet steeped in conventional praise for Establishment values.

The Pindar linkage becomes so completely characterizing that it functions poetically, as metonymy: "Three odes of Pindar were mended, Helen covered about five inches of her embroidery, and St. John completed the first two acts of a play" (224). Asked where her husband is, Helen Ambrose can answer with one word, "Pindar" (152), which has come to represent the man.

Woolf's delineation of Ridley the Pindar scholar is part of her larger, more general presentation of the essential nature of scholarship, which she sees as socially and intellectually remote.[16] We find Ridley sitting "hour after hour among white-leaved books, alone like an idol in an empty church" (170). And Woolf troubles to describe the contents of his study, which is a palpable manifestation of the abstract life of the mind, as he takes Rachel on a guided tour of his sanctuary:

> "Plato," he said, laying one finger on the first of a row of small dark books, "and Jorrocks next door, which is wrong. Sophocles, Swift. You don't care for German commentators, I presume. French, then. You read French? You should read Balzac. Then we come to Words- worth and Coleridge. Pope, Johnson, Addison, Wordsworth, Shelley, Keats. One thing leads to another. Why is Marlowe here? Mrs. Chailey [the housekeeper], I presume. But what's the use of reading if you don't read Greek? After all, if you read Greek, you need never read anything else, pure waste of time—pure waste of time . . . . (171)

Despite Ridley's explicit recommendation of Balzac to Rachel,[17] when Rachel chooses *La Cousine Bette*, she is instructed to "throw it away if she found it too horrible" (172).[18] In this deft insinuation of Victorian moral codes, even so enlightened a scholar as Ridley fears for Rachel's intellectual virginity if it is exposed to Balzac's delineation of the upper middle class's rabid quest for position and money.[19] This world of cyni- cism, corruption, hedonism, intrigue, and base motives is one which Ridley would rather keep from Rachel, his scholarly respect for truth and his opposition to censorship notwithstanding.

Whatever Ridley's limitations and inconsistencies, he is not subject to the disparagement and sharp-edged ridicule, even outright contempt, that surrounds the portrait of that other scholar, William Pepper. Pepper is ludicrously egotistical: the woman worthy of the very special him must "read Greek, if not Persian," be "irreproachably fair in the face, and able to understand the small things he let fall while undressing" (25).

He is testy and rude when giving unsolicited advice upon very nearly every subject: his dinner table "disquisition upon the proper method of making roads" cites the Greeks, the Romans, and the English, then concludes in "a fury of denunciation" (26) against the potholes in the Richmond Park road over which he bicycles every morning. He is, among other things, "an authority" on "vehicular traffic" (19), and he knows "more about separable verbs than any man in Europe" (28). He dabbles in "mathematics, history, Greek, zoology, economics, and the Icelandic Sagas. He had turned Persian poetry into English prose, and English prose into Greek iambics. . . . He was here either to get things out of the sea, or to write upon the probable course of Odysseus, for Greek after all was his hobby" (19). The rhetoric of that passage—if the accumulating content itself has not been sufficient clue to Woolf's wittily malicious intent—is a near parody of the disjointed compartments of knowledge into which William Pepper is split. It has an ironic effect, ultimately: the longer the list of Pepper's desultory dabblings, the less confidence in his depth it inspires.

Pepper's compulsive personality and rigidity of character combine in his habit of scheduling authors to read by the month. Having "done" Petronius in January, he moves on promptly to Catullus-February. This is a secondary detail about a secondary character, but in Woolf's hands, it speaks volumes. The fussy sort of pedant Woolf loved to ridicule, Pepper is smugly overconfident about his intellectual prowess; although a verb commonly used by British intellectuals and students, the word *done* is significant here for its presumptions of finality. Most amazing of all is Woolf's ability to insinuate even Pepper's hidden sexual personality from this scrap of "mere" allusive characterization. The works organized for monthly reading by this overstructured, inhibited gentleman scholar happen to be outstanding examples of classical obscenity. So much for refinement of surface as compared to the grosser predilections of the libido.

Finally the subtleties of Woolf's allusive technique enable her to make significant personality distinctions within the same character type. Pepper's learning lacks those synthesizing, integrative qualities that she found admirable when she found scholarly characters at all admirable. Ridley, for example, works his way "further and further into the heart" (170) of his chosen poet, Pindar; Pepper plays intellectual hopscotch, and when he does "specialize" on the monthly installment plan, he reveals lewd proclivities.

To Pepper also belongs the dubious distinction of quoting classical Greek at the dinner table. He strikes up the famous chorus about mankind from the *Antigone* (45), quoting only those lines which praise man as wondrous. The *entire* choral ode puts human pride into proper perspective, reminding man of his mortality: "Against death alone he hath no resources" (antistrophe 2, l.1). Ironically, at the novel's conclusion, they will all be forced to confront the truth Pepper omitted in his *hubris*, when Rachel Vinrace proves to have no resources against death.[20]

Pepper's quotation—decorative icing on the cake of conversation—reinforces the reader's sense that he is derivative rather than creative. Here is a classical education petrified into extraneous pedantry. The recitation of strange sounds by a pedantic scholar blocks human interaction and emphasizes the speaker's estranged relation to others. Virginia Woolf is *not* ostentatiously displaying an impertinent familiarity with classical Greek. She is making the reader aware of the existential irrelevance of those very intellectual accomplishments which nevertheless command our respect. Her use of the original Greek rather than a transliteration stresses the alien form, not the communicable content, of the *Antigone* quotation. It is an aesthetic decision serving to make the sort of social, intellectual, and psychological points that could not have been made otherwise, for Pepper would not seem so enviable, and Clarissa Dalloway would not be so impressed, if mere understandable English had been chanted at her.

St. John Hirst is yet another of Woolf's variations on the scholarly character. As Pepper's outward appearance was often the subject of her wit, so too is that ugly young man, Hirst, who looks "like some singular gargoyle" (152). Hirst is *symbolically* ugly; that is, his deficiencies of appearance illustrate drastic interior limitations. Like his uncommon intellect, his uncommon ugliness distances him from the warmth of frequent contact; he uses the former to compensate for the latter. His education and intellect limit rather than expand his human wisdom and social development. As one minor character from the lower orders puts it, " 'Oh, he's one of those learned chaps. . . . He don't look as if he enjoyed it' " (138).

Hirst, a fictionalized portrait of Lytton Strachey, is introduced as he sits reading "the third volume of Gibbon's *History of the Decline and Fall of Rome* by candle light" (106). Northrop Frye has written that Gibbon's is "a highly mannered prose . . . [which] continually oversimplifies and oversymmetrizes its material";[21] one might say the same of Hirst. He finds Gibbon "immaculate" (106), and he is given to highly mannered remarks; for example, about nature being " 'a mistake. She's either very ugly, appallingly ugly, or absolutely terrifying. I don't know which alarms me most—a cow or a tree' " (121). Behind this posture of witty bravado is a defensive fear of precisely those things that are beyond being dominated through immaculate writing styles. The masculine claim that factual truth is reality; the rationalist belief that the life of one person or the history of a country can be ascertained with certainty; the assumption that the march of external events reveals more than does the mysterious inner life—these are the beliefs behind Hirst's admiration of Gibbon. They are beliefs that Virginia Woolf, along with many of the female characters in her novels, does not share. Thus it is not surprising when Hirst's suggestion that " 'each member of this party now gives a short biographical sketch of himself or herself' " (143) is countered by Helen Ambrose's wise remark, " 'But of course we've left out the only questions that matter' " (144).

Hirst defines and judges others according to their reading preferences. Far too literally does he believe that books "make a great deal of difference" (164). He is prepared to make them a sufficient criterion for determining the value of a human being. When Rachel challenges this attitude, Hirst's allusive reply only compounds his intellectual arrogance: " 'You agree with my spinster Aunt, I expect. . . . 'Be good, sweet maid'—I thought Mr. Kingsley and my Aunt were now obsolete' " (201). Perfectly in character, the condescending, bookish Hirst mocks the piously sentimental, middlebrow taste of his spinster aunt by quoting pretty Victorian verse (verse, moreover, that counsels ladies to be pious, not intelligent).

For Hirst, Gibbon is the absolute standard of evaluation: " 'He's the test, of course' " (154). Helen Ambrose sees that the shy and retiring Rachel needs to know "the facts of life. . . . What really goes on, what people feel' "; Hirst's response to Rachel's inexperience is " 'I have promised to lend her Gibbon' " (163–64). Indeed, whenever Hirst presumes to educate naive females—and readers should keep in mind the ironic implications of such a situation, presented by a feminist author—Gibbon is ritually invoked. Ultimately even the unworldly Rachel can make fun of Hirst's predictable response by reminding him that "if he were undertaking the education of Evelyn, that [i.e., Gibbon] surely was the test" (306).

When Hirst sends Rachel the prescribed volume of Gibbon, it is accompanied by a brief note, yet another contribution to his characterization by allusion:

> I send the first volume of Gibbon as I promised. Personally I find little to be said for the moderns, but I'm going to send you Wedekind when I've done him. Donne? Have you read Webster and all that set? I envy you reading them for the first time. Completely exhausted after last night. And you? (172)

Not surprisingly, the cerebral Hirst is attracted to the keen and powerful play of Donne's intellect, his learning, paradoxical wit, and complicated

irony. The very phraseology of his stated preferences reflects his admiration for Gibbon: he thinks in oversharp, eighteenth-century categories of
"the moderns" and "sets," which are inclusively accepted or dismissed.
The new element of characterization supplied by Hirst's allusive note is
his appreciation of the likes of Webster and Wedekind. Beneath Hirst's
controlled, even dry intellectuality, a penchant for the sensational and
the violent seems to lurk. It is not the Jacobean drama of Ben Jonson, the
satirical comedies and tragicomedies of Dekker, Marston, Heywood, or
Beaumont and Fletcher, which attract Hirst. He prefers Webster and
"all that set" of, dramatists: the Tourneurs, John Fords, and Thomas
Middletons, whose blood tragedies reek with incest, murder, revenge,
and violence.

In addition to those highly charged Jacobeans, Hirst leans toward
other writers of grotesque technique who stress forbidden, erotic
themes. Wedekind's dedicated exploration of tabooed sexual themes
made him a nonconformist rebel, baiting the respectable world—just the
sort of figure Hirst admires. Carrying Hirst's fascination with sexuality
and nonconformity to ironic planes, Woolf gives us Hirst the Iconoclast
at a very respectable Sunday church service, ignoring Reverend Bax's
sermon and reading "indecent" literature, something identified as the
Sappho Swinburne did (230). By coupling Sappho and Swinburne, that
enfant terrible of Victorian society, Woolf achieves a double-edged allusion whose symbolic unconventionality is quintessential. Forbidden
sexuality, literary eroticism, youth's rebellion against such Establishment
values as orthodox religion—all these are implied. And Hirst's dogmatic
opinion that Swinburne's Sappho is " 'the best thing that's ever been
written' " (230) adds still another dimension: his satisfaction with such
obvious decadence,[22] with Swinburne's padded, hypertensive version of
Sappho, points to a less than cogent literary taste.[23]

The remaining male character of importance is Terence Hewet, the
young man to whom Rachel Vinrace becomes engaged. With his disarming but intricate personality, he is an excellent foil for Hirst. Unlike him,
Hewet has an intuitive capacity to recognize that life is enigmatic. Hirst
hubristically believes that " 'I see through everything—absolutely everything. Life has no more mysteries for me . . . I have a key.' " Hewet
counters with " 'I don't find it simple at all' " (169). These attitudes are
reflected in their literary choices. Although Hewet shares with his friend
an interest in John Donne, his lack of enthusiasm for Gibbon (" 'Not
Gibbon; no,' " 110) matches his description as someone "likely to be at
the mercy of moods which had little relation to facts" (216). Moreover,
he objects to Hirst's intellectually ostentatious behavior at chapel: "Why
go to church, he demanded, merely in order to read Sappho?" (237).[24]

Hewet's preference for George Meredith is yet another significant psychological differentiation from Hirst.[25] In fact, Hewet shares one of Meredith's central concerns, an interest in the psychology of women, in their full humanity as moral beings.[26] His frustration at the inability of men and women to understand each other finds expression in Woolf's fabricated allusion (a quotation-passage from the novel Hewet is writing): " 'Perhaps, in the far future, when generations of men had struggled and failed as he must now struggle and fail, woman would be, indeed, what she now made a pretence of being—the friend and companion—not the enemy and parasite of man' " (297). The plot of Hewet's novel, in which a husband tries to understand the woman he married, a woman who has gone from being his "ideal comrade" to a puzzling and distant wife, has the distinct flavor of Meredith. His fictional couple even " 'shout *Love in the Valley* to each other across the snowy slopes of the Riffelhorn' " (296). Moreover, the ominous atmosphere of mortality in Meredith's work anticipates the conclusion of the novel in which Hewet himself is a character.

Complementing his appreciation of the sharp paradoxes and trenchant psychology that comprise Meredith's exploration of the man-woman relationship is Hewet's admiration for Thomas Hardy's poetry. When he quotes eight lines of a Hardy poem (110), touched by a melancholy wisdom that accepts the brevity of love and the inevitability of death,[27] the Eros-Thanatos conjunction ultimately played out in the novel is reinforced.

Finally and still consistently, Hewet admires the troubled and tentative searchings of Walt Whitman:

> Hewet looked at his book again. . . . and he could see Rachel and hear her voice and be near to her. He felt as if he were waiting, . . . only Rachel too was waiting with him. He looked at her sometimes as if she must know that they were waiting together, without being able to offer any resistance. Again he read from his book:
>
> > Whoever you are holding me now in your hand,
> > Without one thing all will be useless. (267)

In addition to several striking parallels between Woolf's own plot action and the events in Whitman's poem, there are suggestive psychological congruences.[28] The uncertain course of Hewet and Rachel's love; their conflict of freedom and involvement; their fear of losing their separate autonomy; the frustration inherent in their inability to overcome barriers of misunderstanding—all are embodied in Hewet's chosen quotation. And when these difficulties seem insurmountable, causing Rachel to declare " 'Let's break it off, then' " (303), it is in much the same spirit as Whitman's "therefore release me now before troubling yourself any further." Woolf's entire ambiguous presentation of their love is paralleled by the tentative, evasive syntax of the last lines of Whitman's poem: "For all is useless without that which you may guess at many times and not hit, that which I hinted at; / Therefore release me and depart on your way." Neither Woolf nor the poet to whom she alludes presents love as a permanent state obtainable by those who fall, precariously, into its grip.

Hewet's admiration for Whitman, Hardy, and Meredith reflects his willingness to deal with problem areas of life and his intuitive understanding that life is enigmatic. Combined with his rejection of the facile, happy aspects of Thackeray,[29] the collection of allusions adds to our understanding of his character and of what he hopes to achieve by writing a novel called "Silence, or the Things People Don't Say" (220).

Rachel's death becomes the instrument of Hewet's awakening to the reality of suffering and loss. As her condition worsens, Hewet's experience of bereavement and anguish is transformed into a mystic vision of wholeness. He decides that his spiritual union with Rachel will be preserved, perfectly sealed, by death—a feeling that echoes the narrator of *Love in the Valley*, who considers his love "sweeter unpossessed" and believes that "Love that so desires would fain keep her changeless" (l. 47). The impulse behind Hewet's need for *identification* with Rachel is very much akin to the cry of Meredith's narrator: "Let me clasp her soul to know she cannot die!" (l. 168). One critic, sensing the subtle debt that Woolf's deathbed scene owes to Meredith, has called it a presentation of "romantic Richard-and-Lucy love," out of *The Ordeal of Richard Feverel*.[30] But Meredith was not alone in his mystical suggestion that love finds perfect fulfillment in death. Such a belief pervades many of the greatest love stories in literature, especially one of Rachel's favorite novels, *Wuthering Heights*. Feeling that "he seemed to be Rachel as well as himself" (353), Hewet reflects the same intense identification that caused Catherine to declare of Heathcliff: "He's more myself than I am." Because it reiterates past literary presentations of love and death, there is an allusive *weight* to Woolf's episode. Such background resonance deepens the emotional impact and does its rhetorical duty by helping to convince readers that spiritual-mystic attachments count as genuine manifestations of love.

Helen Ambrose, wife of Ridley and guardian to Rachel, is a character second only to the heroine in significance. In her function as educator-guardian, Helen "desired that Rachel should think, and for this reason offered books . . . Defoe, Maupassant, or some spacious chronicle of family life" (124). Helen hopes to mend Rachel's ignorance of actual life by exposing her to Maupassant and Defoe, who share an orientation toward the realistic and the factual.[31] Helen's third choice, chronicles of family life, is consistent with her emphasis on personal relations and her insistence on confronting basic human nature. These recommendations form an interesting contrast to her husband's reluctance to allow Rachel to read *La Cousine Bette*. With greater practical wisdom, Helen realizes that exposure to reality, unpleasant reality if need be, is what Rachel needs.

Helen's perspectives are consistently larger than her role as educator-guardian, wife and mother, would demand. Her intense emotions seem to refer to a generalized rather than a particular situation of foreboding and anxiety. There is, for example, her dramatically exaggerated introduction in the very first chapter, where she is weeping and thinking, "When one gave up seeing the beauty that clothed things, this was the skeleton beneath" (11–12). Her thoughts are often of "far-off things, such as old age and poverty and death" (278). Her pessimism is "not severe upon individuals so much as incredulous of the kindness of destiny, fate"; she hypothesizes "chaos triumphant, things happening for no reason at all, and every one groping about in illusion and ignorance" (221). All of this might make Helen an interesting incidence of morbid personality, the sort of individual who invents imaginary disasters that express her frustration and even perhaps an unconscious sadism,[32] if there were no textual evidence to suggest that she has carefully been structured as a Fate figure. These exaggerated descriptions have mytho-poetic overtones; for example, she is said to rise from her seat "as the moon rises" (160), or when she realizes that "Rachel has passed beyond her guardianship" (287), she mythically departs "behind the curtain" (288). Her prophetic powers are acknowledged and respected by several other characters: Hewet thinks her good sense "like nature's good sense, might be depended upon" (328); Hirst admires "her largeness and simplicity, which made her stand out from the rest like a great stone woman" (135); Rachel considers that "the alarm which Helen sometimes felt was justified" (223).

Moreover, Helen's guidance of Rachel is augmented by similar situations in which she is cast as the arbiter of others' destinies: she advises Hirst to leave Cambridge for the Bar (208),[33] or she seems "to be protecting Terence from the approach of others" (275). She has "presentiments of disaster" (285) about the course of Hewet's and Rachel's love, which do in fact materialize.

The uncanny predictive wisdom that earns Helen her symbolic significance is conveyed to the reader through three devices: her embroidery, her reading of a black philosophy book, and her recitation of "Toll for the Brave" to Hirst (260). This little-known, gloomy poem of Cowper's, sometimes alternately titled "On the Loss of the Royal George," isolates factors of disaster, loss, and death at sea which are analogous to the plot and setting of *The Voyage Out*. Accompanied by no further elaboration, the title itself insinuates that dark destiny which waits to seize the unsuspecting. The frequent references to "a black volume of philosophy" (32–33) give Helen's premonitions, however dire, a context of authority and credibility, for no one else in the novel reads technical volumes on philosophy. The other device suggesting Helen's symbolic importance is her embroidery, "a matter for thought, the design being difficult" (207). The design is in fact a literal "creation" of the future destiny of Rachel and Hewet: it anticipates the actual environment of "a tropical river running through a tropical forest" (33), complete with animals, lush vegetation, and naked natives, in which they are destined to declare their love. As she sews this design, Helen's figure radiates "the sublimity of a woman's of the early world, spinning the thread of fate" (208). Moreover, Helen's embroidery is linked to her philosophic interests, for it is while she works on her "great design" that she reads bits of G.E. Moore's *Principia Ethica* "between the stitches" (33).[34] Even in the closing scenes of the novel, the implication that Helen represents Fate is sustained through the symbolism of card-playing. Against the complacency of the doctor there is the correctness of Helen's intuition: " 'It's no use for him to say that Rachel's better; she's not better; she's worse' " (337). And she is quite right. Thus bolstered by deftly selected images and allusions, Helen Ambrose functions as the embodiment of Fate.

Fate deals its strongest blow to the twenty-four-year-old heroine of the novel, Rachel Vinrace. The voyage out is her voyage; the episodic plot but a sequence of events that modify her personality through their effect on her sensibility. Self-absorbed and unworldly, Rachel is a dissatisfied dreamer who cannot find the meaning of life in conventional Christianity, nor in the political-social values of Richard Dalloway, nor in the historical-factual values esteemed by Hirst. Rather she finds some semblance of meaning in music and literature.

The room of one's own to which Rachel retires to play Bach or Beethoven or Wagner on the piano is a room filled with such books as *Wuthering Heights* and Cowper's *Letters*. Cowper allusions, repeated throughout the course of Rachel's character depiction, come to have a specific meaning of rebellion against parental authority. The *Letters* are the "classic prescribed by her father which had bored her" (35); she finds them " 'rather dull' " (57). She does, however, respond emotionally to the *Letters* at one point, entering into "communion" with "the spirit of poor William Cowper there at Olney" (37).[35] It is a startling if brief brushstroke in Rachel's characterization. The tortured, unhappy, gloomy man who was the Olney Cowper is a markedly strange figure for a young woman on the threshold of life to identify with. Yet allusion to the Olney Cowper deftly anticipates those grim emotional qualities of deranged isolation that will later infuse Rachel's delirium. Then too, the degree to which Rachel Vinrace reflects Virginia Woolf's personality is increased by Rachel's identification with Cowper.[36]

One critic has called *The Voyage Out* the story "of a maleducated and sequestered mind."[37] Certainly Rachel lacks sufficient sense of identity, and she consults literary works as an aid to personality development. But she is subject to the contradictory shaping influence of males: Willoughby has advised Cowper; Hirst bids her read Gibbon; Hewet exclaims " 'Read poetry, Rachel, poetry, poetry, poetry!' " while charging her not to read "antiquated problem plays" (292); Ridley countermands Gibbon, is fearful of Balzac's influence, and offers his own choices (171). Little wonder that in her confusion Rachel strolls about with twin volumes of Gibbon and Balzac, the respective gifts of Hirst and Ridley, in what may be allusively symbolic of the shifting relationship—sometimes complementary, sometimes divergent—between fact and fiction, history and literature. In the context of the strikingly beautiful natural landscape through which Rachel moves, the twin volumes of Balzac and Gibbon embody the juxtaposition of book knowledge to existential reality. There is a world of yellow butterflies beyond literature, where Rachel is awed "by the discovery of a terrible possibility in life," by an unnamed possibility that causes her to gather up her two books "much as a soldier prepares for battle" (176).

Conventional works do not attract Rachel. She finds Jane Austen "like a tight plait" (58)—a simile that captures Austen's impeccable, controlled style and the confinement of her world, where woman's only purpose or ambition was to marry. Rather Rachel is attracted to works that carry the note of rebellion and modernity. She even selects works with a feminist tinge, trying to supplement her anemic sense of self by identifying with the characters: "Then it would be Meredith's turn and she became Diana of the Crossways" (124).

Meredith's full projection of the character of women would of course be especially valuable to Rachel in her search for identity.[38] In "becoming" Diana, Rachel vicariously lives quite a liberated life, for Meredith's Diana Merion sought a divorce when her husband proved incompatible, took to writing novels, became celebrated for her cultural salon, had an affair with a politician, and finally married her faithful suitor. Diana's search for masculine companionship, her fear of sexual possession, and her struggle to achieve independence have pointed applicability to Rachel's problem. Both heroines share the problem of how to reconcile their feminine/sexual nature with individual/intellectual identity.

Equally telling is Rachel's stern concentration on the plays of Ibsen and her absorption in his strong women characters. The effect on Rachel's imagination is profound: "She acted them for days at a time, greatly to Helen's amusement" (123). Taken beyond her personal limitations, Rachel questions life and ponders "the truth of it all" (123) like her role-model Ibsen heroines. As Helen wisely realizes, "It was not all acting . . . some sort of change was taking place in the human being" (124).

Seeking from literature direct insight into the nature of love, Rachel finds that "none of the books she read, from *Wuthering Heights* to *Man and Superman*, and the plays of Ibsen, suggested from their analysis of love that what their heroines felt was what she was feeling now" (223). In their state of painful rebellion against conventional notions of love and marriage, Ibsen's heroines are a poor (because negative) illustration of the emotion of love, and Shaw's play presents love as a condition in which man is relentlessly pursued by woman, nature's aggressive instrument of the Life Force. Between them, Ibsen and Shaw furnish Rachel with exaggeratedly polarized visions of women and love, with heroines either deserting marriage in desperation or maniacally pursuing it. It is not surprising that Rachel can learn little that applies directly to her own predicament.

But in her feeling that the passionate, transcendent love of Cathy and Heathcliff offers no enlightenment, there is a significant if only half-realized irony. Rachel's own love story, like Cathy's, is consummated in death. Despite Rachel's disavowal of congruence with Catherine Earnshaw, their struggle and its final resolution have much in common. Both heroines suffer delirious states in which each fears the self-surrender required by passional love. Each resists the concept of domesticity and the demands of married life; each dies with her deepest capacities for expressing passionate love unfulfilled. Cathy "solves" her dilemma of choosing between Heathcliff and Linton by dying; Rachel finds the same way out of her own problem of independence versus marriage to Hewet.

On the matter of Rachel's death, critics have generally been in a quandary. "It is typical of Mrs. Woolf's indifference to plot that the reason Rachel fell victim to the fever . . . is never made clear," says one.[39] In their search for clear reasons, itself an unproductive approach to Woolf's characteristic evasion of clear reasons, critics are likely to complain of the suddenness of Rachel's death, calling it a failure of aesthetic vision and design that leads to an improbable, arbitrary, unmotivated death.[40] Even if they do not argue that Rachel's death is unconvincing, its significance causes considerable divergence of opinion.

Several commentators approach Rachel's death as simply the natural end of life's voyage,[41] or a triumphant mystic attainment of true reality.[42] Other critics see the death as an insignificant event in the natural order of things, or as a deliberately meaningless existential absurdity.[43] The difficulty with such interpretations is that while none is emphatically "wrong," none is comprehensively "right," for none takes into full account Rachel's personality, which would be largely irrelevant to the illustration of any of those views. Woolf need not have given us such a *conflicted* heroine—a young woman withdrawn from life and fearful of love, who has declared "I shall never marry" (60), yet becomes engaged to Hewet; who finds neither strength nor will to recover from her mysterious, typhoidlike illness, despite the fact that she is on the threshold of life with presumably everything to live for.

In fact Rachel's disease and death have been very deftly related, with full aesthetic consistency, to her character structure and to her primary psychological dilemma. Confused and indecisive, Rachel is too fearful of losing the isolation she calls her "freedom" to enter fully into a demanding love relationship. Her illness and death occur only a few weeks after she becomes engaged to marry Hewet. As James Hafley puts it: "The very thing that is to redeem her—her love for Terence—is also to *cause* her death."[44] Her havens become progressively more detached: she moves from the impersonality of music played in the solitude of her room, to the hallucinatory confinement necessitated by her illness, and thence into the ultimate detachment of death. The delirious hallucinations of her fever are the ultimate expression of her personality tendencies, the ultimate disintegration of the integrity of the outside world, the ultimate loss of identity, the ultimate escape from the complexities of being and loving. Her need for the most radical forms of independence and detachment can find perfect satisfaction only in death.

In the climactic chapter of Rachel's delirium and death, Woolf exploits the full powers of allusion, embedding a quotation from Milton in the opening scene. It is glaringly placed, a veritable trumpet blast, yet most critics apparently do not believe it has anything *significant* to do with Rachel's illness and death. One of them, after identifying the source as *Comus*, has asserted: "The maiden enthralled in a magic spell, as well as the water and thirst parallel, crassly highlight the coming throes of fever."[45] If the *Comus* allusion merely served as an elaborate metaphor for the physiology of fever, it might indeed be "crass." But in reality it is the vehicle of such compacted meaning, crowded with implication, that it cannot be dismissed or ignored.

The atmosphere of Rachel's illness and death is one of vague oppression: shimmering, overheated air; the exhausted breaking of waves upon the shore; white flowers wilting in the merciless sun. Terence Hewet is reading aloud from Milton, after trying several other works, because Milton has "substance and shape" and can "withstand the power of the sun" (326):

> There is a gentle nymph not far from hence,

he read,

> That with moist curb sways the smooth Severn stream.
> Sabrina is her name, a virgin pure;
> Whilom she was the daughter of Locrine,
> That had the sceptre from his father Brute. (326)

The question is simple, if the answer less so: why *this* quotation? Why the insistence that only Milton's *Comus* will do, with its elaborate, allusive diction?

That *Comus* is a masque should alert readers to the growing inappropriateness of realistic standards, to the heavily symbolic and allegorical direction in which Woolf's novel is moving. As Northrop Frye has explained it, a masque "at its most concentrated, becomes the interior of the human mind," a psychic drama of moral conflict and lost direction.[46] Milton's masque pits a licentious, villainous Comus, possessed of magical powers, against a virtuous Lady lost in the wood. It is a battle of sexual indulgence against chastity and abstention, a drama of the trial-by-fire of beseiged virginity.

Early in her portrait of Rachel, Woolf underlined Rachel's conflict of independence and sexual involvement through an allusion to Meredith's heroine in *Diana of the Crossways*. The *Comus* allusion reiterates the same conflict in larger, allegorical terms. Indeed *Comus* is an allusive restatement of Rachel's dilemma: marriage to Hewet would put her virtue—in the sense not only of her chastity but of her inviolate freedom—in jeopardy: "Love vertue, she alone is free" (l. 1019), *Comus* commands. Rachel's refusal to give up her innocent independence is akin to the Lady's imperious resistance to the alluring arguments of Comus: "Thou canst not touch the freedom of my minde / With all thy charms" (ll. 663–64).[47]

Hewet reads aloud the lines describing Sabrina's origin, which are spoken by the Attendant Spirit who defends maidens from harm. Rachel's reaction is intense:

> The words, in spite of what Terence said, seemed to be laden with meaning, and perhaps it was for this reason that it was painful to listen to them; they sounded strange; they meant different things from what they usually meant. Rachel at any rate could not keep her attention fixed upon them, but went off upon curious trains of thought suggested by words such as "curb" and "Locrine" and

"Brute," which brought unpleasant sights before her eyes, independently of their meaning. (326–27)

Locrine and Brute are themselves allusions within the *Comus* allusion. Brute's son Locrine married Gwendolen, but took Estrildis as his mistress, and Estrildis gave birth to a beautiful daughter, Sabrina.[48] Independent of their Miltonic meaning, however, Rachel finds the words *brute*, *Locrine* and *curb* unpleasant—no doubt because they reveal her deepest subjective fears. Milton used *curb* as a noun; as a verb it means restraint and control, the opposite of that unrestricted freedom for which Rachel yearns. *Brute* can mean "a brute"; Rachel has previously exclaimed: " 'Men are brutes! I hate men!' " (82), just as Evelyn Murgatroyd had accused men of having "nothing but their beastly passions and their brute strength!" (247). According to *Comus*, a lustful soul "grows clotted by contagion, / Imbodies, and *imbrutes*" (ll. 467–68, italics mine). *Locrine* contains within it the Latin *crin*, and *hair* has been an emblem of repellent masculinity in this novel. Evelyn says after being kissed,-" 'the disgusting brute—I can still feel his nasty hairy face' " (247); the doctor who first tends Rachel has "very hairy hands" (329), a "hairy wrist" (333), and an "unintelligent hairy face" (338).

These unsavory associations seem almost to *cause* Rachel's mysterious headache:

> Her head almost certainly ached. She was not quite certain, and therefore she did not know, whether to tell Terence now, or to let him go on reading. She decided that she would wait until he came to the end of a stanza, and if by that time she had turned her head this way and that, and it ached in every position undoubtedly, she would say very calmly that her head ached. (327)

What Rachel lets Hewet "go on reading" is the rest of the Attendant Spirit's speech, which details Sabrina's transformation into a Goddess after her death and describes her powers:

> And, as the old Swain said, she can unlock
> The clasping charm and thaw the numbing spell,
> If she be right invok'd in warbled Song,
> For maid'nhood she loves, and will be swift
> To aid a Virgin, such as was herself,
> In hard besetting need. This will I try
> And add the power of some adjuring verse.
>
> (*Comus*, 852–58)

While Woolf does not reproduce these lines for readers, she does have Rachel remain long enough to hear Hewet read the "adjuring verse" with which the Spirit summons up Sabrina:

Sabrina fair,
  Listen where thou art sitting
Under the glassy, cool, translucent wave,
  In twisted braids of lilies knitting
The loose train of thy amber dropping hair,
Listen for dear honour's sake,
  Goddess of the silver lake,
  Listen and save!

But her head ached; it ached whichever way she turned it.
  She sat up and said as she had determined, "My head aches so that I shall go indoors."
  He was halfway through the next verse, but he dropped the book instantly. (327)

After hearing this disguised, symbolic telegraph message to her unconscious, this command to Sabrina to rescue "insnared chastity," Rachel must flee. Hewet is halfway through the next verse, in which the Spirit again repeats his invocation to Sabrina to answer "our summons" and "Listen and save" (ll.888–89).[49] Marriage and motherhood are not the *solution* but the *source* of Rachel's conflicts, as the allusion helps make clear.
  The situation between Terence and Rachel resolves itself thus:

"Your head aches?" he repeated. For a few moments they sat looking at one another in silence, holding each other's hands. During this time his sense of dismay and catastrophe were almost physically painful; all round him he seemed to hear the shiver of broken glass which, as it fell to earth, left him sitting in the open air. (327)

No critic has commented upon this puzzling "shiver of broken glass," possibly because it is so jarringly unrealistic, even hallucinatory. Yet the image is understandable in terms of the meanings that the *Comus* allusion adds to the text. Milton's Comus offered the bewitched Lady a Glass, "this cordial Julep here / That flames" (ll.672–73), entreating her to "be wise, and taste" (l. 813). At precisely that point, the Lady's brothers rushed in, wresting the glass from Comus' hand and breaking it on the ground. In Woolf's masterful symmetry of symbolic analogy, Hewet too hears broken glass fall to earth. The cup of pleasure has been broken. Neither Milton's Lady nor Rachel Vinrace will taste of the sensual delight offered them by seductive men.
  When Rachel retires to her bedroom, the Spirit's plea to Sabrina persists in her mind:

Her chief occupation during the day was to try to remember how the lines went:

23

> Under the glassy, cool, translucent wave,
>   In twisted braids of lilies knitting
> The loose train of thy amber dropping hair;
>
> and the effort worried her because the adjectives persisted in getting
> into the wrong places. (329)

Her effort to remember the lines is her call to Sabrina to break the spell
and deliver her from sexual temptation. Her own "enchantment" (that is,
delirious illness) is about to be broken by Sabrina, the agent of her
redemption:

> The second day did not differ very much from the first day,
> except that her head had become very important, and the world
> outside, when she tried to think of it, appeared distinctly further
> off. The glassy, cool translucent wave was almost visible before her,
> curling up at the end of the bed, and as it was refreshingly cool, she
> tried to keep her mind fixed upon it. (329)

Milton's "glassy, cool, translucent wave" is no longer set off with quotation marks as a "foreign" quotation; it is now thoroughly integrated into
Woolf's own narrative. Not content with mechanical, verbatim repetition, Woolf extends her characteristic strategy of repetition to the allusion, subjecting it to further development and expansion.

On the seventh day of Rachel's illness, hallucinations of escape
trouble her feverish brain, and the Miltonic image undergoes a further
transformation:

> she fell into a deep pool of sticky water, which eventually closed
> over her head. She saw nothing and heard nothing but a faint
> booming sound, which was the sound of the sea rolling over her
> head. While all her tormentors thought that she was dead, she was
> not dead, but curled up at the bottom of the sea. There she lay,
> sometimes seeing darkness, sometimes light. . . . (341)

From Sabrina's cool wave to the sticky pool of fevered delirium—Woolf
moves Rachel closer to her ominous fate. As she becomes progressively
more passive, the wave supports Rachel's voluntary acquiescence: "She
had come to the surface of the dark, sticky pool, and a wave seemed to
bear her up and down with it; she had ceased to have any will of her
own; she lay on top of the wave conscious of some pain, but chiefly of
weakness" (346). Finally Rachel's bed and that wave become synony-
mous: "But for long spaces of time she would merely lie conscious of her
body floating on the top of the bed" (347).

This extended sequence is the penultimate instance of the water
imagery that has been central to the novel's meaning from the beginning.

And that water imagery has often been reinforced by other allusions: to the Sirens, to Cowper's "Toll for the Brave," to Shakespeare's "Full fathom five." That Rachel must escape *under water* from those she calls "tormentors" (341) is given its most forceful expression in the various transmogrifications of parallels to Sabrina, however. The *Comus* allusion integrates previous allusions, figures of speech, and psychology; that is to say, it makes an organic whole of the recurrent water imagery and Rachel's personality conflict. Two particularly revealing incidents anticipate the appearance of the *Comus* allusion; they indicate just how successfully *Comus* finally does come to integrate the separate strands of imagery. In the first:

> He [Hewet] caught her in his arms as she passed him, and they fought for mastery, imagining a rock, and the sea heaving beneath them. At last she was thrown to the floor, where she lay gasping, and crying for mercy.
> "I'm a mermaid! I can swim!" she cried, "so the game's up." Her dress was torn across, and peace being established, she fetched a needle and began to mend the tear. (298)

Considerably in advance of her delirium, this passage reveals Rachel's propensity to escape from normal sexual demands, and to effect that escape by means of the sea. Even in this earlier scene, Hewet already is to Rachel what Comus was to Milton's Lady—the potential violator of her solitary freedom and her virginity, which is symbolized by her torn dress after playing at lovemaking with Hewet.

The other masterful linkage of the *Comus* allusion to Rachel's final hallucination-haunted delirium involves the terrifying dream Rachel had early in the novel, after Richard Dalloway impulsively kisses her. All three incidents—allusion, delirium, and dream—externalize, in surrealistic images, the heroine's innermost world of sexual fears. The bestial appearances of Comus and his company ("a rout of monsters headed like sundry sorts of wild beasts," *Comus*, ll. 92 ff.) are anticipated *more than two hundred pages earlier* in Rachel's nightmare of being trapped with "a little deformed man" whose pitted face was "like the face of an animal" (77). In her delirium Rachel has a similar hallucination of "the movement of an animal in the room" (328). The threatening sexual implications of *Comus* were explicit in Rachel's early dream: "She felt herself pursued. . . . A voice moaned for her; eyes desired her" (77). These "barbarian men" (77) who first disturbed Rachel's sleep with unquiet dreams reappear in *Comus'* suggestive words, *brute* and *Locrine*. Their final manifestation is in "the unintelligent, hairy face" (338) of Dr. Rodriguez, whose medical powers and "spells" cannot save Rachel from her virginal, Sabrinan destiny under the wave of oblivion.

The long damp tunnel in Rachel's dream (77) recurs as "a tunnel under the Thames" (331) in her later delirium, echoing Milton's "smooth Severn stream" (l. 825).[50] In Rachel's dream the tunnel became "a vault" (77); in her delirium the tunnel has "archways" (331). According to *Comus*, the degraded, lustful soul is comparable to the "thick and gloomy shadows *damp* / Oft seen in charnel *vaults*" (ll. 470–71, italics mine). In the original story Sabrina's mother Estrildis was hidden away by Locrine in "a *chamber underground*" (*Historia Regum Britanniae*, 1, 4, italics mine). The full rhetorical power of these intricately interlocking images of tunnels, vaults, archways, and chambers is quite simply unavailable to readers who ignore the strategic *Comus* allusion.

Not only are the lines from *Comus* retroactively related to previous events, images, and allusions,[51] they are also a starting point. Standing at the head of the climactic chapter, they set the tone of, and help to determine, what is to follow. Even the description of the garden setting in which Terence Hewet is reading Milton echoes the setting of *Comus:* red flowers, white wilted blossoms, and the menacing heat of the sun, which suggests Milton's "Sun-clad power of Chastity" (*Comus*, l. 782). Most emphatically not a mere embellishment of style, the *Comus* allusion significantly informs the content and the structure of the novel. In its concern for "the sage and serious doctrine of Virginity" (ll. 786–87), it underscores Rachel's psychic conflict so that it may be even more emphatically perceived by readers. It bears so crucially upon her fate that any interpretation of her illness as *solely* physical, or as a mere accident of random fate, or as evidence of Woolf's alleged lack of literary skill in her first novel, can be seriously challenged.

Comus' conspicuous presence in the chapter necessitates a symbolic interpretation of the heroine's death. It insinuates a larger, latent meaning for Rachel's illness that is not contained in diagnostic symptoms of typhoid, though hints of that disease certainly are present. It invests Rachel's death with an ambiguous dimension that allows readers to propose more inclusive interpretations, which do the novel somewhat more justice than it has received. *Comus* helps us see that Rachel's illness is at least partially psychosomatic, that her death is half-intended self-destruction. If that death is not self-inflicted in the strictest sense, it is nevertheless quite consciously unresisted, for there is a clear absence of any will to recover in Rachel Vinrace at the end. This suicidal personality factor is implied by the *Comus* allusion: "Sabrina, the water spirit, *a lovely death-wish,* has come for her [i.e., Rachel]."[52] Sabrina and her saving wave rescue Virginia Woolf's own Lady from her certain sexual fate of marriage. Rachel's death, like Sabrina's, is the most radical form of purity obtainable and the most uncompromising "solution" of her psychic dilemma.

When Rachel embraces death as her solution and Woolf offers it as her plot resolution, the deviation from the paradigm of Milton's Lady is most radical. Milton's Lady, freed from Comus' immoral sexual threat, lives to relinquish her physical virtue in the lawful context of marriage. But in Rachel there is a pervasive fear of sexual surrender that becomes a denial of sexuality now or in the future. Rachel's virginity is made permanent through death, as was Sabrina's when she "underwent a quick immortal change" to become "Goddess of the River" (*Comus*, ll. 841–42).

Woolf's use of the lines from *Comus* is aesthetically satisfying because it is such a successful subjugation of alien meanings from another work to her own unique and specific narrative purpose. The structural congruences of her heroine to the Lady or to Sabrina are sometimes expressed as parallelism, sometimes as bold antithesis. Woolf recreates and enlarges the reverberations of her chosen allusion so masterfully that *Comus* makes itself felt on all levels—setting, plot, structure, characterization, theme are all deepened by its presence.[53]

Two other quotations are used to establish the ominous mood that hangs over the scene as Rachel's illness worsens unto death. Ridley Ambrose, restless and helpless against her certain fate, takes to his idiosyncratic declamations of poetry, reciting as he paces:

> They wrestled up, they wrestled down,
>   They wrestled sore and still:
> The fiend who blinds the eyes of men,
>   That night he had his will.
> Like stags full spent, among the bent
>   They dropped awhile to rest— (350)

Intensifying the intimations of mortality that pervade the scene, these lines are from Charles Kingsley's ballad of Jane, a maid who dies "a widow and never a bride" (l. 60). They work "into the minds of Terence and St. John all the morning" (350), finally causing the latter to exclaim, " 'Oh, it's intolerable' " (350). And it *is* rather ironically intolerable for him: in less tragic times, he had been the one to disavow Kingsley's pious sentiments.

Ridley progresses from that ballad fragment to:

> stanzas of a long poem in a subdued but suddenly sonorous voice. Fragments of the poem were wafted in at the open window as he passed and repassed.

27

Peor and Baalim
Forsake their Temples dim,
  With that twice batter'd God of Palestine
And mooned Astaroth—

The sound of these words were [sic] strangely discomforting . . .
(351)

Like *Comus*, these lines from Milton's *Nativity* abound in classical and Biblical allusions.[54] Milton calls Peor and Baalim, false pagan divinities, a "damned crew" (25. 228); the phrase is an equally apt description of Comus the Antichrist and his band. They too are false oracles, stilled at last by truth. And because these lines belong to a larger context of purgation, they reiterate *Comus'* ambience of purgation and radical purification.

Hewet and Hirst find the lines "strangely discomforting." Perhaps equally discomforting is the point at which the quotation is cut off, for "mooned Astaroth" was the Phoenician equivalent of Aphrodite. According to Milton, this goddess of fecundity and love "now sits not girt with tapers' holy shrine" (22. 202). Put another way, all hope of love and fertility has fled the scene (along with sensual pleasure, earlier routed in the person of Milton's Comus).[55] As Hewet had read the Spirit's invocation of the saving nymph Sabrina, Ridley now invokes the defeat of other pagan gods before another kind of savior.[56] *All* of Milton's various "*brutish* gods"[57] are now defeated, to trouble Rachel no more. Unfortunately, the gods of sensuality and passion, love and fecundity, are not easily banished: Rachel Vinrace has had *to die* to accomplish their complete dismissal.[58] Woolf's use of allusions from Milton immeasurably deepens the import of her heroine's fate. With his help, Woolf helps readers draw a profound psychological moral from this, her first novel of Eros and Thanatos: the deepest reasons for living or dying are beyond "reasons" like fate, typhoid, or the author's faulty plotting. Inability to love fully is not "freedom." It is death.

As *The Voyage Out* opened with Ridley's four lines from Macaulay, it closes with his four lines from Milton. The use of literary allusion—structurally, symbolically, thematically, has come full circle. And confounding the usual expectations of scholars who like to deal with neat theories of progressively increasing mastery, Woolf has deployed literary allusions in her very first novel with the skill of an experienced master.

two

Jacob's Room

After *The Voyage Out* Woolf wrote *Night and Day*, another of her "novels of fact," and like its predecessor, a lengthy work saturated with literary allusions. Her third novel, *Jacob's Room*, also rich in allusions, is the first of those novels critics like to call "experimental." In it Woolf found a voice, a style, and a point of view distinctively hers. Yet *Jacob's Room* is not a total departure from previous novels. It shares with *The Voyage Out* the archetypal plot of the pilgrimage, and it ends in the premature death of its central character; one critic has called it "the masculine counterpart" of *The Voyage Out*.[1] Bridging the gap between the early novels and Woolf's experimental short stories, *Jacob's Room* truly "marks the beginning of her maturity and her fame."[2]

The language of *Jacob's Room* is figurative, approaching the intensity and concentration of poetry. It is quite likely that Woolf's knowledge of T.S. Eliot's poetry found its way into the novel; some of the striking congruences exist in a kind of limbo somewhere between what one would call general influence and actual allusion.[3] Much the same appears to be the case with Chekhov, whose stories (in translation by Constance Garnett) Woolf had reviewed in 1918 and 1919. An exquisitely sad Chekhovian atmosphere permeates *Jacob's Room;* for example, this observation: "In any case, life is but a procession of shadows, and God knows why it is that we embrace them so eagerly, and see them depart with such anguish, being shadows" (72). Moreover, Woolf and Chekhov share two convictions: that life is essentially an unknowable mystery, and that human communication is extremely difficult, if not impossible. As if to make the similarity explicit, Woolf has one of the characters give Jacob a volume of Chekhov's stories.

In her essay "Modern Fiction," which predates *Jacob's Room*, Woolf had discussed Chekhov's "Gusev." There is in the "Gusev" story a "huge bull's head," which matches the recurring sheep's skull in *Jacob's Room*, and Gusev is a soldier who suffers the same inconsequential death in battle as Jacob. The thematic resolution of both the Chekhov story and the Woolf novel is that one life is over, but Life goes on. Woolf focuses on the objects in Jacob's room after he dies; Chekhov describes the clouds, sky, and ocean immediately after Gusev's body is consigned to the sea. In fact Woolf's comments on "Gusev" show us exactly how to read her own novel:

> We are given a few scraps of their talk and some of their thoughts; then one of them dies . . . The emphasis is laid upon such unexpected places that at first it seems as if there were no emphasis at all; and then, as the eyes accustom themselves to twilight and discover *the shapes of things in a room* we see how complete the story is, how profound, and how truly in obedience to his vision Tchekov has chosen this, that and the other, and placed them together to compose something new.[4]

Scraps of talk, unexpected emphases, the shapes of things in a room—of such stuff is *Jacob's Room* made. Readers soon learn to accept its large doses of uncertainty and irony, and they learn that the unseizable, enigmatic qualities of the work in general apply to the matter of literary allusion in particular.

For example, the technique of characterization through allusive naming considerably enriches the ironic texture of *Jacob's Room*. A teasing significance is implied; the names "have reference, but no meaning. . . . Virginia Woolf exploits semantic satiation to indicate this."[5] There are evocative names like Seabrook, and the implicit irony of names like Mrs. Grandage and Miss Wargrave; Jacob's friend, Richard Bonamy, is an Anglicized version of a *bon ami*.[6] A few of the given names and several of the surnames Woolf bestows upon her minor characters are encapsulated allusions, conjuring up actual literary figures or fictional characters. The hero's surname evokes the battlefield of Flanders, foreshadowing his death in World War I, and his first name introduces Biblical dimensions, most of which are decidedly ironic.

As the Biblical Jacob was favored of God[7] and one of the heirs of divine promise (Heb. 11:9), so Jacob Flanders has "a sense of . . . himself the inheritor" (45). And like his Biblical counterpart, Woolf's Jacob becomes a wandering pilgrim hoping to preserve his birthright. But the Biblical Jacob's quest was a religious one in which he declared, "for I have seen God face to face, and my life is preserved" (Gen. 32:30); his persistent struggles culminated in a divine blessing for himself and that which he represented, the nation of Israel. Jacob Flanders's life struggle with the angel of mortality ends in an obscure death, an empty room, and a pair of shoes—themselves something of an ironically resonant symbol for piety, poverty, and humility. Woolf's Jacob never sees personal and national importance, the special love of God, or the success of his worldly struggles. His demise invites comparison with the gloomy vision of the victory of the heathen, who "have devoured Jacob, and laid

waste his dwelling place" (Ps. 79:7). Modern civilization is life-destroy-
ing; it cannot be revitalized by young Jacobs. They cannot supplant the
treacherous Esaus of this world and achieve their rightful spiritual inheritance; their wholeness is frustrated by a fragmented culture that
brings about the untimely deaths of its promising young men.[8] Woolf
even capitalizes upon the physical "props" associated with the Biblical
Jacob—grape vines and ladder—in the following incident: " 'There's
another bunch higher up,' murmured Clara Durrant, mounting another
step of the ladder. Jacob held the ladder as she stretched out to reach the
grapes high up ,on the vine" (62).[9] The scene can be read as manifest
evidence of the love Clara feels for Jacob,[10] but it also has an ironic
resonance related to its Biblical dimension—Jacob is no patriarch capable
of founding a nation, no tragic hero capable of ascending to extraordinary heights: he is not even the one climbing the ladder and picking the
grapes.

While such extensive use of allusive naming may be a new refinement of Woolf's technique, allusive characterization (of a raft of secondary characters) is not; she continues to project personalities via literary
allusion. Jacob's friend, Bonamy, that Lytton Strachey figure[11] who is
indifferent to women and whose "peculiar disposition [was] long ru-
mored among them" (154), is introduced much as his ancestor St. John
Hirst was—reading. Perhaps his book is Keats,[12] perhaps it is about "the
Holy Roman Empire" (43)—and in that suggestion of Gibbon resides
another similarity to Hirst. Eventually we learn that the book *is* Keats
(43) and that Bonamy likes to read "all those Frenchmen" (72), while
information as to which Frenchmen and which works is withheld.[13] In
conversation with his friend, Jacob defends "poor old Tennyson" (72), so
presumably Bonamy does not like that distinguished Victorian's works,
but which works and why not remain a mystery. Bonamy is possessed of
"a Wellington nose" (69, 85); that statesman was extravagantly praised in
Tennyson's *Ode on the Death of the Duke of Wellington*. In fact Tennyson's
"last great Englishman" of "long-enduring blood. . . . Whole in himself,
a common good" is mocked in Bonamy, whose nose is the sole basis of
comparison.

Bonamy likes "books whose virtue is all drawn together in a page or
two" and "sentences that don't budge though armies cross them" (140).
There is, then, a certain justice in his preference for the fabled lucidity
and precision of French literature; but there is also his admiration for a
passionate sensualist like Keats. The inconsistency is compounded by his
condescension to Jacob for having "this romantic vein" (140) in him.
Woolf is here using her characterizing allusions in such a way as to
complement the novel's theme of the mysterious unknowability of
others.

There is quite a gallery of minor female characters, allusively sketched. One of them, Mrs. Sally Duggan, is "putting the life of Father Damien into verse" (153), exactly as Terence Hewet's aunt "put the life of Father Damien into verse" (*The Voyage Out*, 141).[14] In both instances, Woolf uses the reference to suggest an unwholesome obsession with religious values. Hewet considered his aunt "a religious fanatic" (*The Voyage Out*, 141), and the narrator of *Jacob's Room* informs us that Mrs. Duggan "had lost everything—everything in the world, husband and child and everything, but faith remained" (153).

Somewhat like Mrs. Flushing and Mrs. Thornbury in *The Voyage Out*, who (respectively) hated and revered Shakespeare, Lady Hibbert in *Jacob's Room* declares: " 'I had all Shakespeare by heart before I was in my teens' " (86). Mrs. Papworth, a rather salty domestic, uses a Biblical allusion as a simile when she observes "Sanders [i.e., Flanders, Jacob] and Bonamy like two bulls of Bashan driving each other up and down, making such a racket" (102). The image suggests Mrs. Papworth's slightly shocked sense of sexuality and is perhaps an ironic comment upon the potency of Bonamy or Jacob. A certain Lady Charles comes home from the opera, "sighs sadly as she ascends her staircase,[15] takes down Thomas a Kempis," and cannot sleep for asking "Why? Why? Why?" (68). The Kempis reference complements the other Biblical allusions in the novel, keeps "spiritual" issues in the reader's mind, and deepens Woolf's ironic undercutting of just those significant issues which she has evoked. Mrs. Durrant, another sleepless lady who resorts to reading, marks "certain lines in the *Inferno*" (77). The narrator leaves unspecified *which* lines, but visions of a journey through Hell and the landscape of sin and punishment have been evoked.[16]

Julia Hedge, the feminist ("death and gall and bitter dust were on her pen-tip," 106) inhabits the reading room of the British Museum. Contemplating the names of the great men that circle the dome, she cries out " 'Oh damn . . . why didn't they leave room for an Eliot or a Bronte?' " (106). In that angry yet poignant question all of Virginia Woolf's own feminism is lodged. Julia has invoked half of that company of women writers whom Virginia Woolf considered "great."[17]

Then there is Miss Umphelby, who lectures on Virgil. Although she "sings him melodiously enough, accurately too," her lectures are "not half so well attended as those of Cowan" (42). Professor Cowan at his worst is a mere technician of strict scholarship, "ruling lines between names, hanging lists above doors" (42). Miss Umphelby at her worst is a caricature of the feminine impulse to reduce large issues to subjective triviality, so that Virgil becomes a matter of " 'But if I met him, what should I wear?' " (42).

The narrator observes of a Mrs. Norman, who occupies the same train compartment as Jacob, "Nobody sees anyone as he is, let alone an elderly lady sitting opposite a strange young man in a railway carriage. They see a whole—they see all sorts of things—they see themselves. . . . Mrs. Norman now read three pages of one of Mr. Norris's novels" (30–31). With the help of this allusion, the reader is placed in the same frustrating relationship to Mrs. Norman as she is to Jacob. Mrs. Norman can no more fathom Jacob's character from the few trivial clues of his physique, loose socks, and shabby tie (30) than the reader can fathom *her* character from the teasing clue of Norris novels. Which Norris is Mrs. Norman reading? which novel of which Norris? which three pages? The reader might make a proper guess only if he were armed with *extrinsic* knowledge of Woolf,[18] but having just the text before him, he finds that he must settle for the narrator's "One must do the best one can with her report" (31).

Quite a few of the secondary women characters have a direct bearing upon Jacob's life. Indeed we see Jacob largely through the eyes of the *women* who know him. His mother, Betty Flanders, is a relatively rare phenomenon in Woolf fiction—a character bereft of literary allusion, except for the unidentified fairy tale she tells to the infant Jacob. Protecting her son against the threatening intrusion of a storm brewing outside, she pits her fairy-tale defense, a feminine re-creation of a nicer, less dangerous world.

The girls of dubious reputation with whom Jacob later consorts epitomize the inner emptiness of outwardly exciting metropolitan life. He meets Florinda at the Guy Fawkes bonfire; she is wearing "the conical white hat of a pierrot" (74, 77), which suggests her frivolity and rather sarcastically implies her Pierrette superficiality as a clown-lover. He is astoundingly naive and sentimental about her: he thinks prostitutes have "an inviolable fidelity. Then he saw her turning up Greek Street upon another man's arm" (94). The reference to Greek Street, added to Florinda's virginal name, only compounds the irony. Jacob, who reveres the Greeks, has mistakenly supposed Florinda to be an embodiment of the spirit of Greek culture, "free, venturesome, highspirited" (76). She is, in fact, "ignorant as an owl" (79). She assays literature thus: "First she washed her head; then ate chocolate creams; then opened Shelley. True, she was horribly bored. What on earth was it *about?*" (78).[19]

Jacob recovers from the disaster of Florinda with an artist's model, Fanny Elmer. She too pines for literary enlightenment, albeit with greater ambition and capacities than Florinda: "She . . . would learn Latin and read Virgil. She had been a great reader. She had read Scott; she had read Dumas" (121).[20] The contrast between her might-be reading of Virgil in Latin and her actual reading of Scott and Dumas makes a satiric point of its own. Scott is probable, but Dumas seems even more likely. There is of course the problem of the deliberately imprecise allusion: which Alexandre Dumas, *père* or *fils?* In *père*, Fanny would find exciting narratives of adventure and romance; in *fils* a preoccupation with sex and money. *La Dame aux Camélias* is not exactly without relevance for a latter-day courtesan like Fanny.

Fanny reads Fielding with much the same effect that Shelley had upon Florinda: "This dull stuff (Fanny thought) about people with odd names is what Jacob likes" (122). She decides that she would have liked *Tom Jones* "if I had been educated" (122), and does not hesitate to profess a dishonest admiration of the work to Jacob. When he announces that he is going to Greece, Fanny, feeling deserted, "thought it all came from *Tom Jones*" (123, 124). She sees in Fielding's hero an unfortunate paradigm for Jacob of picaresque adventures and a crowded amorous career.

Indeed Jacob advances to that stage of a male's amorous adventures which entails falling in love with an older married woman. In Greece he meets the vain Sandra Wentworth Williams, who studies her beauty in mirrors, poses dramatically against ruins, and imagines herself to be made in the heroic image of Grecian womanhood. There are repeated ironic-Homeric descriptions of her: "She stood, veiled, in white, in the window of the hotel at Olympia" (141–42); or, "Sandra rode opposite, dominant, like a victory prepared to fling into the air" (147). Woolf makes *her* the reader of those "stories by Tchekov" (141), in which she discovers "something very profound . . . about love and sadness and the peasants" (143). Sandra's Chekhov stories are in "a little book convenient for travelling" (141), and her volume of Balzac is merely part of her evening costume—yellow dress with purple spots, black hat, matching book (145).

Sandra judges Jacob to be "credulous as yet" (161) and suspects him of being "a mere bumpkin" (153).[21] She addresses herself to his mysterious personality in allusive terms:

> "He is," she mused, "like that man in Moliere."
> She meant Alceste. She meant that he was severe. She meant that she could not deceive him . . . .
> "He's a small boy," she said, thinking of Jacob.
> And yet—Alceste? (169)

Through Sandra's comparison of Jacob to Alceste, Woolf reiterates Jacob's paradoxical complexity, his innocent foolishness combined with intellectual severity. Sandra finds Jacob "severe," and the narrator notes "something caustic" (159) in him; this certainly makes him kin to the hero of Molière's *Le Misanthrope* and his opinions of society's hypocrisy.

There is Jacob's furious response to literary censorship; his merciless opinion of the toadying Everard Benson, who gave "tea parties in his rooms (which were in the style of Whistler, with pretty books on tables), all this, so Jacob felt without knowing him, made him a contemptible ass" (104); his admiration for achievement and courage: " 'Shakespeare had more guts than all these damned frogs put together' " (126). And when Jacob bids a ticket-collector to " 'Go and get drunk' " (170) on his half-crown tip, he is the quintessential misanthrope.

Just as Alceste's desire to be sincere and genuine was distorted by his enormous egotism, Jacob too can be blindly egocentric, "boastful, triumphant," feeling he had "read every book in the world; known every sin, passion, and joy" and believing that he and Timmy Durrant " 'are the only people in the world who know what the Greeks meant' " (76). Yet he and Timmy quote Greek at each other quite heedlessly: "Durrant never listened to Sophocles, nor Jacob to Aeschylus" (76). Despite his high praise for Shakespeare's plays, Jacob has never "managed to read one through" (47). Despite his reverence for Greek literature, "Jacob knew no more Greek than served him to stumble through a play" (76). And despite Jacob's admirable qualities, the narrator is not unaware of "endowing Jacob Flanders with all sorts of qualities he had not at all . . . half of what he said was too dull to repeat; much unintelligible" (73).

Like George Eliot's idiot-Jacob, who could distinguish between good and evil, Jacob is "convinced of . . . the clear division between right and wrong" (44). He believes "the future depends entirely upon six young men. And as Jacob was one of them, no doubt he looked a little regal and pompous" (107). Looking "regal and pompous" and contemplating his part in changing the future of the world, Jacob echoes Alceste's hubristic belief that his personal honor can transform society's vices. But his intentions are defeated by the prevailing *Zeitgeist*, which shatters his personal fulfillment by killing him in its war. Finally Woolf has chosen her allusive metaphor so well that not only is Jacob analogous to Alceste, but Sandra is roughly equivalent to Celimène, Molière's flirtatious and vain coquette.

Clara Durrant is another woman in Jacob's life. Not surprisingly, a young woman whose name invokes *claritas* or pure radiance is the exact opposite of Fanny and Florinda. Clara is "a flawless mind: a candid nature; a virgin chained to a rock" (123); she lives a life of stifling conventionality.[22] When an unsuccessful suitor writes verses addressed to Chloe, the literal-minded Clara thinks him a "ridiculous young man" (85). She is uninspiringly "typical"; the reference to Chloe, that cliche name for maidens and shepherdesses in poetry, catches just that quality.[23]

However, it is not as cliche Chloe but in a more specifically mythological context that the narrator places Clara. While she is walking her dog, her companion Mr. Bowley observes that she looks "like a huntress . . . some pale virgin with a slip of the moon in her hair" (166). In this sly evocation of the cold, chaste Diana, even that goddess's attendance by dogs has not been overlooked.[24]

By far the most interesting woman in the novel is the narrator, who assumes the role of a character. This intrusive, garrulous female, who is thirty-five years old and addresses us directly, has been vividly described by one critic as "a sort of super-jackdaw who deposits in the reader's lap bright fragments of description, summaries, catalogues, tiny morsels of dialogue, brief flashes of characterization, hints and hieroglyphs."[25] Her linguistic repertory includes rhetorical questions, revelatory asides, vivid figures of speech, and allusive observations like "it is generally agreed that wit deserted beautiful lips about the time that Walpole died" (68).[26] This Walpole allusion prepares readers for the narrator's subsequent mini-essay on letters (92–94), in which Byron and Cowper are offered as prime examples of writers who composed immortal poetry, but who also chose to write mortal letters ("the sheet that perishes"), addressing themselves "to the task of reaching, touching, penetrating the individual heart."

In another glancing remark that perhaps is not strictly an allusion, the narrator speaks of "the old pageant of armies drawn out in battle array upon the plain" (163), using images strongly reminiscent of those with which Matthew Arnold closes "Dover Beach." And she notes Bonamy's fierce expression while reading Keats, to ask, "Why? Only perhaps that Keats died young—one wants to write poetry too and to love— oh, the brutes! It's damnably difficult" (44).[27] The narrator calls Shakespeare's plays and Shelley's *Adonais* "sovereign specifics for all disorders of the soul" (78), repeating this brace of allusions, in reverse order, on the next page. Shelley's elegy is relevant to several aspects of Woolf's novel. The poem, itself allusively named, is an elegy on the death of John Keats, himself one of the allusions in *Jacob's Room*. Since Adonais symbolizes the young man of promise who dies tragically young, the comparison applies not only to Keats but Shelley himself, and to Jacob Flanders. Moreover, the narrator often uses diction and images out of Shelley; for example, "Draw the veil thicker lest I faint with sweetness" (118) and "We start transparent, and then the cloud thickens. All history backs our pane of glass" (49).

Or we find the narrator commenting on "the Greek myth":

First you read Xenophon;[28] then Euripides. One day—that was an occasion, by God—what people have said appears to have sense in it; "the Greek spirit;" the Greek this, that, and the other; though it is absurd, by the way, to say that any Greek comes near Shakespeare. The point is, however, that we have been brought up in an illusion. (138)

Jacob considers Greece "the height of civilization" (164), and he hopes to find direction, identity, and fulfillment there, but his odyssey is futile because it is prompted by illusory idealizations and false expectations of perfection.

The narrator returns to Shakespeare in the scene in which Jacob and his friend Timmy Durrant are sailing to the Scilly Isles: "What's the use of trying to read Shakespeare, especially in one of those little thin paper editions whose pages get ruffled, or stuck together with sea-water?" (47). Because of the insistent metonymy, Shakespeare is felt as a *presence* ("with Shakespeare on board"), which represents the highest and best. When the volume falls into the water—its fragility having been carefully established by the narrator's description—the event becomes a cultural loss sustained by careless modern society: "Shakespeare was knocked overboard . . . and then he went under" (48).

In another Shakespearean incident (88), Jacob and Clara hear the last stanza of "Who Is Sylvia?" sung at a party. The lines help to suggest Clara's personality—that of a beauty who is "holy, fair and wise" and somewhat unapproachable—and they supplement the Diana allusion by presenting Clara as a goddess who "excels each mortal thing" and deserves the tribute of garlands. Then too, the song's interrogatory quality reinforces the strains of doubt and uncertainty that pervade this novel: who is Sylvia? who is anybody? how can we ever know one another?

In addition to straightforward comments on literature, the garrulous narrator makes allusive remarks about the various settings of *Jacob's Room*. There is a reference to Waverley in which she disavows the very allusiveness summoned up by the name: " 'Waverley,' the villa on the road to Girton was called, not that Mr. Plumer admired Scott . . . but names are useful" (33).[29] In one passage the elements of the scene described include a man "reading half a page of *Lothair* at the bookstall" (113). This gratuitous observation is not so arbitrary or irrelevant as might be supposed. In Disraeli's *Lothair* the central character searches for self-realization in modern society, and ultimately finds his identity in religious duty.[30] If we add the *Lothair* allusion to Jacob's Biblical associations, the ironic and religious dimensions of the novel are expanded. In a description of the Italian landscape, the narrator invokes classical literature:

"There were trees laced together with vines, as Virgil said. . . . Virgil's bees had gone about the plains of Lombardy" (135).

When Jacob goes to the British Museum to read Marlowe, the narrator offers the following reason:

> Youth, youth—something savage—something pedantic. For example, there is Mr. Masefield, there is Mr. Bennett. Stuff them into the flame of Marlowe and burn them to cinders. Let not a shred remain. Don't palter with the second rate. Detest your own age. Build a better one. (107)

This passage has been misread by critics who attribute to Jacob the expressed sentiments of our literate narrator.[31] In any case the error is understandable, for the opinions echo Woolf's own on the mediocrity of Bennett and Masefield.[32]

When she describes the British Museum where Jacob is working, the narrator represents it as a monument to intellect in which the life of the mind is vividly manifest. The Museum shelters "the visions and heat of . . . Plato's brain and Shakespeare's" (109); the literature of "Rome, Greece, China, India, Persia" (107) is sequestered here; the names on the dome include Plato and Aristotle, Sophocles and Shakespeare, Macaulay and Gibbon. Most often invoked as the personification of that "enormous mind" which is the Museum are Plato and Shakespeare: each is mentioned six times within a few pages (107–9) and they are paired three times on one page alone (109). Christopher Marlowe, the subject of Jacob's investigations, is mentioned five times within this section. Thus does Woolf make palpable for readers "this density of thought, this conglomeration of knowledge" (108).[33]

The narrator's respect for the intellectual quest is apparent in the description of the British Museum. But praise for the *agents* of learning—scholars, professors, the assorted researchers in the Reading Room—is scarce. The three middle-aged Cambridge dons in *Jacob's Room* stand accused by the narrator of perpetuating fragmentation, trivia, facile classifications, and oversimplified facts. They have broken the vital linkage of life to thought and feeling. Professor Erasmus Cowan is "Virgil's representative among us," but Virgil would scarcely recognize himself: "What if the poet strode in? '*This* my image?' he might ask, pointing to the chubby man" (41). The noble study of Virgil does not redeem the professor's timidity: "And as for arms, bees, or even the plough, Cowan takes his trips abroad with a French novel in his pocket, a rug about his knees, and is thankful to be home again in his place, in his line" (41). Professor Huxtable has a brain "populous with ideas" (40); one suspects the reference to his "great full brow" (40) may be an ironic invocation of the Greek meaning of *Plato*. He cannot, however, subdue the frightening complexities of reality with his rigorously controlled intellect; he sits "gripping the arm of the chair, like a man holding fast because stranded" (40). Huxtable is a man so learned that he writes "all his letters in Greek" (108), yet no literary allusions comprise his characterization. Professor Sopwith, who cuts chocolate cake for visiting undergraduates, is also bereft of allusions. This allusive poverty is deft indication of the professor's inability to unite personal and intellectual qualities, a subtle illustration of that divorce of life from literature which so distressed Woolf.

It is the bookshelves of George Plumer that provoke the narrator's most severe censure: "Books were on his shelves by Wells and Shaw; on the table serious sixpenny weeklies written by pale men in muddy boots—the weekly creak and screech of brains rinsed in cold water and wrung dry—melancholy papers" (35). Presumably such literary fare suits George Plumer's "cold grey eyes" and the "abstract light" (35) in them. Shaw and Wells symbolize "the triviality and intellectual poverty of Mr. Plumer's mind," as do the scorned sixpenny weeklies.[34] Indeed more than one dozen different newspapers and magazines are named in *Jacob's Room*. Like the purely literary allusions, they contribute (ironically) to an intensification of the epistemological theme. Amid this glut of attempts to communicate—telephones, newspapers, letters—there is only the reality of our *failure* to decipher others. The essential mystery of personality forever eludes us, and the various forms of mass communication leave us more isolated than ever.

The only other character to rival the female narrator in interest and complexity is the hero himself. Along with the narrator and the other characters in the novel, readers must engage in a Biblical search: we are all "them that seek him, that seek thy face, O Jacob" (Ps. 24:6). The quest, aided all along the way by Woolf's allusiveness, may be discontinuous, but it is chronological, for it follows Jacob from childhood to premature death.

Trailing ironic clouds of Biblical glory behind him, Jacob grows into adolescence. When the scholarly Reverend Floyd allows the three Flanders brothers "to choose whatever they liked in his study to remember him by" (21), Jacob, whose mother finds him her most disobedient son, a "naughty little boy" (10), selects "the works of Byron in one volume" (21–22). One critic has called this Byron allusion Woolf's first "masterful use of condensed symbols,"[35] noting that several of Jacob's character traits—"love of learning, admiration for Greece, a rebellious nature, . . . the effect he had on women, especially rather stupid or uneducated women unable to stand up to him"[36]—are symbolized by his early identification with Byron.

Byron was for Woolf very nearly as ambivalent a figure as Jacob is for readers. Woolf was skeptical, resistant, even mocking of Byron. She could say she "would not cross the road" to dine with Byron,[37] or complain that Byron seemed "tawdry and melodramatic,"[38] yet she felt compelled to acknowledge in Byron's "confident, dogmatic" manner a "superb force . . . a thoroughly masculine nature."[39] When Jacob chooses Byron he chooses a masculine stance; a sarcastic, mocking manner; a particular relationship to the world (rebellious, nonconformist, and "shocking" by middle-class standards). He chooses to adopt what Woolf's father called Byron's "indignant revolt against the whole system of effete respectability."[40] He chooses the life of a wanderer and adventurer, with extensive travels and extensive love affairs with diverse types of women. Jacob's tours of Italy and Greece, his several loves, his too-early, war-connected death parallel situations in Byron's own life. Perhaps most important is the way in which Byron is an ideal analogue to that combination of lucidity and feeling, classicism and romanticism, which exists in Jacob.

Jacob's Byronic rebelliousness breaks through when he is confronted by George Plumer's bookshelves full of Wells and Shaw and sixpenny weeklies. The narrator laments "how miserable it is that the *Globe* newspaper offers nothing better to Jacob Flanders!" (98), and Jacob himself finds it " 'Bloody beastly!' . . . Had they never read Homer, Shakespeare, the Elizabethans?" (35). He thinks of "the world of the elderly—thrown up in such black outline upon . . . reality; the moors and Byron" (36). The allusive counterpoint of Wells/Shaw versus Byron dramatizes the conflict of the prosaic mentality and the poetic temperament, the clash of modern materialism with the romantic quest for being. Jacob's task is to distinguish between what is unworthy and what is significant and true, and he must persist in his obstinate search, even though "the Plumers will try to prevent him from making it. Wells and Shaw and the serious sixpenny weeklies will sit on its head" (36).

By now it is quite clear to readers that Jacob's literary interests are among the essential clues to his enigmatic personality; thus his room at Cambridge assumes paramount importance. Indeed there is an uncanny commingling of Jacob Flanders and his room. This interpenetration of character and scene is not a new approach: there was the carefully contrived presentation of Rachel Vinrace's room and Ridley Ambrose's study in *The Voyage Out*. But the intensification of the strategy is such that one critic has declared that "the entire burden of *Jacob's Room* rests upon Jacob's identity with his 'room.' "[41]

Amid the paraphernalia of furniture, photographs, and pipes in Jacob's Cambridge room, "there were books enough" (39). Aside from dictionaries and textbooks and some works of philosophy, there are "very few French books" (39), a fact that contrasts him with Bonamy, who has read "all those Frenchmen" (72). The works that are enumerated have about them the same deliberate imprecision and studied generality encountered elsewhere in the novel: "the works of Dickens . . . all the Elizabethans. . . . The works of Jane Austen, too, in deference, perhaps, to some one else's standard. Carlyle was a prize" (39).[42]

Woolf wrote often of her beloved Elizabethans; we know what qualities she meant to suggest as fascinating to Jacob—"the characteristic Elizabethan extravagance . . . the hyperbole, . . . [the] freshness and audacity."[43] The clue that Austen's works may be on Jacob's shelves in deference to someone else's taste[44] strengthens our awareness that it is to the extravagant and highly dramatic gesture that Jacob responds, not to the contained aesthetic brilliance and the smaller world of Austen.

The works of Dickens would also appeal to Jacob for their exuberant, larger-than-life qualities.[45] Because Dickens created extreme types in a spirit of exaggeration, Woolf considered him one of the "character mongers and comedians";[46] the narrator of *Jacob's Room* refers to "the highly respectable opinion that *character-mongering* is much over-done nowadays" (154, italics mine).

As for Thomas Carlyle, his savage, almost apocalyptic style is not altogether foreign to Elizabethan writers, especially the Jacobean playwrights. Moreover, the allusion relates not just to Jacob's characterization but to the novel's theme. Carlyle's denunciation of materialism and industrialism as destructive of human personality is echoed in this novel's negative attitudes toward society and war. In *Heroes and Hero Worship*, Carlyle discussed the Hero as divinity, prophet, poet, priest, man of letters, and king. Jacob Hero is an ironic reflection of the Hero as priest, king, and divinity via the Biblical allusiveness of his name; of the Hero as poet and man of letters in his efforts to write polemical essays; of the Hero as prophet in his wish to make speeches in Parliament and in high-handed thoughts of leadership like, "Why not rule countries in the way they should be ruled?" (150). But Jacob cannot fulfill his implied mission: the "perfect mastery of machinery" (155), in the guise of war, destroys him, exactly as Carlyle had anticipated in another work, *The French Revolution*, when he spoke of modern battles "transacted by mechanism . . . in an artificial manner." In fact the whole of *Jacob's Room* becomes a pointed illustration of Carlyle's contention in *Sir Walter Scott*: "The uttered part of a man's life, let us always repeat, bears to the unuttered, unconscious part a small unknown proportion. He himself never knows it, much less do others."

The reverberations from the Carlyle reference, along with the allusion to Disraeli's *Lothair*, augment the political and social dimensions of *Jacob's Room*. Carlyle and Disraeli shared "the same sense of perplexity, the same unsureness about fundamentals, and the same dissatisfaction with conventional answers on the ground that they are shallow."[47] The two writers are even linked historically: in 1874 Disraeli offered Carlyle a baronetcy, which he refused.[48] Woolf knows what she is about, even when she offers several seemingly unrelated allusions.

The only *named* work in Jacob's room is "the *Faery Queen*," yet another representative of the richly vivid Elizabethan age. Spenser's grand vision embraced history, politics, and philosophy—thus Woolf's judicious choice of that allusion manages to keep such issues floating in the background. Because Woolf's novel shares with the *Faerie Queen* the quest motif, Jacob's adventures and romances echo Spenser's declared intention to portray "fierce warres and faithful loues" (*FQ*, 1.1, 9). The cutting edge of irony is that Jacob is not one of Spenser's brave knights of Holiness, Temperance, Chastity, Friendship, Justice, and Courtesy, any more than he was Carlyle's Hero. Because he falls short of meeting the standards these allusions imply ("possibly," the narrator suggests, promising young men "look into the eyes of faraway heroes, and take their station among us half-contemptuously," 117), the novel becomes a mock-epic of Jacob Flanders on the picaresque-heroic path of knightly honor. As Spenser never completed his projected twelve books of the *Faerie Queen*, so Jacob's life is only half realized. His premature death in war leaves readers with Spenser's sense that "life is wretchednesse" (*FQ*, 3.14, 9). Both Spenser and Woolf compare present time to "the image of the antique world" (*FQ*, 5.1, 2), and Spenser's conclusion is strikingly similar to the one reached by the end of *Jacob's Room:*

> Me seemes the world is runne quite out of square,
> From the first point of his appointed sourse,
> And being once amiss growes daily wourse and
>   wourse.
>
> (FQ, 5.1, 7–9)

Jacob's Cambridge room, then, harbors the "best" literature, as compared to Shaw, Wells, and sixpenny weeklies. One critic has put it succinctly: "If to have a room means, as Virginia Woolf herself says, to have the power to think for oneself, then to have a room full of classics means to think about the lasting and the real."[49]

On the table in Jacob's room is an essay entitled "Does History Consist of the Biographies of Great Men?" (39). We see now why Carlyle was "prized," for Jacob's essay is clearly influenced by, if not derived from, a distinctly Carlylean conceit. The question that serves as the title of Jacob's essay was answered in the affirmative by Carlyle, who declared: "The History of the world is but the Biography of great men" (Lecture I, "The Hero as Divinity," *Heroes and Hero Worship*). Further-

more, it was Carlyle who declared: "There is no life of a man, faithfully
recorded, but is a heroic poem of its sort" (*Sir Walter Scott*). This idea is a
subtle commentary upon the structure of Woolf's novel, which in its
own way is a mock-heroic poem upon the life of a would-be hero.

At Cambridge Jacob and his friend Simeon discuss Julian the Apostate. If we consult Gibbon (also alluded to in this novel) we find a
portrait of that Roman emperor as "philosophic warrior" and "specula-
tive soldier," which begins to suggest further ironic analogues to Jacob.
Although Julian's edict of tolerance is in ironic tonal contrast to Jacob's
slashing, intolerant essays, both were killed in action in war. Struck by a
javelin, Julian "fell senseless from his horse" (*Decline and Fall*, 1, chap.
24); this bears an intriguing connection to Jacob's various falls from
horses and to the riderless horse incident discussed below. Jacob died
anonymously and without glory; Gibbon makes it clear that Julian died
"with the firm temper of a hero and a sage" (chap. 24), discussing the
nature of the soul with two philosophers at his bedside.

Woolf undoubtedly drew upon Bloomsbury Group associations for
the Cambridge sections of this novel. Jacob's "essay upon the Ethics of
Indecency" (78) is curiously reminiscent of a paper entitled "Art and
Indecency," which Lytton Strachey had delivered circa 1908 at one of
several Cambridge societies to which he belonged.[50] Lines are mentioned
in a midnight conversation between Jacob and his Stracheyan friend,
Bonamy, which Jacob "had been seeking all day" (69); they are not in
Virgil, as Jacob first suspected, but in Lucretius. At Cambridge, Lytton
Strachey had been "an ardent disciple of Lucretius."[51] True to Woolf's
larger novelistic strategy of the enigmatic allusion, *which* lines in the melancholy and philosophic poetry of Lucretius remain a mystery. Perhaps it
was some striking comment upon the permanence of matter and the infinity of the universe (*De Rerum Natura*, book 1). Perhaps the arguments
Lucretius offers as proofs of the soul's mortality or his thoughts on the
folly of fearing death (book 3); or his violent condemnation of the passion
of love (book 4); or his comments on the creation of man and the development of civilization (book 5) claimed Jacob's attention. The "answer" is to
be found *somewhere* in Lucretius, for the Roman poet expressed the metaphysics of *Jacob's Room* when he wrote, "There is in all things a void, and
to know this assists apprehension / And leaves you not wandering in
doubt . . . There is intangible space, / A void and a room."[52]

Jacob's essay on indecency has been prompted by a professor's
heavily censored edition of Wycherley, which Jacob considers "an out-
rage, . . . a breach of faith; sheer prudery; token of a lewd mind and a
disgusting nature. Aristophanes and Shakespeare were cited. Modern life
was repudiated" (70).[53] This reaction to the handiwork of Professor Bulteel, whom Jacob labels a " 'damned swine!' " (69), is quite Carlylean in

its angry contempt and passionate fury, its intense concern for truth, its insistence that falsity be decried.[54] Jacob knows, however, that this noble gesture, this iconoclastic essay on indecency, will be rejected by the *Contemporary*, the *Fortnightly*, and the *Nineteenth Century*, despite the fact that what he has written is "the truth," according to the narrator (70). Those detestable serious weeklies which represent effete respectability cannot tolerate the unvarnished, indecent truth.

Given Jacob's rebelliousness and fierce intellectual integrity, it is fitting that he would oppose censorship and rush to the defense of a sardonic, sometimes savage playwright who did not hesitate to excoriate the selfishness, lust, affectation, and duplicity of man. However, "in spite of defending indecency, Jacob doubted whether he liked it in the raw," the narrator informs us. "He had a violent reversion towards male society, cloistered rooms, and the works of the classics. . . . Then Florinda laid her hand upon his knee" (82). We are twice told that "the problem is insoluble" (81, 82). Epitomized by Florinda's touch and the classics,[55] the insoluble problem is the standard dilemma of philosophic dualism. "The body is harnessed to a brain" (81); Jacob's mistress is "a stupid woman" (82) who cannot possibly fulfill his need for intellectual and emotional companionship. Sex, beauty, "indecency" are not enough. Interestingly, the problem is also stated in Lucretius, perhaps in the very lines for which Jacob searched: "The intellect cannot spring up / Alone, outside of the body, or live far from blood and sinews."[56]

When Jacob transcribes a passage from Marlowe in the British Museum, his effort is judged to be "incredibly dull" (107) because it is an unoriginal and uncreative task, which reduces the flame of Marlowe's genius to a matter of collated editions. Marlowe is not justly represented by such petrified scholarship, any more than Virgil would have recognized himself in Professor Cowan's activities.

Jacob discovers that of all the world's literature, "It's the flavour of Greek that remains" (75).[57] When he and his friend Durrant quote Sophocles and Aeschylus back and forth to each other, the narrator remarks: "What is Greek for if not to be shouted on Haverstock Hill in the dawn?" (76). Woolf believed that Sophocles and Aeschylus suffer from "being read privately in a room, and not seen on a hillside in the sunshine."[58] Where Sophocles demands a large background, Plato is cerebral room-reading.[59] Thus we find Jacob reading Plato alone in his room, late at night.

Jacob's participation in the timeless *nowness* of great thought and in the difficult search for truth is established by the allusion to Plato.[60] Woolf's own deep commitment to literature and to philosophic pursuits enabled her to render such nondramatic scenes as Jacob reading in his room with unusual vividness, even with intensity.[61] Jacob's intellectual activity comes significantly alive when Woolf places his reading process within the larger metaphysical context of the (intrusive) world:

> Meanwhile, Plato continues his dialogue; in spite of the rain; in spite of the cab whistles; in spite of the woman in the mews behind Great Ormond Street who has come home drunk and cries all night long, "Let me in! Let me in!"
>
> In the street below Jacob's room voices were raised.
>
> But he read on. For after all Plato continues imperturbably. And Hamlet utters his soliloquy. . . . Plato and Shakespeare continue. . . . (109)

Outside the great mind (be it British Museum in general or dialogue of Plato in particular), the march of events continues. But great thought also is a continuing presence which must be cherished and protected: "The night-watchmen, flashing their lanterns over the backs of Plato and Shakespeare, saw that . . . neither flame, rat, nor burglar was going to violate these treasures" (109).

Jacob has been reading the *Phaedrus*, and "Plato's argument is stowed away in Jacob's mind" (110). Because the argument of the dialogue concerns the reasons why a philosopher should welcome release from the body, in the certainty that the soul is immortal, such details add to our sense of the underlying thematic concerns of the novel. We can infer that Jacob has "stowed away" the proofs Socrates uses to convince his friends that his soul will not die with his physical body. Spirit, like ideas, is imperishable. It is a weighty issue Jacob has been pondering at length in his Cambridge room, for if in Plato's argument the soul is immortal, in Lucretius it is declared mortal.

Jacob's dogmatism about literature causes him to declare that beyond Marlowe and Shakespeare, Fielding is the only suitable choice, "if you must read novels" (122). Jacob's favorite novel being *Tom Jones*, we may note a few resemblances. While Jacob is intellectually oriented and Fielding's Tom is not, like Tom he is not self-reflective; he never reveals the motivations behind his thoughts and deeds—that task is left to the talky narrators Fielding and Woolf have invented, and each of them contributes numerous interruptive essays. Both Jacob and Tom have several amorous adventures, but more significantly, the saga of both of these young men is a tale of pilgrimage and growth toward genuine identity of self. Once again, the final analogues are ironic and belong to that mock-heroic strain of allusion which persists in this novel. At the conclusion of Fielding's novel, Tom's goodness and virtue triumph over disastrous circumstances, a comic happy ending mocked by the loss, grief, and death that conclude *Jacob's Room*.

In another of the several literary conversations reported in the

novel, Jacob's friend Cruttendon announces that he is about to name
" 'the three greatest things that were ever written in the whole of literature' " (126) and recites "Hang there like fruit my soul."[62] Jacob's choice
is " 'The devil damn you black, you cream-faced loon!' " (126), quite a
contrast to the romantic enthusiasm of Cruttendon's selection. Mallinson
the painter offers " 'hey diddle diddle, the cat and the fiddle' " (126) to
puncture Cruttendon's high spirits, for " 'He's a bit of a fool' " (127).
Jacob then mentions " 'this man, Pierre Louÿs now' " (127), dropping
the allusion as abruptly as he offered it. We never discover his opinion of
this French prose-poet and novelist, whose most insistent theme is sexuality in general, lesbianism in particular. Louÿs is a "shocking" writer
whose effect upon a reader might well reveal something significant about
the reader's character. But the nature of Jacob's reaction is withheld, and
the allusion becomes another proof of Jacob's tantalizing unknowability.

Because he cannot escape her solicitude, Jacob reads Sandra Wentworth Williams's "cursed book" (144) of Chekhov stories and retaliates
with his own gift, "the poems of Donne" (160). Sandra observes that Jacob
"had marked the things he liked in Donne, and they were savage enough"
(161), a judgment consistent with her comparison of Jacob to Molière's
Alceste. Obviously pertinent to the novel's theme and to Jacob's characterization is Donne's search for an integrated identity, his exploration of
those conflicting parts of the self that give rise to human variety and
complexity, his obsessive preoccupation with the private world of the self.
Indeed Woolf saw Donne as one of three "keepers of the keys of solitude"[63] and respected his troubled, "queer individuality."[64]

Jacob is no Donne, but he is a complex paradox—highly individualized, yet without a distinctive self-identity; unseizably enigmatic, yet
representative; a historical prototype of the educated pre-1910 English
male whose promise was cruelly snuffed out by the war, like such sol-
dier-poets as Rupert Brooke and Siegfried Sassoon, who also abruptly
left empty rooms behind them.

Jacob is "descended on his mother's side from a family of the greatest
antiquity" (70–71). Woolf even uses the formal title of courtesy after
Jacob's full name, referring to him as "Jacob Alan Flanders, Esq." (90); *Es-
quire* denotes a member of the English gentry ranking just below a knight.
His good breeding, apparent in the facts of his birth, is also demonstrated
by his reading of the finest literature. Woolf carefully stresses his uncommon sensibility and his distance from the average: "Only Jacob, carrying
in his hand Finlay's *Byzantine Empire*, . . . looked a little different; for in
his hand he carried a book, which book he would . . . open and study, as
no one else of all these multitudes would do" (66).

Jacob's aristocracy of birth and taste is exemplified in and by a collection of literary allusions that themselves insinuate the "gentleman" motif of this novel. It is first made explicit in an early exchange between Jacob and Timmy Durrant on their mutual acquaintance, Masham:

> "He's a gentleman," said Jacob.
> "The Duke of Wellington was a gentleman," said Timmy.
> "Keats wasn't."
> "Lord Salisbury was."
> "And what about God?" said Jacob. (51)

Jacob's room contained several *Lives* of Wellington, whom he admires. His recognition that Keats was neither Duke nor gentleman is a pointed reminder of the way in which Keats's critics used the class issue in their attacks, commanding him to abandon poetry for pharmacy, or sneering at him as a disciple of Cockney poetry, "the most incongruous ideas in the most uncouth language."[65] It remained for that highborn gentleman Shelley to transform his indignation over the condescending treatment Keats received into the high art of *Adonais* (which like *Jacob's Room* is an elegy on the premature death of a young man of promise).

Many other allusions used to characterize Jacob emphasize the gentleman motif with varying (usually ironic) degrees of applicability: Lord Byron; Emperor Julian; that parentless foundling of low birth, Tom Jones; the aristocratic snob, Alceste; that upper-class trend-setter of the mid-eighteenth century, Horace Walpole;[66] the titular hero of Disraeli's *Lothair*, who undertakes "an *aristocrat's* quest for his true role."[67] The only named literary work to grace Jacob's Cambridge room is an allegory on the making of a man of nobility, about which Spenser declared: "The general end therefore of all the books is to fashion a gentleman or noble person in vertuous and gentle discipline."[68]

Jacob's gentlemanly breeding relates to the larger hero and quest motifs inherent in his characterization. The persistent perfume of irony in this novel is a function of the accumulating mock-heroic analogies of Jacob to his Biblical namesake, to Byron, to a Carlylean hero, to Tom Jones, to a Spenserian knight, to the Emperor Julian, to Alceste, to Lothair, and so on. To these parallels one more ironic component should be added: the Greek allusions, which create a pseudo-Homeric significance.

Like a Greek god, Jacob is regarded by others as remote, handsome, and somehow "significant." Dick Graves considers him "the greatest man he had ever known" (111); Helen Askew thinks him a "hero" (111).

He is ceremoniously garlanded with paper flowers and glass grapes (75), the latter simultaneously invoking both classical and Biblical dimensions. Florinda likens him to a statue (80); Sandra sees his head "exactly on a level with the head of the Hermes of Praxiteles" (145); Fanny Elmer's "statuesque, noble" idea of Jacob is compared to "the battered Ulysses" (170). Because contemporary British culture provokes his rebellion and contempt, Jacob hopes to find identity and fulfillment in Greece, which he considers "the height of civilization" (164). But his odyssey is futile because it is prompted by illusory expectations, by "the governesses who start the Greek myth" (137). Jacob has been "brought up in an illusion" (138) of antique perfection; he reacts by becoming gloomy and pessimistic. Comparing modern society to an idealized classical civilization must of necessity leave contemporary society belittled and unsatisfactory. Measured against Greek heroes like Ulysses the pilgrim and the rebel Achilles, Jacob himself falls ridiculously short of the mark.

The heroic precedent Jacob would follow is the performance of courageous acts of individual daring. Unlike Achilles, however, modern man follows impersonal orders that force him into battle as one of many anonymous soldiers fighting someone else's (usually the politicians') war. Death in modern Trojan Wars is ironic or merely pathetic, not heroic.

Jacob's analogue in the *Iliad* fulfills his destiny and wins fame, whereas Jacob's death renders him even more obscure. Paralleling the *Iliad* in its dramatization of the conflict between society's dictates and personal integrity, Woolf's novel gives us a Jacob/Achilles who perceives that his society is inadequate and corrupt and refuses to compromise his personal honor, preferring instead to withdraw. Achilles sulked in his tent; Jacob reads Plato alone in his room or writes never-to-be-published essays upon civilization, "a comparison between the ancients and moderns, . . . something in the style of Gibbon" (136). Because he cannot actualize his classical ideals or his present potential, Jacob becomes a mere *symbol* of the hero. A plaster hero stranded on his pedestal, Jacob is essence, not existence, "fixed, monolithic" (165). He is unable to transform his nation or culture for the better. He reads the *Daily Mail* and *knows* "something ought to be done about it" (138), just as Sandra's husband knows "there never was a time when great men are more needed" (143), but he experiences a paralyzing loss of faith: "He would go into Parliament and make fine speeches—but what use are fine speeches and Parliament, once you surrender an inch to the black waters?" (139).

Perhaps the most striking dramatization of the failed hero theme occurs in the slyly written Hyde Park scene. There Clara Durrant is walking her dog, which just happens to be named Troy. She is conversing with Mr. Bowley, who just happens to be making remarks like

" 'England seems all right' " as they just happen to be standing near a "statue of Achilles," while it just happens that "a horse galloped past without a rider" (167). In Jacob's room there was a copy of "a Manual of the Diseases of the Horse" (39),[69] and we know he "rode to hounds— after a fashion" (155). The nation needs a leader to mount the horse of England, but it cannot look to Jacob for such leadership: he has "galloped over the fields of Essex, flopped in the mud, lost the hunt" (101). That undermines his effectiveness both as gentleman *and* hero. Little wonder that having measured Jacob against the ideal aristocrat-hero, the narrator reminds us: "The problems of civilization were solved . . . by the ancient Greeks, though their solution is no help to us" (149).

Prophetically, Julia Eliot, who has also seen the riderless horse gallop by, passes the statue of Achilles and thinks that the present "seems like an elegy for past youth and past summers, and . . . she saw people passing tragically to destruction" (168).

Woolf gives readers her final variation on the gentleman theme at the close of the novel, when Jacob is reobserved by the Reverend Floyd, who recalls, " 'I gave him Byron's works' " (173). Byron could scarcely be more appropriate to the interlocking hero-artistocrat-gentleman-rebel motifs in this novel. Here is a Romantic Hero who mocked his role even as he played it, who began his masterpiece with the cry:

> I want a hero; an uncommon want,
>   when every year and month sends forth
>   a new one,
> Till, after cloying the gazettes with cant,
>   The age discovers he is not the true one . . .
>   (*Don Juan*, 1.1. 1–4)

In form and content, the allusive circle is now complete. Jacob entered and exits with the assistance of Byron, who was "in the shade of the Greeks," and Jacob "is a shadow of this shade."[70]

In its serious lyric moments, *Jacob's Room* is an elegy for a lost hero, which captures an ambiance Woolf was to sustain even more purely and brilliantly in the Percival character in *The Waves*. But in the final analysis the novel is also an ironic and rather pessimistic lament for the would-be hero. Jacob Flanders neither led a hero's life nor died a hero's death. The one-page chapter that concludes the novel, a masterful distillation of thematic motifs, is one in which literary allusions are absent. And rightly so, because the search for Jacob Flanders (made by Jacob himself, the other characters, the narrator, and the reader) has not disclosed *him*, only the *objects* in his room. Only forms, dumb silent shapes, survive—

the room itself, "a bill for a hunting crop" (one last reminder of the gentleman-aristocrat theme), flowers in a vase, and "a pair of Jacob's old shoes" (176), the very last reality, forlornly noted by Jacob's mother, in the very last line of the novel. There are also some letters, but a letter is "this phantom of ourselves" (92), another symbol of the unseizable self, evidence of "the power of the mind to quit the body" (92). Moreover, the letters are not even Jacob's letters, which were "about art, morality, and politics" (94); they are letters written *to* him, and therefore unable to reveal his psyche. The existence of these letters teases us, as did the literary allusions applied to Jacob: they give a very limited access to his personality, enough to encourage us to persist in trying to define him, not enough to fathom his character. Each person's past is truly "shut in him like the leaves of a book known to him by heart; and his friends could only read the title" (64–65). Literature is like life's quest: "In search of what? . . . What do we seek through millions of pages?" (97).[71]

To the cry of his brother Archer in the beginning of the novel, Bonamy's " 'Jacob! Jacob!' " is added at the end. The answer is silence "in an empty room," while outside his room, where there is "confusion," "a harsh and unhappy voice cried something unintelligible" (176). Jacob Flanders remains an undisclosed riddle. The dilemma of personal identity, the problem of the unknowability of others, has been dramatized and *deliberately* left unsolved. Readers and critics who find Jacob's incorporeality and obscurity a weakness in the novel have missed the point of Woolf's deliberate enigma. She has done exactly what she wanted to do in this much underrated novel, not what we might have preferred her, more positively or solidly, to do. She has demonstrated the final mystery of self to self and self to others. Through the defeat of Jacob Hero at the hands of the unpredictable forces of life and death, she has made us experience the disparity between ideal and real. She has evoked the poignancy, that mixture of sorrow, irony, and regret, which surrounds the defeat of young promise. Jacob's vagueness, the empty room he leaves behind, the confused and warring society glimpsed beyond his solitary room, are in fact Virginia Woolf's palpable success.

Now that her voice as a novelist was her own, more and even better were to come.

three

Mrs. Dalloway

Contiguities and juxtapositions sufficed for *Jacob's Room;* indeed they were properly expressive of the content of that novel, but Woolf's next work required a more complex and organic structure, in which space and time are more narrowly focused. Significant reality in *Mrs. Dalloway* is not the phenomenological world of things encountered in *Jacob's Room*— letters, books, a pair of shoes—but an inner psychological truth.

As different as it is from *The Voyage Out* and *Jacob's Room, Mrs. Dalloway* nevertheless belongs to a recognizable continuum in which "logical" progress and development of Woolf's craft is evident. For instance, the significance of the room as a symbol of the inviolable essence of personality, its function as a sanctuary-retreat from life's intrusions, persists. What one critic has called the "elegiac tone"[1] used to describe Jacob Flanders, his rebellion against society, and the relation of war to his life and death—all reappear in a subtly transformed way in the Septimus Warren Smith of *Mrs. Dalloway*. And characters from the earlier novels come to life again in this novel: Mrs. Hilbery from *Night and Day;* Mrs. Durrant, Clara, Mr. Bowley, and Moll Pratt from *Jacob's Room*. Clarissa and Richard Dalloway themselves first appeared in *The Voyage Out;* Clarissa figured in short stories Woolf wrote at Rodmell in the summer of 1922. Four brief sketches having to do with this insistent character were published in *A Haunted House and Other Short Stories*. The story "Mrs. Dalloway in Bond Street," published in the *Dial* in 1923, anticipated the novel, and there were various drafts of such stories as "Ancestors" and "The Introduction."[2] Virginia Woolf was painstakingly working out her own unique solutions to the unique aesthetic problems presented by this novel.

She refined and deepened the experimental strategies of *Jacob's Room*, but she did not abandon allusiveness in *Mrs. Dalloway*.[3] Although a rare critic can recognize that the allusions in this novel have a "suggestiveness which adds a further dimension to the meaning as in poetry," resistance to the technique dies hard.[4] Reuben Brower has singled out "the super-literary, pseudo-Homeric similes which adorn various pages of *Mrs. Dalloway*," calling such "Homeric horseplay" dramatically and narratively irrelevant "elaboration for its own sake."[5] Many of us see these "irrelevant" adornments as valuable mock-heroic additions to the meaning, however.[6] For example, there is the mock-heroic diction of the passage in which Clarissa's maid is said to handle her parasol "like a sacred weapon which a Goddess, having acquitted herself honourably in the field of battle, sheds, and placed it in the umbrella stand" (43–44). This sarcastically diminished suggestion of Clarissa-as-goddess becomes bitterly ironic when applied to her psychological double, Septimus Warren Smith, who in his madness believes himself to *be* God.

Mythological allusions (often mixed with mock-heroic overtones) figure prominently in *Mrs. Dalloway*, where they are used for purposes of characterization or to enlarge the symbolic dimensions of the novel. Doris Kilman, an embittered spinster and religious fanatic hired by Richard Dalloway to tutor his daughter, radiates those qualities of death, sterility, and repressed hostility which her last name implies. Clarissa finds in Kilman "the power and taciturnity of some prehistoric monster armoured for primeval warfare" (190) and hates her.[7] Images of "twigs cracking" and "hooves planted down" (17) add up to an "allusion to the satyr,"[8] and in this case the satyr reference applies both to Kilman and to Clarissa's hatred of her, a hatred that is "this brutal monster" (17), a primitive emotion that belies the cultivated life she leads.[9]

A crucial contribution to the symbolic theme of *Mrs. Dalloway* is made when the narrator speaks of the "prying and insidious . . . fingers of the European War," a war that has "smashed a plaster cast of Ceres" (129).[10] Woolf accomplishes much with this brief invocation of the Goddess of the Corn, a symbolic opposite to the sterile, deathly qualities of war. Ceres is presented as a shattered-by-force, benevolent female deity, which underscores Woolf's feminist concept of war as a belligerent perversion of the oppressive sexual energy of males. It offers an intimation of the personality traits of Septimus Smith, whose own spiritual and sexual potency is broken by the war, and whose relationship with his wife, ironically enough, cannot be saved by that goddess who is the traditional protectress of marriage and family life. The allusion is directly relevant to the life-death antithesis that pervades the novel. The myth of Ceres/Demeter and her daughter Proserpine/Persephone deals in the antinomies of life and death, earth and underworld, growth and decay, brightness and gloom, death and resurrection. In its archetypal rebirth pattern, the myth anticipates the story of Christ's resurrection, and Septimus in his madness supposes himself to be a Savior, "the Lord who had gone from life to death" (147).

Nor do the Ceres connections end there. Part of the education of Septimus Smith consists of his contact with Miss Isabel Pole, a lecturer on Shakespeare. The color of Miss Pole's dress, but a minor detail in a minor character, is in fact highly significant. Septimus sees her "one summer evening, walking in a green dress in a square" (128) and goes off to war remembering "Miss Isabel Pole in a green dress" (130). The fertility myth explicit in the Ceres allusion is restated through this character's name and green dress,[11] for the spirit of vegetation was always leaf-clad, and "the unripe or green corn was personified as the Green Demeter."[12] Indeed "Demeter herself bore the title of Green."[13] Clarissa too partakes of this debased fertility myth—she has a *green* party dress that shines in artificial light, but loses its color in natural sunlight (55).

As for Isabel's last name, the rites of Demeter involved the harvested sheaf of corn, which was often fastened to a *pole*.[14] Jane Harrison, the classical scholar with whose works Woolf was familiar, wrote: "The Maypole or harvest-sheaf is halfway to a harvest Maiden; it is thus . . . that a goddess is made."[15] In traditional English celebrations, the May-Pole is decked with leaves to resemble a flowering tree; Septimus makes his own fertility goddess out of Miss Pole when she passes by in her green dress and he reacts thus: " 'It has flowered,' a gardener might have said, had he opened the door" (128–29).

Septimus' wife Rezia is also an ironic diminution of the Ceres figure. Significantly, Rezia is Italian, and Woolf has used the Latin name of the goddess rather than the Greek equivalent. Rezia misses the fertile gardens of her homeland and the Italian streets, "crowded every evening with people walking, laughing out loud, not half alive like people here, huddled up in Bath chairs, looking at a few ugly flowers stuck in pots" (34).[16] In one of his hallucinations her husband sees her as "a flowering tree" (224). As a diminished Ceres figure, Rezia's desires help precipitate her husband's severe breakdown: "She must have a son like Septimus" (134). Septimus' impotence and suicide are her answer; Ceres has indeed been "smashed" beyond repair. Immediately after Septimus leaps to his death from the window, Rezia's traumatized mental wanderings take on a mythic quality entirely in keeping with her allusive significance. She remembers that she "ran through cornfields," and she hears "stirrings among the dry corn" (228). Even the diction of the final description ("strewn she felt, like flying flowers over some tomb," 228) sustains the allusive significance Woolf has so discreetly established.

Characterization in mock-heroic terms or by mythological allusions is of course in addition to more straightforward allusive methods. *Mrs. Dalloway* does not abandon the sort of allusive characterization found in earlier novels. The Richard Dalloway of this novel descends from the Dalloway who kissed Rachel Vinrace in *The Voyage Out;* his Establishment values of success, prestige, and conformity remain. His prosaic, factual mind is expressed in his wish "to write a history of Lady Bruton's family" (167). He has what his wife calls an "adorable, divine, simplicity" (182), but he is remote and insecure (a man who "doubted his own taste," 173) and unable to express emotion, especially sex-linked emotion: "He could not bring himself to say he loved her [Clarissa]" (179). He allows Clarissa to remain isolated in her attic room where she can sleep "undisturbed" (46). A single Shakespearean allusion reveals much about him: "Seriously and solemnly Richard Dalloway got on his hind legs and said that no decent man ought to read Shakespeare's sonnets because it was like listening at keyholes (besides the relationship was not one that he approved)" (113).

This dismissive intolerance recalls the Dalloway of *The Voyage Out* who condemned Shelley and his set, and even Mr. Grice from that novel, who thought the sonnets "too passionate." Presumably, what strikes Richard Dalloway as "indecent" is the "plot" of the sonnets, with its *menage à trois* situation of Shakespeare's infatuation with a woman and his devotion to a male friend. It is not surprising that Dalloway's conventional mind is shocked and frightened by what he finds in those poems. Sonnet 20, for instance, in which Shakespeare refers to "the master-mistress of my passion," with its graphic references to anatomy ("But since she [Nature] prick'd thee out for woman's pleasure"), would of course be totally unacceptable to Dalloway. Scholars continue to debate the exact nature of Shakespeare's "love" for his male friend and to offer nice interpretations of individual sonnets, but their conclusions—even Virginia Woolf's, if we knew her exact opinion—are less important than the fact that Shakespeare's sonnets are an especially apt example of provocative literature. They function as a kind of litmus paper, colored by the sexual maturity, fears, and biases of their readers, revealing *their* latent sexual orientations as readily as they do Shakespeare's. That Richard Dalloway cannot approach these "dangerous" sonnets on any terms, that he must defensively refuse to encounter them at all, is a masterful revelation of the deeper levels of his character.

In the character of Hugh Whitbread there is an intensification of the worst qualities of Richard Dalloway: "Dim, fat, blind, past everything he looked, except self-esteem and comfort" (288). Hugh has embraced Establishment values so completely that his own individuality is totally absorbed in servility to authority. Significantly, he is bereft of allusion; he aspires only so far as to help Lady Bruton write her letters to the *Times*—the same Lady whose family history the equally unimaginative Richard Dalloway wishes to write.

Sally Seton and Peter Walsh despise what such worldly careerists as Dalloway and Whitbread represent. Peter thinks Hugh "a positive imbecile" (8) and Sally observes contemptuously, " 'He's read nothing, thought nothing, felt nothing' " (110). Whitbread's job at Court provokes Walsh's malice: "He [Whitbread] blacked the King's boots or counted bottles at Windsor" (288). Peter's sharp tongue (remarked upon twice by Sally, 288, 292) is in perfect harmony with his expressed preference for Pope. His opinion of Whitbread's official position is akin to Pope's estimation of the Court: "Folly, my son, has still a Friend at Court" (*Dunciad*, 1; 300). And Walsh's contempt for Hugh's toadying could find no better parallel than in the sharp wit of Pope, who penned several scathing lines upon ,obsequious opportunists, perhaps none more scathing than the two lines that constitute his "Epigram Engraved on the Collar of a Dog"—"I am his Highness' dog at Kew; / Pray tell me, sir, whose dog are you?"

Clarissa finds Peter "a little cranky," inclined to give himself "airs," and "bookish" (237); all of these evaluations are thoroughly consistent with his admiration for the cantankerous poet who was the wicked wasp of Twickenham. She observes that he "knew better than anyone" (192) Pope and Addison.[17] This duo of eighteenth-century rationalists helps convey that quality in Peter which one critic called "the absolutism of his thinking."[18] For example, Sally Seton observes that "Peter did not agree that we know nothing. We know everything, he said; at least he did" (294). This has all the smug rationalism of such Age of Reason dogmatisms as "One truth is clear, WHATEVER IS, IS RIGHT" (*Essay on Man*, Epistle 1; 294).

Peter strikes those who meet him as "the perfect gentleman, the fascinating, the distinguished" (239); his taste for Addison complements this image. Virginia Woolf called Addison part of "that little fraternity," presumably including Pope, which was discriminating and highly critical. For her, Addison was "on the side of sense and taste and civilisation";[19] fittingly, Clarissa realizes that Peter had taught her the true meaning of the word "civilised" (54).

Walsh reveres English civilization; it is English *society* he finds unworthy. The collocation of Peter and Clarissa expresses not only the conflict of independence and conformity but also the antithesis of intuition and reason, female and male psyches, which is present in every one of Woolf's novels. It is through Peter's (and Sally's) critical eyes that we view the pretenses, the shallow values, the unsatisfying life Clarissa lives. Even his habit of fondling his horn-handled penknife in Clarissa's presence, an act filled with sexual implications, is an emblem of his "lacerating her with criticism."[20] In his antagonism toward Clarissa, Peter remains true to the eighteenth-century writers he most admires. Many of Addison's essays stress "the foibles of women,"[21] as does much of Pope's poetry, especially *The Rape of the Lock*, that "satire upon feminine frivolity" which Woolf's father declared the prototype supplying "Addison and his colleagues with the materials of so many *Spectators*."[22]

Peter Walsh has much in common with Sally Seton, who is vital, unconventional, and adventurous. They possess a value system in contradistinction to the world of the Dalloways. Because they prize intellectual and personal freedom, spontaneity and honesty, they are set off from less admirable characters by their common interest in literature; indeed, Walsh once gifted Sally with "a little Emily Bronte" (285).

Sally smokes cigars, runs naked down hallways, supports the suffragette movement, and reads radical literature.[23] When she gives Clarissa William Morris to read, it is "wrapped in brown paper" (49), a detail that nicely captures the suppressions of Victorianism. Sally reading Morris has the same kind of symbolic value as Hirst and his Swinburne in *The Voyage Out*: youth in rebellion against the convention-bound older generation and its middle-class values. The Morris who wrote *News from Nowhere* and *Chants for Socialists* complements Sally's "daring" personality, for she is filled with plans on how "to reform the world" and intends "to found a society to abolish private property" (49). It is true that Sally's later life and marriage seem to be "an apparent repudiation of her youthful radicalism."[24] Daring young ladies who read Morris may nevertheless conclude by marrying a bald industrialist. Woolf's added touch of making Sally's husband own "cotton mills at Manchester" (277) is an especially apt irony: Morris was a fervent socialist with a deep disgust for an industrialized England. His hopes for reforming the fabric of society seem to come to a mocking end in Lady Sally Rossiter. Yet there is a sense in which Sally has *not* betrayed her literary idol. Morris's works project an idealized joy and hope in their treatment of strong, handsome, and serene men and women. When readers last see Sally, at Clarissa's party, she is in "the softness of motherhood" (284), having given birth to five sons. She quickly observes that Clarissa "lacked something" (287), that she "was at heart a snob" (289). Sally is still, at least partially, an outsider critical of Clarissa's "party" values and personal maturity. And although Sally once went about decapitating flowers—with all of the latent sexual meanings of that act—she now raises plants: "hydrangeas, syringas, very, very rare hibiscus lilies . . . beds of them, positively beds!" (290).

As for the characterization of Lady Bruton, the allusions used to suggest her personality are reinforced by her last name, which suggests *brute* and *Briton*. The essence of Lady Bruton is to be found in these two qualities of Amazonlike force and nationalistic pride. Indeed her first name, Millicent, also has *militant* associations. This "strong martial woman" (164), who has fantasies about being "a general of dragoons" (159) and "could have worn the helmet and shot the arrow" (274), is reminiscent of some Amazon warrior. She has, moreover, the sententious patriotism of Richard Dalloway in *The Voyage Out.* "More interested in politics than people" (160), Lady Bruton's fierce nationalism is very different from Peter Walsh's love of British civilization. Walsh admires Pope and Addison; Lady Bruton is proudly aliterary. Walsh wished to write imaginative literature; Lady Bruton is not only incapable of imaginative fiction but unable to write even her own letters to the *Times* telling of her various patriotic projects.

When she speaks of England as "this isle of men, this dear, dear land," her imprecise approximation of the language of *King Richard II* makes the point that thinking about England "was in her blood (without reading Shakespeare)" (274). By ironic analogy Lady Bruton has much in common with the soldier-politician who speaks those lines.

There is a vine in Lady Bruton's garden "which either Lovelace or Herrick—she never read a word poetry of [sic] herself, but so the story ran—had sat under" (159). One critic has devoted considerable comment to this secondary allusion, arguing that it has a "purely rhetorical purpose, as a means of transition from Richard's mind to Lady Bruton's."[25] He asserts that the information that Lady Bruton never read poetry is an unjustified authorial interruption because "Lady Bruton's literary taste is of no significance."[26] But such a judgment misses both the fine stroke of characterization involved and the implicit social criticism that follows from it. Lady Bruton is a representative of that upper-class society toward which Woolf is consistently critical in this novel. Bruton is *unread*, and to have a nonliterate sensibility is a very serious deficiency in Woolf's world of values. There is sarcasm, not merely a plot-serving technical device, in Woolf's insistence that to such people, mere literary gossip ("The famous poet Robert Herrick sat here" or "Richard Lovelace once sat there"), not the phenomenon of creativity, matters. The name of either poet, *any* poet, will suffice for an amusing little story to be told over high tea. As Lady Bruton herself admits, "The difference between one man and another does not amount to much" (157). Lady Bruton's professed love of England excludes comprehension of her nation's great literary sons, Herrick, Lovelace, Shakespeare, et al. Thus the claim that a character's literary taste is extraneous is tantamount to an admission by that critic that he has not grasped one important means by which Virginia Woolf not only reveals but actually judges (however obliquely) her characters. The sympathetic characters read literature, or at the very least are respectful of its influence—for example, Rezia tries to share her husband's literary enthusiasm: "Could she not read Shakespeare too? Was Shakespeare a difficult author?" (135). Unsympathetic characters are almost always presented as unsusceptible to literature. Miss Kilman, beyond the touch of life-giving rain in her ugly raincoat, is also isolated from the human emotion of imaginative literature. It is history she knows, and the books she gives to Elizabeth are "law, medicine, politics" (198). Finally the true villains of this novel, the doctors Holmes and Bradshaw, are hostile and immune to literature.

The incompetence and tyranny of Holmes and Bradshaw result directly in the impulsive suicide leap of Septimus Smith. As upholders of a narrow masculine rationality that excludes an intuitive grasp of the complexity of life, they propagate rigid standards empty of humanity. It is neither insignificant, irrelevant, nor an accident that these men of science are aggressively antiliterary. Dr. Holmes in a visit to Septimus "opened Shakespeare—*Antony and Cleopatra*; pushed Shakespeare aside" (138). In Bradshaw the Philistinism is even more explicit: "There was in Sir William, *who had never had time for reading*, a grudge, deeply buried, against cultivated people who . . . intimated that doctors . . . are not educated men" (147, italics mine).

To epitomize the evil that resides in Bradshaw, Virginia Woolf invents a mythology of two sister goddesses who owe a great deal to the classical counterparts from which they are derived. This rhetorical move makes possible a comprehensive metaphor through which the horrifying extent of Bradshaw's didacticism and his will-to-power are exposed. As "the priest of science" (142), Bradshaw is empowered to make it "impossible for the unfit to propagate their views until they, too, shared his sense of proportion" (150). The mad Septimus, whose extreme hypersensitivity clearly lacks the required proportion, becomes Bradshaw's most important human sacrifice.

Woolf's "proportion, divine proportion" (150) descends from the Greeks' *sophrosyne*, a kind of internal concord or harmony representing the ideal of moderation best epitomized in the Delphic advice "nothing in excess."[27] Midway between unbridled instinct and repressive self-control, *sophrosyne* was the way to avoid those excesses of pride, ambition, and violence that were the downfall of so many protagonists in Greek tragedy.[28] Perhaps because Woolf subverted this concept from the Greek literature she so admired, her authorial insistence that Proportion is an evil Goddess put to evil use is somewhat less than convincing.

Proportion has a "sister, less smiling, more formidable" (151), the goddess Conversion. "She feasts on the wills of the weakly, loving to impress, to impose, . . . [she] offers help, but desires power; smites out of her way roughly the dissentient, or dissatisfied" (151). Conversion is a devious deity, a hypocrite whose tyranny is masked by "some venerable name; love, duty, self sacrifice" (152). Conversion sanctions the movement from moderation to oppression, from Bradshaw's decision that "this is madness; this sense" (151) to suppression of all differences. As

Bradshaw's goddess of Conversion makes Septimus and Nature itself submit to Science, so too does it mold his wife into the required pattern. In a brilliant Platonic metaphor, Woolf has Lady Bradshaw produce shadows, that is, those mere imitations of reality called photographs. And she is thoroughly oppressed by her tyrant husband: "There had been . . . only the slow sinking, water-logged, of her will into his. Sweet was her smile, swift her submission" (152).

Like her sister goddess, Conversion is a distortion of the Greek *peitho* or persuasion, who began as Aphrodite's handmaiden and ended by becoming the Greeks' means to political harmony.[29] And like the notion of moderation, persuasion is a recurrent, even noble concept in Greek thought, but Woolf has transformed Peitho, the wooer of opinion, into Conversion, a goddess who coerces it. Septimus Smith is the polar opposite to these uncreative sister deities who represent the norm by which he is judged.

The novel that bears Mrs. Dalloway's name has been called "a novel of such inner consistency that each detail sheds additional light on her character and experience."[30] As an emblem of the surface world of society, Clarissa properly lacks force and originality; her disinterest in the intellectual life is reflected in the fact that she is not well read. However, she did have a passing interest in literature when she was young. Influenced by Sally Seton, "she read Plato in bed before breakfast; read Morris; read Shelley by the hour" (49).[31] There are intricate interconnections in this named trio. Shelley, whose poetry is filled with Platonic ideas, is relevant to the thematic motifs of this novel and to Clarissa's characterization. William Morris's *Earthly Paradise* is based on a Platonic "symposium device."[32] The metaphysics of *Mrs. Dalloway* is in part rendered through sun imagery, which functions in Woolf's novel as in Plato's *Republic:* it symbolizes reality, truth, and knowledge. When Septimus feels "the heat wave" and imagines he can "see into the future" (102), this suggests the Platonic myth of the cave and the man who emerges from illusory darkness into the sunlight of truth. Indeed Septimus' madness is presented as a visionary gift, a deeper insight into reality than others can achieve—a classically Platonic conception. Then too, reference to Plato has the structural function of linking Clarissa and Septimus together.

Rigid suppression of deep emotion characterizes Clarissa's lifestyle.[33] Fearful of her instincts and threatened by passion, Clarissa denies two especially intrusive emotions—religion and love. Her hatred of religion finds its outlet in hatred of Miss Kilman, and her proper Victorian upbringing has left her with strong sexual inhibitions. Her sexual

ambivalence is at the root of her personality structure, and those fundamental fears are often projected with the help of literary allusions. By
choosing to marry Richard Dalloway rather than Peter Walsh, Clarissa
avoided the intimate demands she knew Peter would make: "With Peter
everything had to be shared; everything gone into. And it was intolerable" (10). But her attraction to Walsh (as well as her fears) remains,
preserving her conflict in perfect parity.

The extended scene in which Peter and Clarissa confront each other
(59–71) is ironically analogous to "The Sleeping Beauty."[34] Clarissa
feels "like a Queen whose guards have fallen asleep and left her unpro-
tected" (65). By itself the Queen simile might only be an instance of an
inflated, glorified self-image, yet a deeper level of interpretation emerges
if parallels to the Sleeping Beauty fable are explored. Clarissa is sewing
when Walsh arrives; her needle and scissors recall the circumstances of
the fairy tale, in which the Princess's hand is pierced by a spinning
needle, and the wound causes her to fall into an enchanted, hundred-
year slumber. The Princess was shut up in a castle enclosed by trees,
thorns, and *brambles;* so Clarissa is secluded in her solitary attic room,
"where she lies with the *brambles* curving over her" (65, italics mine).[35]
The Prince climbed the staircase and entered Sleeping Beauty's bedchamber; Walsh bounds up the stairs and bursts in upon Clarissa (59).
The Princess was awakened to love by the Prince's kiss; in *Mrs. Dalloway*, Peter kisses Clarissa's hands (60) and later, in a gesture of rather
maternal pity, Clarissa kisses Peter (69).

Clarissa's psychic virginity is comparable to that of the slumbering,
sexually unawakened Princess of the fable. And like another enchanted
heroine evoked by Woolf—the Lady in Milton's *Comus*, whose relationship to the virginal Rachel Vinrace was ultimately one of ironic divergence—the congruence of the frigid Clarissa Dalloway with Sleeping
Beauty is fraught with a final ironic dissimilarity. Peter Walsh is as
much her antagonist as her Prince Charming; Clarissa feels she must
"beat off the enemy" (66). Rachel Vinrace's fate was not to encompass
the marriage that awaited Milton's Lady, and Clarissa's permanent fears
prove stronger than that erotic but erratic attraction to Walsh that sometimes can cause her to think impulsively, "Take me with you" (70).
When Peter leaves "without looking at her" (71), the possibility that our
heroine might be awakened to passionate love is mocked by Clarissa's
ever-watchful repressions.[36]

Two allusions in particular help illuminate Clarissa's marriage,
which like that of Septimus is a union of emotional convenience, not
passion. One of them illustrates the emotional logic of her choice of a
tranquil husband, and the other shows how, having made the safe
choice, she cannot be truly happy with her truncated emotional life.

Given Clarissa's sexual inhibitions, it is not surprising that she concurs with Richard's opinions about the "indecent" love relationships suggested by Shakespeare's sonnets. But that part of her which still longs for intense emotional fulfillment, the part that wanted to marry Peter Walsh, resents the sexual cowardice necessitated by her fears. In Clarissa's attitude toward her good, safe husband there is something deprecatory, even hostile. It was present from the very beginning: "Dalloway had come over; and Clarissa called him 'Wickham'; . . . Clarissa got his name wrong. She introduced him to everybody as Wickham. At last he said 'My name is Dalloway!' " (92). Here is psychological insight so incisive and accurate that Freud himself might have applauded it.[37] Clarissa's mistake reveals how slight an impression Richard made upon her. It is no innocent phonetical error, for neither his first nor last name sounds remotely like "Wickham." The slip betokens a deeper, hidden reaction to the man. George Wickham is the villain of *Pride and Prejudice;* personable and charming as he is, his activities include dissipation, lying, blackmail, and elopement with the fifteen-year-old Lydia Bennet, of whom he quickly tires. In Wickham's elopement and dissipation we may read an ironic disparagement-by-comparison of Dalloway's tepid masculinity. Moreover, the Clarissa-Peter-Richard triangle is an echo of the triangle formed by Elizabeth Bennet, Wickham, and Darcy. Elizabeth Bennet has the same sort of choice to make as Clarissa;[38] she finally realizes her error and acknowledges her love for Darcy, whereas Clarissa marries her "villain" after rejecting her "hero." Years later, when Clarissa gives the party with which the novel concludes, Sally Seton Rossiter remembers that Clarissa "had called Richard 'Wickham.' Why not call Richard 'Wickham'?" (285). This allusive recapitulation, over 190 pages later, reminds us of Clarissa's original attitude of distaste and dismissal toward her husband. Moreover, the unrepentant bravado of Sally's question makes it clear that her critical stance toward Dalloway's world persists.

Fearing as she did heterosexual passion with Peter Walsh, Clarissa construes her girlhood relationship to Sally Seton as "falling in love" (48). We have already seen how temperamentally alike Sally and Peter are; Clarissa's frustrated feelings for Peter find a devious outlet in an intensity of feeling for Sally. In her isolated attic room Clarissa can free herself from her repressions, abandon propriety and her social *persona*, letting her pessimistic preoccupation with death and her latent traits of masculinity emerge.

The physical setting of Clarissa's attic room (45–46) is masterfully projected and has symbolic significance. It radiates literary overtones. One might compare the attic room with its narrow bed, tight-stretched sheets, and half-burnt candle to the "bridebed, childbed, bed of death, ghost-candled" in Joyce's *Ulysses*. One critic has offered an allusive interpretation of the bed sheets, "tight-stretched in a broad white band" (45), as an analogue to "the sail of Theseus."[39] The half-burnt candle of life is of course a familiar metaphor, perhaps most powerfully expressed in the Macbeth speech beginning "Out, out, brief candle!" Then too, shortly before she retires to her attic room, Clarissa thinks of the line from *Cymbeline;* the description of Imogen's bedchamber in that play (2.2) curiously resembles Clarissa's setting—both heroines are in bed, reading, beside a half-burnt taper.

What Clarissa is reading in this isolated room with its intimations of futility, old age, and death is expressly contrasted with more positive moments of illumination and epiphany:[40] "against such moments . . . there contrasted . . . Baron Marbot" (47). It assuredly adds a different dimension to Clarissa's character to learn that her attic-room reading is *Memoires du général baron de Marbot.* That a supposedly thoroughly feminine woman should be interested in belligerently masculine war memoirs is suggestive enough.[41] But when the narrative does in fact progress from Marbot's intimations of the manly life style, from his concern with power, glory, and heroism, to Clarissa's identification with "what men felt" (47), the revelatory function of the thrice-repeated allusion (46, 47, 205) becomes clear.

Earlier we had been told that Clarissa "scarcely read a book now, except memoirs in bed" (11). Woolf once speculated about what the reader of memoirs sought: "Is it love or ambition, commerce, religion, or sport? It may be none of these, but something sunk deep beneath the surface, scattered in fragments, disguised behind frippery."[42] Clarissa Dalloway seeks thus:

> The candle was half burnt down and she had read deep in Baron Marbot's *Memoirs.* She had read late at night of the retreat from Moscow. . . . Richard insisted, after her illness, that she must sleep undisturbed. And really she preferred to read of the retreat from Moscow. He knew it. So the room was an attic; the bed narrow. . . . (46)

Marbot's descriptions of the Russian campaign, particularly of Napoleon's ignominious retreat, are harrowing. The battlefield was covered with "thirty thousand corpses half devoured by wolves"; soldiers died of exposure to the freezing cold or of starvation, despite eating their horses. When one of the bridges over the Beresina River broke under the combined weight of men, horses, and wagons, those who were not crushed or drowned were killed by Russian guns firing "upon the wretches who were struggling to cross the river." Nearly 25,000 men were lost.[43]

This tale of agony and suffering, death and defeat, is Clarissa's chosen reading in her attic room. The extremely negative emotions of such a precisely designated allusion must—unless Woolf is assumed to be an inept writer—be the objective correlative of Clarissa's own psychic state. The Marbot allusion links, metaphorically, the retreat from Moscow to Clarissa's retreat from sexuality. That retreat has resulted in the quality of "virginity preserved through childbirth which clung to her like a sheet" (46). Napoleon's failure at Moscow is the analogue of Clarissa's failure of Richard: "She had failed him. And then at Constantinople, and again and again" (46).

Clarissa's recognition of having failed Richard leads her directly to thoughts of loving Sally Seton (48–53). She certainly cannot share with her husband her feeling that the most entrancing love experience is homosexual, especially when that husband has found the sexual relationships in Shakespeare's sonnets indecent and intolerable. To Clarissa "the most exquisite moment of her whole life, [was] passing a stone urn with flowers in it. Sally stopped; picked a flower; kissed her on the lips" (52). Her latent lesbianism is established beyond doubt by an allusion to *Othello*, which she invokes to explain her feelings about Sally.[44] Recollecting her sensation of "going cold with excitement" (51) over Sally's proximity, Clarissa remembers feeling "as she crossed the hall 'if it were now to die 'twere now to be most happy.' That was her feeling—Othello's feeling, and she felt it, she was convinced, as strongly as Shakespeare meant Othello to feel it" (51). Woolf's insistent rhetoric—in which we are given quotation, author, and character—stresses the allusion's total context. This play, dealing with the theme of sexual jealousy, is one in which the leading character "loved not wisely, but too well" (5.2.344). The quoted lines are contained within Othello's rapturous speech upon beholding Desdemona; Othello kisses Desdemona immediately afterward. The kiss Sally bestows upon Clarissa is their analogous consummation. Iago then intrudes upon the intimacy of Othello and Desdemona (2.1.200–203), as Peter Walsh intrudes upon Sally and Clarissa (53). In this speech Othello expresses "content so absolute" that he would willingly die "most happy"; thus the allusion reinforces the love-death motif in the novel.

The *Othello* allusion occurs once more, when Clarissa hears of the suicide of Septimus Smith. (Othello too was a suicide for love's sake.) She wonders: "But this young man who had killed himself—had he plunged holding his treasure? 'If it were now to die, 'twere now to be most happy,' she had said to herself once, coming down [the stairs] in white" (281). Now the allusion is juxtaposed to the concept of *treasure*, of something preserved "that mattered" (280). The "treasure" Septimus preserves by killing himself should, like Othello's and Clarissa's, involve love. And since Clarissa has applied the lines from *Othello* to a lesbian love-object, we might expect her counterpart's "treasure" to be a similarly homosexual love. And it is. In the largest symbolic or archetypal sense, the search for treasure often brings death to its seekers; in this novel as well, only death keeps love's treasure from the destruction of time.

There is yet another Shakespearean allusion that makes its contribution to the characterizations, themes, and structure of this novel. " 'Fear no more the heat o' the sun / Nor the furious winter's rages,' " a quotation from the Song in *Cymbeline*, has prompted more explication than any other single allusion discussed in this study, yet even it lacks the accurate, universal attention it deserves.[45] The quotation is central to the novel's structure and contains within it most of the novel's key metaphors. To appreciate the novel fully, we need to appreciate the way in which new meanings accrue to the lines as they are repeated five times throughout the novel.

They first appear when Clarissa passes Hatchard's book-shop window and sees several books: "Jorrocks' *Jaunts and Jollities;* . . . *Soapy Sponge* and Mrs. Asquith's *Memoirs* and *Big Game Shooting in Nigeria*" (13).[46] It is not merely that Woolf revels in small, odd details like the assorted book titles in a shop window.[47] Together the allusions reveal the pastimes of the privileged ruling class: the memoirs of a titled lady, and hunting books by gentlemen who can afford to indulge their taste for the escapist sport of killing animals, foreign or domestic. Surtees's caricature of John Jorrocks projects the typical English sportsman in sketches that reveal what Woolf's father characterized as "the coarse convivialities of the boozing fox-hunting squires."[48] Through Woolf's deft evocation of a few "social" literary allusions we see the tone of a time and a class. Moreover, Clarissa embodies this social order in all its superficiality[49] and substitution of mere vivacity for intensity and depth. She is Woolf's oblique but definite criticism of the social system. One critic has observed that a passage referring to the *Tatler* "quite devastatingly defines the attitudes by which Clarissa Dalloway measures her social triumph,"[50] but the bookshop allusions are encountered even earlier in the novel, and they accomplish just that purpose.

Amid these literary relics of privileged triviality, Clarissa spies one other book, open to the lines, " 'Fear no more the heat o' the sun / Nor the furious winter's rages' " (13). The two opposing concepts in that Shakespearean imperative, in all their possible variations (heat-cold, summer-winter, light-darkness, passion-frigidity), constitute the fundamental metaphors of the novel. The sun, perhaps *the* most crucial image in the novel, is first invoked in this allusive form. Shortly before Clarissa read the lines, she had mused upon the meaning of life and death (12). Immediately after reading the refrain she thinks: "This late age of the world's experience had bred in them all, all men and women, a well of tears. Tears and sorrows; courage and endurance; a perfectly upright and stoical bearing" (13). In other words, the times require exactly that stoical bearing which Shakespeare's song urges upon mankind. And we learn that Clarissa "admired most" (13) Lady Bexborough, who remained undefeated by war and death and carried on even "with the telegram in her hand, John, her favorite, killed" (5).[51]

In the first appearance of the *Cymbeline* lines, Clarissa *does* in fact fear loss of life, the passage of time, and growing old. On one symbolic plane, the heat of the sun is Clarissa's enemy, embodying life's energies at their most intense and passionate. We should recall that the crucial allusive passage in *The Voyage Out* also presented the sun's heat as a (sexual) menace that attracted Rachel even as she feared it. The lines relate to repressed feelings Clarissa has to face; they remain suspended in her mind. After she reads the command in Hatchard's window, she returns to her house, which is, in telling contrast to the sun's heat, "cool as a vault" (42). The situation is quite literally reminiscent of the Song: "Thou thy worldly task hast done, / Home art gone, and ta'en thy wages."[52]

Clarissa's wages turn out to be disappointment at being excluded from Lady Bruton's luncheon invitation. Her reaction is: " 'Fear no more,' said Clarissa. Fear no more the heat o' the sun; for the shock of Lady Bruton asking Richard to lunch without her made the moment in which she had stood shiver . . . she feared time itself, . . . the dwindling of life; how year by year her share was sliced" (44). She feels separated from the emotional crutch of her husband Richard, who in his own tepid way protects her from the sexual heat of a more demanding man like Peter Walsh.[53] Feeling suddenly "shrivelled, aged, breastless" (45), Clarissa fully realizes the truth of the next two lines of the Song: "Golden lads and girls all must / As chimney-sweepers, come to dust." She cannot banish her sense of mortality. The attic-room sequence, with the Marbot allusion, her sense of failing her husband, and her love for Sally Seton, follows this catalytic quotation.

Somewhat later Clarissa is sewing the green folds of a silk dress. The tear in her dress represents the same thing as Rachel Vinrace's torn dress (sexual experience), and both women mend the tear in a symbolic attempt to attain an asexual, virginal state. Serene content descends upon Clarissa as the allusion is repeated for the third time: "The heart in the body which lies in the sun on the beach says too, That is all. Fear no more, says the heart, committing its burden to some sea, which sighs collectively for all sorrows, and renews, begins, collects, lets fall" (58–59). This passage has been much praised; one critic, himself a poet, called it a kind of "*vers libre:* in the daring and fullness of the metaphors it has a remote indebtedness to Homer."[54] Certainly it is "large" enough to relate Clarissa's individual ego to external reality. Moreover, it is complex enough in its ambiguity to symbolize "both freedom from fear and the fear of interruption,"[55] as demonstrated by the scene that follows, wherein the intrusive Peter Walsh unexpectedly violates Clarissa's solitude. Freedom from fear can be found in the committing of the heart's burden to the sea, thus releasing Clarissa from anxiety. Beautiful as this image may be, it nevertheless implies the same death wish as did Rachel Vinrace's watery images of peace.

The fourth appearance of the *Cymbeline* allusion occurs within the mind of Septimus Warren Smith, who needs to be seen as a character in his own right before his function as Clarissa's double can be fully understood. The comedy of manners and the narrative irony inherent in the treatment of Clarissa Dalloway is eschewed in the portrayal of Septimus. His embodiment of the themes of war, madness, and suicide constitutes the polar element of tragedy. That he symbolizes war and death is established in part by the allusion to Ceres—the dead were frequently described as "Demeter's people."[56] His is the fate of the too-sensitive man in a brutalized, warring world bereft of love and compassion. The Ceres allusion is the vehicle of the tragic irony of Septimus' destiny: he is himself powerless to establish or perpetuate the universal love for which he continually pleads in his madness.

How is Septimus' portrait augmented by allusions? His madness, for one thing, has a mythological ambiance. He fancies that sparrows sing "in voices prolonged and piercing in Greek words, from trees in the meadow of life beyond a river where the dead walk, how there is no death" (36). His suicide has congruences with classical myths of the dying god, "the scapegoat, the eternal sufferer" (37), whose life is offered to redeem humanity. Such rebirth and resurrection motifs suggest analogues to Christ as well as to mythology, but classical rather than Christian parallels seem to be the ones most intricately sustained within the novel.[57] Septimus' insanity is also rather Shakespearean: his vow that "he would not go mad" (215) is akin to Lear's plea, "Ó, let me not be mad, not mad, sweet heaven! / Keep me in temper: I would not be mad!" (1.5.49–50).[58]

Septimus Smith's name needs close attention. If we suspect some irony in the resolute ordinariness of the name Smith, we have Woolf's own substantiation. In her essay on the larger-than-life Elizabethan view of reality, she comments that modern society is "based upon the life and death of some knight called Smith."[59] Woolf yokes this deliberately ordinary name to a most uncommon given name: "London has swallowed up many millions of young men called Smith; thought nothing of fantastic Christian names like Septimus with which their parents have thought to distinguish them" (127). *Septimus* confronts readers with the sacred number *seven*, highly significant in mystic, esoteric lore, and entirely appropriate to the novel's intimations of pagan and Christian religious concepts. It is, for example, in the seventh book of *The Republic* that the Platonic metaphors of the sunlight as knowledge and darkness as ignorance are developed. Even more telling is the significance of the number *seven* in Dante, whom Septimus reads obsessively. More about Dante later.

"One of those half-educated, self-educated men whose education is all learnt from books borrowed from public libraries" (127), Septimus is a would-be writer. We are not given any actual examples, but we are told the themes of his apocalyptic scribblings. He composes poems about Miss Isabel Pole, the Shakespearean lecturer with whom he is infatuated—and she in her position as his teacher dutifully corrects his love poems "in red ink" (128). His table drawer is "full of those writings; about war; about Shakespeare; about great discoveries; how there is no death" (212). There are "odes to Time; conversations with Shakespeare" (224), and because his madness deprives him of the reassuring objective structure of time,[60] the subjects take on added poignancy. He invents stories about the hated doctor Holmes "reading Shakespeare—making himself roar with laughter or rage" (213), for to Septimus the spectacle of that Philistine doctor reading Shakespeare is a terrible travesty.

Owing to Miss Pole's influence, he finds himself "devouring Shakespeare, Darwin, *The History of Civilization*, and Bernard Shaw" (129). When Miss Pole muses, "Was he not like Keats?" (128),[61] we experience an intricately interlocking allusive reinforcement of the death and rebirth theme, via the Adonis myth, here applied to Septimus by Woolf as it had been applied to Keats by Shelley. The comparison of Keats to Septimus completes the web of meaning, and that meaning is in part ironic, for Woolf considered Keats one of the great androgynous writers,[62] and Septimus' tortured, divided psyche cannot possibly attain such integration. Nor should we forget that the relationship of Septimus to Miss Pole is a student-teacher-lover relationship, whose implications are in harmony with both the Shakespearean and the Platonic echoes in this novel.

In his most paranoid delusions of grandeur, Septimus believes himself "called forth in advance of the mass of men to hear the truth, to learn the meaning, which now at last, after all the toils of civilization—Greeks, Romans, Shakespeare, Darwin, and now himself—was to be given whole" (101–2). When Septimus volunteers to go to war, he does so "to save an England which consisted almost entirely of Shakespeare's plays and Miss Isabel Pole in a green dress" (130). The poignancy and irony of Septimus' reverence for Shakespeare is largely the result of Shakespeare's symbolic significance (in Virginia Woolf's value world) as the whole human being, the androgynous mind *par excellence*.[63] Whether Shakespeare or Keats is the example, this androgynous ideal of a multiplicity of selves, made from a unity of masculine and feminine qualities, is clearly beyond the deranged capacities of Septimus Smith.

Woolf combines the meanings of Shakespeare and Miss Pole with impressive artistry—it is Miss Pole who gives Septimus "a taste of *Antony and Cleopatra*" (128). Thus the war smashes not only the fertility of Ceres, but the importance to Septimus of Isabel Pole (whose last name symbolizes the debased fertility ritual of the Maypole), and the significance of *Antony and Cleopatra*. The later reference, seemingly a minor allusive element, is in fact part of the convincingly particularized reality of Septimus' madness. It functions as a profound if indirect barometer of Septimus' sexual maladjustments. And it has a fitting counterpart in Clarissa's sexual problems, which relate to *her* Shakespearean allusion (*Othello*). Like Shakespeare's sonnets and Richard Dalloway's reaction to them, *Antony and Cleopatra* and Septimus' changing response to it reveal the depths of his psyche. And like the sonnets, this play is undeniably concerned with sexual love. It is a play of mature, adult passion that is uninhibited and even licentious—that is important, because it increases the degree to which Septimus finds it threatening. If we were to substitute some seemingly equivalent Shakespearean play—for example, *Romeo and Juliet*, the love story of two overheated adolescents—we would realize at once the wisdom with which Woolf has chosen this particular play.

The imagery of *Antony and Cleopatra* associates sun and fire with the intense and complicated passions the play depicts; this is totally in keeping with the existing metaphors of Woolf's novel. Cleopatra's "I am fire and air" (5.2.292) corresponds to Septimus' feeling that "over Miss Pole; [and] *Antony and Cleopatra*" there flickered "a red gold flame" (128).[64] But war and the homosexual affection of an officer named Evans have intervened. "O, wither'd is the garland of the war, / The soldier's pole is fallen!" (4.15.64–65)—such lines seem to be a cruel pun on Septimus' situation. When he returns from the war and tries to reread the play, he finds that "that boy's business of the intoxication of language—*Antony and Cleopatra*—had shrivelled utterly" (133). He cannot now face this passionate play. "The message hidden" in the play is that "Shakespeare loathed humanity—the putting on of clothes, the getting of children, the sordidity of the mouth and the belly!" (133–34). Of course there is no such message in *Antony and Cleopatra*;[65] indeed sexuality at its most positive in the plays is usually *associated* with procreation. There is only Septimus' desperate psychological need to justify his personal inadequacies by projecting them onto Shakespeare. He has made the play the objective correlative of his disgust with humanity in general, with heterosexuality in particular. "Love between man and woman was repulsive to Shakespeare. The business of copulation was filth to him before the end. But, Rezia said, she must have children" (134)—in Woolf's masterful juxtapositions, we see that Septimus' rejection of Miss Pole and *Antony and Cleopatra* embodies, synecdochically, his rejection of heterosexuality, which in turn implies his latent homosexuality.[66]

Septimus' allusion to *Antony and Cleopatra*, like Clarissa's *Othello* reference, reveals its respondent's sexual conflicts; it also subliminally reinforces the larger love-death theme in the novel. Both plays involve the classic opposition of Eros and Thanatos. Othello, Antony, and Cleopatra are all suicides, their destruction provoked by love's passion. Cleopatra's self-confessed "immortal longings" (5.2.284) are echoed in Septimus' and finally Clarissa's acceptance of oblivion. The novel shares with Shakespeare's play the sense of death as love's consummation; for example, Antony declares: "But I will be / A bridegroom in my death and run into't / As to a lover's bed" (4.14.99–101); Cleopatra's simile is: "The stroke of death is as a lover's pinch, / Which hurts, and is desir'd" (5.2.298–99).

Through the use of allusions, Woolf manages to suggest the progressive disintegration of Septimus' psychological integrity. Before the war and officer Evans, literature was a glorious experience. Afterward Septimus finds "the secret signal which one generation passes, under disguise, to the next is loathing, hatred, despair. Dante the same [as Shakespeare]. Aeschylus (translated) the same" (134). Aeschylus' *Oresteia* trilogy is ironically relevant to Septimus, who like Orestes goes mad and is pursued by his own Furies. The invocation of Dante, however, is far more important. We are told that Septimus, even in the extremity of his insanity, "could read, Dante for example, quite easily" (133). We have already seen in *The Voyage Out* and in *Jacob's Room* that the symbolic journey or quest is a staple of Woolf's fiction; no better illustration of the mode exists than the *Commedia*. One critic has justly declared that "the whole movement of the *Divine Comedy* provides a model for Septimus' experience."[67] But Woolf precisely limits the allusion: " 'Septimus, do put down your book,' said Rezia, gently shutting the *Inferno*" (133). It is to that arena of lost souls that Woolf directs our attention.

Septimus' descent into his own particular inferno is the result of his increasing failure to make contact with other human beings, which is manifest in his disintegrating marriage and in his professed inability to feel. Because Septimus is mad, he is quite literally one of Dante's "fallen people, / souls who have lost the good of intellect" (*Inferno*, 3.17–18).[68] In his madness Septimus is outside time and beyond hope, for hope assumes the possibility of *change*, and Dante's infernal scene is an eternity of suffering without end. *Lasciate ogni speranza, voi ch'entrate*, says the chilling final line of the harsh inscription on the Gate of Hell.

The allusion to Dante's *Inferno* supplies the single most illuminating explanation of Septimus' strange first name. Behind Dante's use of the number *seven* loomed the collected rhetorical power of the seven deadly sins and the seven sacraments. *Purgatorio* has seven ascending terraces and seven sins repented. The seventh sin in the seventh terrace is sexual (lust) and it is punished in flames. In Dante's geography, the true torments of Hell begin beyond the vestibule of Hell and Limbo, with the punishment of sins of sexual passion.[69] Fittingly enough, one member of that roaring, unlit whirlwind is "sense-drugged Cleopatra" (5.64). The seventh circle is the first one in Lower Hell, where sins of violence and bestiality are punished. Only after readers realize that *the circle that is Septimus is the circle of punishment for war, suicide, and sexual perversion*, can they fully appreciate the dazzling rightness of the allusion.[70]

The seventh circle is guarded by the Minotaur, a monster conceived in a sodomitic union, which feeds on the flesh of seven youths and seven maidens. Across the river of boiling blood in which the great war-makers of the world are punished is the second round (of the seventh circle), the wood of the suicides. The suicides have been turned into trees. Septimus' hallucinations, as we know, have a good deal to do with trees: God's revealed message to him is "Do not cut down trees" (224); he has written of "how the dead sing behind rhododendron bushes" (224); he thinks "the supreme secret . . . [is] that trees are alive" (102); he is in fact introduced to readers as he beholds "a curious pattern like a tree, . . . and this gradual drawing together of everything to one centre before his eyes, as if some horror had come almost to the surface and was about to burst into flames, terrified him" (21).

The leaves on Dante's "unnatural trees" (13.15) are eternally wounded and eternally bleeding souls, eternally eaten by "the odious Harpies" (13.10). Septimus has characterized "Amelia What'shername" as "a leering, sneering obscene little harpy" (135), and Clarissa speaks of "the depths of that leaf-encumbered forest, the soul" (17).[71] Rezia's image of Septimus is of "that hawk or crow which being malicious and a great destroyer of crops was precisely like him" (225)—a destroyer bird implies exactly those elements of violence and sterility found in the birds of the *septimus* circle.[72]

In addition to being devoured by Harpies, the souls of the suicides are torn apart by packs of savage dogs (13.126–29). Septimus has had a vision of human beings as "lustful animals" who "hunt in packs. Their packs scour the desert and vanish screaming into the wilderness. They desert the fallen. They are plastered over with grimaces" (135). Moreover, his drawings of detestable people "naked at their antics" (135) suggest the *Inferno's* "torn and naked wraiths" (13.117). His "Toms and Berties in their starched shirt fronts oozing thick drops of vice" (135) and his vision of "women burnt alive" (136) seem to come from Hell itself.

In the third round of the seventh circle, upon a desert of burning sand and under an eternal rain of fire, there are three types of scorched sinners: blasphemers, sodomites, and usurers. To the extent that Septimus has renounced humanity via his images of disgust and loathing, he is one of Dante's sinners who "blasphemed God, their parents, their time on earth, / the race of Adam, and the day and the hour / and the place and the seed and the womb that gave them birth" (3.100–102). Dante's sodomites are alienated from human nature; Septimus, feeling himself to be so alienated, tried to make Shakespeare a co-hater of human nature; he considers Holmes representative of "horrible" human nature (213). His recurring conviction is that "he had committed an appalling crime and been condemned to death by human nature" (145), that "the verdict of human nature on such a wretch was death" (138). It is all entirely appropriate to the unflinching fatalism of Dantesque ethics, which exiled sodomites for their violence against ordinary human nature.

Dante's sodomites rove in bands, running endless futile circles. For their unnatural and sterile sin they are punished in a barren desert where no natural fertilizing rain ever falls; instead there is an unending stream of fire. Septimus' terror that "the world wavered and quivered and threatened to burst into flames" (21) thus takes on an added significance. So do his hallucinations of *blood-red* flowers growing through his flesh and his *bloody* death and the *red roses* upon his wallpaper and Holmes's "*blood-red* nostrils" (139) and the fact that his true love-object, officer Evans, has *red* hair. All make minor but effective subliminal contributions to the accruing significance of the color. The third round of the septimus circle is quintessentially *red:* fires flame down from above or rage upward from the desert; the suicides' wood has a *blood-red* rill; Dante says "it ran so red / the memory sends a shudder through me still" (14.74–75).

Woolf's threefold repetition of "falling down, down . . . into the flames" (100, 213, 216) exploits Dantesque symbolism of descent-as-fatality. Septimus' sensation that "the bed was falling; he was falling" (131) is comparable to Satan's fall from heaven, and he feels himself to be as reviled for his sins as Satan himself, "so pocked and marked with vice that women shuddered when they saw him on the street" (137–38).

This descent into his own subjective hell of insanity, into the chasm that yawns before his disordered mind, is yet *even more* precisely projected by Woolf: we read that Septimus "descended another step into the pit" (136). According to Dante's geography, "another step into the pit" would go beyond the Wood of the Suicides to the waterfall that plunges over the Great Cliff into the Eighth Circle. It was at this point that Dante had to remove the cord tied around his waist, for the extremity of the drop required that he and Virgil fly down from the precipice on the back of Geryon, the monster of fraud. To this we might compare Septimus' drawings of "zigzagging precipices with mountaineers ascending roped together" (223). Dante's intensification of the descending action has a crucial symbolic significance: the seventh circle was the Hell of the violent and bestial; the eighth is a blacker Hell of the fraudulent and the malicious. Virginia Woolf's use of the noun *pit* is entirely appropriate: the eighth circle is divided into ten concentric ditches, where sin and guilt are further intensified into prison pits of torment. Septimus too has descended from violence to the greater sin of fraud. Enumerating his own fraudulent crimes he lists "how he had married his wife without loving her; had lied to her; seduced her; outraged Miss Isabel Pole" (137). There remains only the manner of Septimus' death to complete Woolf's mastery of sustained allusive relevance. When he commits the sin of suicide by leaping "vigorously, violently down on to Mrs. Filmer's area railings" (226), that final plunge becomes the ultimate expression of his Dantesque essence.

The flight from the heat of life is also a movement away from the sun of God's love and warmth. This novel's thematic polarities of life and death, rising and falling, communication and isolation, light and darkness, rebirth and annihilation mingle in its Dante and Shakespeare allusions.[73] The two references combine in Septimus—he believes that Nature reveals her meaning through "Shakespeare's words" (212), and because his concept of *treasure* ("every power poured its treasures on his head," 211) relates back to the *Inferno*,[74] it establishes his link to a covert homosexual love-object, just as Clarissa's allusion to *Othello* did. The notion of *treasure* occurs to Septimus shortly before he takes his own life. Later on, Clarissa's question about his fate will be: "Had he plunged holding his treasure?" (281). Shakespeare occurs to Septimus shortly before his suicide: "Fear no more, says the heart in the body; fear no more. He was not afraid" (211). And since he considers the doctors Holmes and Bradshaw to be his persecutors, death will certainly put Septimus "past the tyrant's stroke," past "slander, censure rash," past "joy and moan."

Such is the unremitting, interlocked allusive structure of this novel.

When Clarissa's recurring phrase occurs in the consciousness of Septimus Smith, connections are forged between the two characters that are not merely formal. They are also symbolic and thematic. The shared allusion establishes something more important than spatial contiguity; it establishes their psychological kinship. Septimus lacks the bookshop window in which Clarissa first saw the lines from *Cymbeline*, but their appearance in his own meditations establishes virtual identity with Clarissa. However much some critics may complain that characterization by allusion is trivial or highbrow or unconvincing, none has seriously questioned the rhetorical success of *this* piece of allusiveness. It works and it is nothing short of brilliantly realized.

When Dr. and Lady Bradshaw bring the news of Septimus' suicide to Clarissa's party, she feels "her dress flamed, her body burnt" (280), as once earlier she had felt "drenched in fire" (255). This vicarious reaction now unites in her, as it did in Septimus, the Shakespearean sun imagery with the burning flames of the *Inferno*. She believes his suicide "was her disaster—her disgrace. It was her punishment" (282). The word *punishment* recalls the *Inferno*, just as the word *treasure* linked Septimus and Clarissa, first to the *Inferno* and then to each other.

Septimus' defiantly willed death releases him from failure to communicate. Thus his death is not a negation, but "reaching the centre" (281). It is the "embrace" (281) denied one during one's lifetime—the "criminal" (that is, homosexual) love-embrace Clarissa experienced with Sally Seton. She therefore sees Septimus' suicide as an affirmation: liberation from a conflicted consciousness, preservation of values that life sullies or forbids.

It is only after a sequence involving her vicarious experience of Septimus' suicide, her interpretation of death as defiance, communication, and embrace, an admission that "there was in the depths of her heart an awful fear," and personal acceptance of disgrace and punishment, that the line from *Cymbeline* recurs, for the fifth and last time, to Clarissa (280–82). Leaving her party for a moment, Clarissa observes from her window an old woman in the room opposite her: "And the words came to her, Fear no more the heat of the sun" (283).

If "the depth of our insight into Clarissa's character is dependent upon our having grasped the relationship between Clarissa and Septimus,"[75] then it is also dependent upon our having grasped the functions of the *Cymbeline* allusion, which is part of their relationship. They share the allusion and the symbolism of its imagery. Through his death Septimus has become the sunlight of self-illumination for Clarissa, who has confronted the dark side of her own inner being. "Fear no more" serves to reveal Clarissa's unconscious desire for death by connecting her with her death-embracing double. The life and death instincts, the sane and insane worlds, are thereby joined.

There is a satisfying symmetry in the first and last appearances of the *Cymbeline* lines. Clarissa began by admiring Lady Bexborough for confronting mortality and carrying on with her duties as required. She ends by confronting the inevitable fact of mortality herself and carrying on: "She must go back to them [the party guests] . . . she must go back" (283–84). Her vicarious death-through-Septimus leaves her free from fear of the heat of the sun; she can return to her party. The final repetition of the allusion embraces both Clarissa's death wish and her transcendence of annihilation. This paradox is also present in the original source, for the *Cymbeline* Song is a dirge that attempts to reconcile man to his fate by characterizing death as the lifting of life's burden, rest, peace, "quiet consummation." But the song is also the beginning of a rebirth to new life, sung over an Imogen who is only apparently dead. Like Imogen raised from death (in a classic archetypal resurrection myth), Clarissa returns, revitalized, to her party.

In the final appearance of the *Cymbeline* allusion, Clarissa gains a transcendent awareness of the paradox of existence, its mingling of the realities of life and death. As Clarissa and Septimus comprise a divided personality now made psychologically whole, they are also a philosophic unity, having shared an illumination in keeping with what E.M. Forster called the "shimmering fabric of mysticism"[76] that pervades the novel. They have rejected the narrower confines of personal individuality for an awareness of their oneness with the vast universe. In the assumed after-life of the spirit, which has broken free of time, resides the immortality myth; its life-death-rebirth sequence is woven into the very fabric of *Mrs. Dalloway*. The lines from *Cymbeline* and the reference to Ceres give it expression, but the Adonis myth (implicit in the allusions to Keats and Shelley) is an equally strong manifestation.

While Shelley's elegy on Keats is not alluded to in *Mrs. Dalloway*, lines from *Adonais* are a significant part of the story from which the novel was born. In "Mrs. Dalloway in Bond Street," Clarissa muses:

> And now can never mourn—how did it go?—a head grown grey. . . . From the contagion of the world's slow stain. . . . have drunk their cup a round or two before. . . . From the contagion of the world's slow stain! She held herself upright. But how Jack would have shouted! Quoting Shelley, in Piccadilly! (in McNichol, p. 22)

The phrases "can never mourn" and "the world's slow stain" are repeated throughout the story. Not only does this relate the Clarissa of that story to the fully developed Clarissa of the novel, it also links these two Clarissas to the earlier Mrs. Dalloway who made her appearance in *The Voyage Out*, quoting exactly that stanza of *Adonais* and repeating exactly that line about "the contagion of the world's slow stain" which continued to fascinate Woolf through revision after revision of the Clarissa Dalloway saga.

The spirituality of Shelley's poem is most appropriate to Woolf's presentation of mystic beliefs. Woolf called Shelley one of the "priests" whose lines were "to be laid upon the heart like an amulet against disaster."[77] Clarissa need fear no more in the midst of Shelley's confident idealism:

> The One remains, the many change and pass;
> Heaven's light forever shines, Earth's shadows fly;
>
> Life, like a dome of many-coloured glass,
> Stains the white radiance of Eternity,
> Until Death tramples it to fragments.—Die,
> If thou wouldst be with that which thou dost seek!
> (*Adonais*, 52.460–65)

We have seen how Clarissa and her counterpart seek to penetrate through the veil of ordinary life to reach the radiant mystic center. They are in agreement with Shelley's counsel to "no more let Life divide what Death can join together" (53.477).[78] Moreover, *Mrs. Dalloway* shares several key metaphors with *Adonais*. For instance, truth-seeking consciousness is likened to "something which has soared beyond" (42) in *Mrs. Dalloway;* in *Adonais* Keats's spirit is said to have "outsoared the shadow of our night" (40.352). Woolf's simile of rumors "passing, invisibly, like a cloud, swift, veil-like upon hills" (19–20) uses characteristically Shelleyan images. Most significant of all is the analogue of Septimus to Shelley's own analogue of Adonis-Keats. Adonis was pursued by the boar he wounded; in Shelley's poem, Keats is hounded by bestial critics who are called "herded wolves" (28.244) or "obscene ravens" (line 245) or "the monsters of life's waste" (27.243). As Keats is "a herd-abandoned deer struck by the hunter's dart" (33.297), so Septimus is hounded and persecuted by his bestial doctors with blood-red nostrils who "hunt in packs" (135). Shelley's hunted-hunter metaphor for Keats and the critics is echoed in Septimus' feelings about "human cruelty—how they tear each other to pieces. The fallen, he said, they tear to pieces" (213).

Again the "Bond Street" story shows how closely connected the *Adonais* allusion was to the "Fear no more" refrain in Woolf's characterization of Clarissa: "From the contagion of the world's slow stain. . . . Fear no more the heat o' the sun. . . . And now can never mourn, can never mourn, she repeated, her eyes straying over the window; for it ran in her head . . . " (McNichol, p. 23). The novel came to be permeated by these earlier resonances from Shelley's elegy. Even after explicit quotations from *Adonais* were abandoned, Shelley remains a powerful presence called up by shared mystic affirmations or by similar images and phrases.[79]

In the world of *Mrs. Dalloway*, character is revealed not by action but through memory, and allusions are an important part of that special method of characterization. These echoing allusions sometimes substitute for plot action as well, in the sense that they maintain sequence and a continuity of past and present. Furthermore, they often function as gradually enlarging metaphors, eliciting the central theme. As they expand in significance, they progressively disclose the core concerns of the novel in which they have been invoked.

four

Orlando

After *Mrs. Dalloway* Woolf continued her lyric exploration of consciousness in *To the Lighthouse*, probing even deeper into reverie and memory—that of her characters and even her own memory of her parents. Then, almost as if she had had too much of demandingly serious, broodingly poetic novels, she next produced something predictably unpredictable: a brilliant comic fantasy, the mock-biography, *Orlando*. Where *Mrs. Dalloway* dealt with one day in the life of its protagonist, *Orlando* spans more than three centuries, from the late sixteenth century to midnight, October 11, 1928. There were brief evocations of centuries of time passing in *Jacob's Room*, even the suggestion of a comic narrative mode in that novel, and certainly its challenge to conventional novelistic form predates *Orlando's* nonconformity. But in *Orlando*, that quintessential symbol, Rachel's room of autonomy and protection, which became Jacob's room at Cambridge, then Clarissa's attic room, is a many-chambered mansion.

Orlando is a literary hybrid that defies attempts to fit it into one genre: it combines biography, history, fantasy, fiction, poetry, and allegory. It resembles, in passing, the quest novel, the picaresque novel, satire, the fairy story, the feminist pamphlet, the *Bildungsroman*, and a history of English literature told in metaphors. Its idiosyncratic nature has dampened somewhat the critical urge to find influences and precedents, but those critics who feel they must find a forerunner of *Orlando* do manage a rare consensus by consistently nominating Laurence Sterne.[1] Several of them remind us that Lytton Strachey had once advised Woolf to write a *Tristram Shandy* sort of work.[2] Woolf does do Sternesque things in *Orlando*, for example, leaving blank spaces (in chapters 4 and 5). But to overstate Woolf's indebtedness to *Tristram Shandy* is to underestimate the originality of *Orlando*.[3] Moreover, if Woolf "appropriated" anything from anywhere, it was from Vita Sackville-West's *Knole and the Sackvilles*.[4] Indeed *Orlando* has been called "a tract with a key,"[5] the key being *Knole*. Woolf drew some of the descriptive details of Orlando's unnamed estate from the account of Knole: the heraldic leopards, the tapestries, the gilded furniture, the depth of mirrors, the "vulgar" silver in the King's bedroom, the list of furnishings shipped in July of 1624 to Knole, and several names of the household staff.[6] Woolf also borrowed the fifty-two (for weeks in a year) staircases and the 365 (for days in a year) rooms from Knole Castle, and she offers a portrait of Edward Sackville, fourth Earl of Dorset, as the frontispiece of Orlando as a boy.

The accumulation of such details, however, is far less important than the larger fact of Woolf's use of some 350 years of Sackville family history. By alluding to *Knole*, Woolf can construct a portrait of Orlando that has significance on the personal, national, and cultural levels. Orlando embodies nothing less than an English family, England herself, and England's literature. Woolf obviously shared Vita Sackville-West's conviction that the Sackvilles were "representative. From generation to generation they might stand, fully equipped, as portaits from English history . . . each as the prototype of his age" (*Knole*, p. 28). Her fictional Orlando, first male then female, is equivalent to the prototypal Sackville temperament, manifested in the Elizabethan, Thomas, Lord Buckhurst, and persisting through Vita Sackville-West into the twentieth century.

Being in part a history of English literature, *Orlando* is of necessity a rather "erudite fantasia," which conspicuously displays its literary learning.[7] It has been called "a comic survey course, complete with stylistic parodies, in English social and literary history."[8] The use of allusion is mandatory in such a work; yet one critic, who considers *Orlando* a "colossal pun" and "an inspired joke, a joke charged with meanings," wonders if, being "packed with reference," it is not "too esoteric—for one not in the enchanted circle—to be universally valid."[9] *Orlando* is not, I think, dismissable as an esoteric in-joke, but neither is it for lazy readers, and those who wish to savor every drop of its wit and humor need to pay close attention to its brilliant use of allusion.

Orlando begins with a Preface which is signed "V.W." It names some dead but "illustrious" writers who are called "friends"—another small but telling indication of Woolf's emotional involvement with the tradition of English letters. The Preface declares: "No one can read or write without being perpetually in the debt of Defoe, Sir Thomas Browne, Sterne, Sir Walter Scott, Lord Macaulay, Emily Bronte, De Quincey, and Walter Pater—to name the first that come to mind" (5).

These are characteristic choices. Woolf believed, for example, that Defoe represented the prosaic pole in English novel writing,[10] and Emily Brontë the poetic.[11] Along with Defoe, Sterne and De Quincey dabbled in pseudo-biography or autobiography.[12] As for the rest of the writers mentioned in the Preface, Woolf had read "Scott's life and letters" by the age of twenty.[13] Macaulay's historical sense makes him an appropriate inclusion; Woolf spoke of his "vivid partisanship,"[14] as Vita Sackville-

West had pointed out his "picturesque and vivid pen" (*Knole*, p. 138). Walter Pater's significance could perhaps be explained to full satisfaction only by Woolf herself, but his essays on such writers as William Morris, Browne, Lamb, and Shakespeare indicate their similarity of taste. Pater's four *Imaginary Portraits* and his *Appreciations*, a volume on English literature, are akin to Woolf's own approaches to fiction and the essay. Finally, two biographers, Harold Nicolson and Lytton Strachey (then alive), are mentioned in the Preface. Strachey's Preface to *Eminent Victorians* anticipates Woolf's own attitudes. However, *Orlando* outdoes Strachey in its assumptions and execution and may possibly be a sly parody of the historical biography that goes Lytton one better.

These names scattered about Woolf's Preface are more than token acknowledgment of literary debts. They are evidence of the considerable tradition out of which even so singular a work as *Orlando* springs. They establish a *context* and impart to this high-flying fantasy some sense of stability and reality. However, the tone of the Preface is not so much serious as mock-solemn. Pope and Dryden are nowhere in evidence, and the omission of Shakespeare is glaring. Alert readers begin to divine the humor of Woolf's capricious choices, delivered in disarming, deadpan prose. So seemingly reasonable, yet so totally arbitrary beneath it all, the Preface is a hodge-podge of great writers, Bloomsbury friends, and relatives—all ploddingly enumerated in that spirit of high scholarship which must include *everyone*, however unimportant and disparate. The tone, content, and form of pedantic biographies are ridiculed in Woolf's sly duplication of the ritual gratitude of the scholarly biography, reeled off in long lists of helpers. She closes with a light touch of malice:

> Finally, I would thank, had I not lost his name and address, a gentleman in America, who has generously and gratuitously corrected the punctuation, the botany, the entomology, the geography, and the chronology of previous works of mine and will, I hope, not spare his services on the present occasion. (6)

Like the Preface, *Orlando* as a whole either frustrates or mocks the reader's conventional expectations. Allusive naming of characters, for instance, takes on an added playfulness; so often the surnames—by some "sheer coincidence" in which we cannot quite believe, knowing Virginia Woolf—just happen to be the surnames of relatively obscure English authors. Woolf's fanciful names for Orlando's husband, the Russian princess, the Archduchess, and the leader of the gipsy band are also allusive. Most significant is the naming of Nick Greene, the writer-critic figure who first appears in the Elizabethan era.

One critic has declared Nick Greene a comic figure with enough credibility "as an unnamed type to render unnecessary any curiosity about the model that inspired it."[15] But surely recognition of the literary source of Greene's name adds another dimension to his character. There is both purpose and point to the narrator's gratuitous observations of "how common the name of Greene was" (55) and "how some Greens spelt the name with an e at the end, and others without" (56). The writer with whom Nick shares his surname was an Elizabethan author-critic notorious for having slandered Shakespeare.[16]

By far the greatest extension of meaning through allusive naming occurs in the name Orlando, which comes out of a rich literary background it would impoverish enjoyment to ignore. It captures the essence of the medieval romance hero in French and Italian literature.[17] Indeed we find several of Woolf's plot incidents echoing their Italian sources. In Ariosto's *Furioso* Orlando has a sword named Durendal; Woolf's opening sentence has Orlando "in the act of slicing at the head of a Moor" (7). A bit later in her tale, Woolf has Orlando fall twice "in sheer abstraction, from his horse" (54), recalling the original Orlando's horse, Brigliadoro, from which he too fell while in combat with the Saracen Mandricardo.

If not in literary name, in character and personality Orlando is an "allusion" to his/her real-life model, Victoria Sackville-West. However, I do not believe the correspondences are so absolute that readers should conclude that "in her [Vita] alone it [*Orlando*] reaches its destination."[18] A good deal of Virginia Woolf herself is invested in the character of Orlando; for example, one product of her own adolescence was a "*history* of my own family—all very longwinded and *Elizabethan* in style."[19]

The interpenetration of novel and biography, fantasy and realism that is the essence of *Orlando* requires paradoxical comic techniques to express the tensions between inner and outer realities. *Orlando*'s stance toward conventional biography must be one of satire or parody because its underlying assumption is that biographers cannot adequately render the inner life—only the poet or novelist is capable of revealing that sort of complexity. Hence the comic insufficience of our biographer-narrator, who persists in using his ridiculously limited genre to describe the diffuse complexity of Orlando, his/her literary compositions, and his/her journey through 350 years of English history. The ludicrous inadequacy of this prim biographer, armed with pedantic facts, fussy details, and pompous asides, becomes more evident as the narrative progresses, but he maintains his scholarly exactitude to the very end, where readers are presented with an Index as irrelevant as it is incomplete.

Like the Preface, its inclusions and exclusions are totally arbitrary.

It lists some of the allusions and omits others; it offers only seven page-references for *The Oak Tree*, which is mentioned dozens of times;[20] it includes gratuitous items like "Railway, the, 178" and "Marshall and Snelgrove's, 196," to identify a department store. It indulges in oblique sarcasms like "Greene, Nicholas (afterwards Sir)"; it supplies information not to be found in the text at all, for example, the identification of the mysterious shabby poet as none other than Shakespeare, and it lists "Othello, 35" for those who could not identify the play and quotation in the episode on that page.

The biographer-narrator of *Orlando* is an extension of that busy, interruptive narrator first encountered in *Jacob's Room*. Not simply the *victim* of Woolf's deadly wit, he is the *vehicle* through which she implements her satirical method. The mock-biographer who created Jacob Flanders out of bits and scraps of information has become the more stuffy and pretentious narrator of *Orlando*. His slavish devotion to "facts" results in such stultifying pieces of redundant precision as:

> It was now November. After November, comes December. Then January, February, March, and April. After April comes May. June, July, August follow. Next is September. Then October, and so, behold, here we are back at November again, with a whole year accomplished. (174)

The biographer's style, which is nothing if not pompous, is littered with personifications like "Ambition, the harridan, and Poetry, the witch, and Desire of Fame, the strumpet" (52), and pseudo-Homeric extravagances about "the wine-blue purple-dark hill" (177). He is even Miltonic, endeavoring "to compare great things with small" (173).[21] Through this self-appointed "historian of letters" (73) we glimpse the evolution of English literature, especially its changing critical views and the role of the man of letters in successive ages.

It all begins in the Elizabethan era,[22] Woolf's favorite literary period.[23] She paints a vivid picture of the vigorous action, energy, and extravagance that characterized the age, praising even the "danger and insecurity, lust and violence, poetry and filth [which] swarmed over the tortuous Elizabethan highways and buzzed and stank" (147). Her sentences become as short and blunt as their content: "Violence was all. The flower bloomed and faded. The sun rose and sank. The lover loved and went. . . . Girls were roses, and their seasons were short as the flowers. Plucked they must be before nightfall; for the day was brief" (16). Such sexual metaphors echo a favorite conceit of the Cavalier poets, as in Herrick's familiar "To the Virgins, to Make Much of Time," or

Lovelace's line in "Love Made in the First Age": "lads indifferently did crop / A flower, and a Maiden-head." Because Orlando follows "the leading of the climate, of the poets, of the age itself" (16), his initial gender is symbolically appropriate. The passionate, flamboyant, and virile Elizabethan age requires masculinity; for Woolf this was an undeniable assumption.[24]

Orlando, male, Elizabethan, sixteen years old, is first seen slicing at a Moor's head with his sword—an echo of the mock-heroic behavior of his namesake in Ariosto and Boiardo.[25] He lives a passionate life of adventure, "feeding on the same sustenance of experience as provided matter for Shakespeare's plays and Dekker's satires."[26] Since the Elizabethans "had none of our modern shame of book learning" (18), and since the women of that time were important only in imaginative literature,[27] Orlando combines life and art by writing poems about allusively named lady loves: "It may have been Doris, Chloris, Delia, or Diana, for he made rhymes to them all in turn" (17). The names are true to Sackville family history as well as literary convention. Though not an Elizabethan, Charles Sackville, the sixth Earl of Dorset, wrote several verses to Chloris,[28] and himself protested the frequent recourse to that name in his own lines, "Methinks the poor town has been troubled too long, / With Phyllis and Chloris in every song."[29] Orlando is indeed expressing the Elizabethan *Zeitgeist* by addressing his sonnets to women whose classical names have built-in resonance.

The great romance of Orlando's Elizabethan tenure is with the beautiful Princess Marousha Stanilovska Dagmar Natasha Iliana Romanovitch, alias Sasha. She provokes Orlando into compulsive image-making and extravagant hyperbole. He compares her to "snow, cream, marble, cherries, alabaster, golden wire" (29), to "a melon, a pineapple, an olive tree, an emerald, and a fox in the snow" (23), giving Woolf an opportunity to parody the florid extravagance of the Elizabethan conceit. Their love affair allows for enriching parallels to Renaissance paradigms. As smitten as ever Ariosto's Orlando was with his Angelica, this Orlando and his Sasha fittingly talk "of Moor and Pagan" (28). And, allusively enough, Orlando comes to realize that "all extremes of feeling are allied to madness" (28).[30] Woolf's plot situations in this chapter repeatedly echo the *Furioso*. Her Orlando discovers "Sasha seated on the [Russian] sailor's knee" (32); Ariosto's Orlando discovered "his faithless mistress and her paramour" (*Furioso*, 23.893). Violently angry at Sasha's deceit, Orlando runs "wild in his transports" (29), and when Sasha does not meet him at the appointed rendezvous, he is "past reasoning" (38), much like Ariosto's "hapless Orlando, with his wits destroy'd" (*Furioso*, 29.329). "The riot and confusion" of the scene by the Thames in which Orlando beholds flood victims "in the utmost agony of spirit" (39) is Woolf's materialization of

Orlando's psychic torment. It is also an effective parallel to those bizarre acts of madness that Ariosto's Orlando commits when he rends his clothes and runs naked through the countryside, fighting with herdsmen and killing their beasts (*Furioso*, 23–24). After the turmoil Orlando, "seeming to recollect himself" (40), curses Sasha roundly for her treachery; this is equivalent to the restoration of wits experienced by Ariosto's Orlando, when "heal'd of every love-sick care" he comes to "scorn those charms He held so dear before" (*Furioso*, 39.488, 491). Even Orlando's revival from a faint by brandy (32) has its parallel in the *Furioso*, in which Orlando's sanity returns after he sniffs the contents of a vessel (39.455–59).

Before the disillusioning end of the Sasha affair, however, Orlando is temporarily reconciled to his Princess. They attend a theatrical performance in which "a black man was waving his arms and vociferating. There was a woman in white laid upon a bed" (35). Orlando is intoxicated by "the astonishing, sinuous melody of the words" (35), some of which remain in his memory: "Methinks it should be now a huge eclipse / Of sun and moon, and that the affrighted globe / Should yawn—" (36). Woolf has taken these lines, spoken by the anguished Othello shortly before he smothers Desdemona, and supplied a singularly masterful new context. They are the correlative of Orlando's feelings about his *genuinely* unfaithful Sasha: "The frenzy of the Moor seemed to him his own frenzy, and when the Moor suffocated the woman in her bed it was Sasha he killed with his own hands" (35–36). Even the eclipse in the quotation nicely correlates with the plans of Orlando and Sasha to flee "on such a night as this" (36). Moreover, the *Othello* allusion supplements the themes of jealousy and love's madness already invoked by the *Furioso*.

Orlando has written some "twenty tragedies and a dozen histories and a score of sonnets" (14). At the tender age of sixteen, he composed " 'Aethelbert: A Tragedy in Five Acts' " (9). His Elizabethan counterpart, Thomas Sackville, was co-author of the first English tragedy, *Gorboduc*; he wrote sonnets and produced a five-act tragedy when quite young (*Knole*, pp. 32–33). Both Orlando and Sackville selected elevated themes and royal protagonists, the better to grandly combine history and nobility;[31] both tended to use allegorical figures.[32]

Woolf adapts her allusive techniques to the fantastic mode of *Orlando* by having several English writers appear as actual characters. In the first chapter Orlando sees "a rather fat, rather shabby man" (12) lost in thought, and he cannot forget "the shabby poet and the great Queen" (13): Shakespeare and Elizabeth.[33] The vision of Shakespeare at work, pen in hand, remains with Orlando;[34] for him and for his creator, Shakespeare is the supreme symbol of that ideal unity which resides in the androgynous human being.[35]

In the second chapter, Orlando, disillusioned over Sasha and exiled from Court, retires to his country house to live "in complete solitude" (42). The gloomy Jacobean age is an appropriate atmosphere for his brooding melancholy.[36] The Sackville Orlando most resembles at this point is the Jacobean Richard, who also lived in solitude. The sudden seven-day trance into which Orlando falls, waking "graver and more sedate in his ways than before" (43), is compared to "death in small doses" (44), and a symbolic rebirth is suggested: "Had Orlando . . . died for a week, and then come to life again?" (44). The metaphor of sleep/ death has many literary sources, originating in Greek mythology, in which Sleep and Death are twin brothers. It also appears frequently in the literature of the period Woolf is gently satirizing; for example, Thomas Sackville's "heavy *Sleep*, the cousin of Death,"[37] and Browne's "Sleep is a death; oh, make me try / By sleeping, what it is to die."[38]

His trance having rendered Orlando pensive and rather morbid, he takes "a strange delight in thoughts of death and decay" (45). The atmosphere reeks of "bat or death's head moth" (45), coffins in the ancestral crypt, skeletons and skulls (46). One critic has remarked that Orlando "broods like Hamlet,"[39] and it is not difficult to see in the rampant skulls and Orlando's ruminations on mortality a sly parody of the churchyard grave-digging scene (5.1.ff.) in *Hamlet:*

> Orlando, stooping his lantern, would pick up a gold circle lacking a stone, that had rolled into a corner . . . and the eye which was so lustrous shines no more. "Nothing remains of all these Princes," Orlando would say, indulging in some pardonable exaggeration of their rank, "except one digit," and he would take a skeleton hand in his and bend the joints this way and that. "Whose hand was it?" he went on to ask. "The right or the left? The hand of man or woman, of age or youth? Had it urged the war horse, or plied the needle? Had it plucked the rose or grasped cold steel? (46)

However, it is not in Shakespeare that Orlando finds a perfect complement to this mood, but in Thomas Browne, "a doctor of Norwich, whose writing upon such subjects took his fancy amazingly" (46).[40] In his solitude Orlando has chosen a writer whom Woolf called one of the "keepers of the keys of solitude."[41] Proceeding to parody the subjects and styles of Jacobean writers as she earlier parodied Elizabethan styles, Woolf has Orlando "investigate the delicate articulation of one of the doctor's longest and most marvellously contorted cogitations" (47). Such diction skillfully reproduces Browne's Latinate vocabulary and his learned, exotic style.[42] Browne is a particularly suitable allusion[43] because he complements Orlando's pessimistic preoccupation with the brevity of human life and the gloomy fact of mortality. Browne's interest in skulls, bones, and the accoutrements of burial, as expressed in *Hydriotaphia: Urn Burial*, is echoed in Orlando's tour of his family sepulchre. And the concept of *diuturnity* appears in Browne as well. By referring to "brevity and diuturnity" (64), Woolf allusively presents the time dialectic of *Orlando:* the ephemeral versus the enduring, the past persisting in the present. When the narrator observes that Orlando's ponderous conclusions about diuturnity "might have been reached more quickly by the simple statement that 'Time passed' " (63), it is undoubtedly a sly allusion by Woolf to one of her own works: Part 2 of *To the Lighthouse* is called "Time Passes."

Browne is responsible for Orlando's contraction of "the disease of reading," which leads to the more fatal "scourge which dwells in the ink pot and festers in the quill. The wretch takes to writing" (48). Orlando composes forty-seven prose and poetical works before he reaches the age of twenty-five; "There was scarcely a single drawer that lacked the name of some mythological personage at a crisis of his career" (49).

Having been initiated into the mysteries and agonies of literary composition, Orlando recollects that "rather fat, shabby man who sat in Twitchett's room ever so many years ago" (51). In the recurring image of Shakespeare, the ultimate role model for Orlando, the themes of immortality and tradition that are central to the work are personified. Orlando concludes that his ancestors' deeds are "dust and ashes, but this man [Shakespeare] and his words were immortal" (53). Shakespeare also serves as the basis for Woolf's introduction of a favorite thesis, "How No Aristocrat Can Write a Book."[44] Being an aristocrat, Orlando must conquer the built-in problem of "how difficult it is for a nobleman to be a writer" (52). Shakespeare is Orlando's amulet, renewing his determination to write.

In the grip of his intense literary ambition, Orlando contacts Nick Greene, "a very famous writer at that time" (54). When Orlando names his five "favorite heroes" (57), Greene disposes of them instantly:

> Shakespeare, he admitted, had written some scenes that were well enough; but he had taken them chiefly from Marlowe. Marlowe was a likely boy, but what could you say of a lad who died before he was thirty? As for Browne, he was for writing poetry in prose . . . Donne was a mountebank who wrapped up his lack of meaning in hard words. The gulls were taken in; but the style would be out of fashion twelve months hence. As for Ben Jonson—Ben Jonson was a friend of his and he never spoke ill of his friends. (57)

The real Robert Greene's attack on Shakespeare now finds a parallel in the fictional Nick Greene's contention that Shakespeare plagiarized Marlowe, an opinion that reflects the belief of some scholars that Marlowe wrote all or parts of Shakespeare's plays. And it is a reverse-image of his real-life namesake's tendency to "imitate" his own peers.[45] Nick's opportunistic attention to what is in or out of fashion is an echo of his Elizabethan namesake's policy of writing to please the public; it helps explain his superficial, not to say Philistine, judgment of Browne and Donne. To Woolf, Donne was an original, atypical poet, "more remote, inaccessible, and obsolete than any of the Elizabethans."[46] His self-analytic "desire for nakedness in an age that was florid"[47] would surely offend and threaten a crowd-pleaser like Greene.

Woolf's Nick, nearly as sanctimonious toward Marlowe as Robert Greene was in his *Groatsworth of Wit*, condescends to "Kit Marlowe, . . . rather drunk, . . . [saying] silly things . . . killed in a drunken brawl" (58). Robert Greene cast himself as a repentant sinner rejecting the evil example of friends like Marlowe, whose conceit and atheism he righteously disavowed.[48] Yet the actual jealousy behind Nick's slighting remarks is as plain as was Robert Greene's jealousy, for he "could not let Marlowe alone, or forgive him his success."[49]

Under the circumstances, Nick's disavowal of speaking ill of friends takes on the color of hypocrisy,[50] especially after he projects his own money-making attitude onto Shakespeare, whom he accuses of writing "any trash that would sell" (57). Woolf lets the smug Nick betray his own stupidity with the prediction that Shakespeare and the entire Elizabethan age will be a forgotten period in English literature (58). Pointing out "the faults" of *Hamlet*, *Lear*, and *Othello* (59), Nick is an absurd figure.

Like the sort of short-sighted critic Woolf intensely disliked, Greene has contempt for the literature of the present and praise for the dead past: "The more he denounced his own time, the more complacent he became" (58). He could only "say the finest things of books provided they were written three hundred years ago" (59). To him, literature's great age was the Greek, when writers "cherished a divine ambition which he might call La Gloire (he pronounced it Glawr . . .)" and did not indulge in "wild experiments" (57).

Greene's wish-fulfillment dream is to "lie in bed every morning reading Cicero" and "imitate his style so that you couldn't tell the difference between us" (58). His taste for Cicero is complement to that profound unoriginality that results in his need to counterfeit other writers to the point of identity. The allusion to the great Roman statesman and orator carries a touch of pomposity altogether appropriate to Nick Greene's glorified self-image; it has intimations of nationalism and rhetorical bombast, as when Nick persists in talking of "Glawr and Cicero and the death of poetry in our time" (67). It was Cicero of course who set the standards for the English gentleman's education. His influence reached even into the eighteenth-century prose of Gibbon and Johnson; Queen Elizabeth, under the instruction of Ascham, read nearly all of Cicero by the age of sixteen. Such a prestigious precedent could hardly fail to influence someone like Nick Greene, who is already so susceptible to "imitation."

Orlando gives Greene a copy of his play on Hercules and a quarterly pension (61). Greene responds with a scurrilous satire, which cites "wordy and bombastic" (62) passages from Orlando's work, "Death of Hercules."[51] Nick's satire is a financial success that brings in enough cash to pay the expenses of his wife's latest pregnancy, much as Robert Greene the hack wrote to turn "an honest penny to bury himself with."[52] Thus is Greene's treachery against fellow writers symbolized by and in the allusive surname he shares with the maligner of Shakespeare.[53]

Orlando concludes that literary ambition is a vain farce. He burns "fifty-seven poetical works, only retaining 'The Oak Tree,' which was his boyish dream and very short" (62). As an Elizabethan boy, Orlando sat under the huge oak tree which has become the title of his sole surviving work. This subject suggests, almost in a punning way, those concepts of ancestry and genealogy (that is, a family tree, one's roots) with which the novel is concerned.[54] It captures the weight of the facts of nature, of the thingness of things, which Orlando's poem celebrates. And because it survives the fire of reality's disillusionments, it is on its way to becoming the novel's most effective symbol—barring only Orlando him/herself—of stability persisting through change, permanence in a transitory world, the timeless immortality of nature and art. Orlando continues to sit "under his favorite oak tree" (63) and to work on "The Oak Tree, A Poem" long hours into the evening—thus do poem and reality, art and nature sustain him.

Orlando's great house, like his poem, recalls him from depression. It represents generations of anonymous effort by "obscure noblemen" like "Richards, Johns, Annes, Elizabeths" (69).[55] As his historical counterpart Edward Sackville had done, Orlando refurbishes and expands his estate, gives banquets, participates in political life, and is adored by women. And like Richard Sackville, third Earl of Dorset, who befriended Beaumont and Fletcher, Ben Jonson, and Michael Drayton (*Knole*, p. 59), Orlando patronizes the arts and finds himself the recipient of fulsome dedications from grateful poets.

Orlando's Russian Princess returns, transmogrified into a Roumanian Archduchess from "Finster-Aarhorn and Scand-op-Boom" (74).[56] Orlando feels "the beating of Love's wings" (75), and there follow some brilliantly wrought, allusive variations upon this metaphor. Up close, the beautiful bird of love has the creaking call and "coarse black wings" (76) of a crow. It is "Lust the vulture, not Love, the bird of Paradise," and

Lust the vulture is that most disgusting of birds, the harpy, the "dung-bedraggled fowl" (76) out of epic tradition and the depths of Hell by way of Dante. Since harpies are pictured in legend as greedily snatching at food, their insatiable hunger is an apt metaphor for lust.

In the third chapter Orlando is granted a Dukedom by King Charles, and there is a party to celebrate the event. To give us the "facts," the biographer resorts to the usual trappings of scholarship—letters, diaries, newspapers of the period. And within the larger parody of the plodding biographer's style, there occur two other parodies: the "long-winded" diary of the naval officer, John Fenner Brigge, and the personal letter of a Miss Penelope Hartopp.

Brigge records in his diary the incidents he witnessed when he climbed "into a Judas tree, the better to observe" (83). Woolf's cunning choice of tree suggests the diarist not just as reporter of gossip but as Judas-betrayer of the secrets of others. Brigge's account is full of uninspired cliches ("packed like herrings in a barrel"); overbearing Imperialist attitudes ("it impressed upon them [the natives of Constantinople] . . . the superiority of the British"); and degeneration into such purely personal trivia as "the rest of the entry records only his gratitude to Providence (who plays a very large part in the diary) and the exact nature of his injuries" (83–84). It is a deft comic touch, totally in keeping with the spirit of an age that produced Samuel Pepys's *Diary* (in which Pepys wrote of Charles Sackville's affair with Nell Gwyn).

Miss Penelope Hartopp's "much defaced" letter to "a female friend at Tunbridge Wells" (84) captures the gushing, scatterbrained sentimentality of feminine correspondence at its worst. Supposedly a letter giving information about the celebration, it is actually shallow palaver about how lovely "Mr. Peregrine said I looked" and how handsome Orlando was, replete with triple exclamation points.

The morning after his party, Duke Orlando is discovered to have sunk into his second "profound slumber" of seven days (86). The prim biographer confides his extreme reluctance to record the shocking event, but "Truth, Candour, and Honesty, the austere Gods . . . of the biographer" (87–88) oblige him to continue. The presence of this trinity turns the biographer's report of Orlando's trance into an allegorical conflict between his biographical gods and the three allegorical figures who enter Orlando's bedchamber—Purity, with her snow-white hair; Chastity, wearing "a diadem of icicles"; and Modesty, "frailest and fairest of the three" (88).[57] The Ladies speak at some length against the protesting "silver trumpets" (88) of Truth, making the elaborate ritual of Orlando's transformation a parody of an outmoded Restoration masque; that is to say, an outmoded form is suitable for harboring outmoded sexual prudery and ignorance.[58]

Purity finds she cannot "cover vice and poverty" with her deceitful veil; Chastity would rather destroy Orlando, "freeze him to the bone" (88), than let the dreaded sexual result of his trance stand. Both are banished by trumpet peals, which announce the triumph of truth. Modesty, whose virgin eyes are covered so that she cannot see "Increase [which is] odious to me" (89), is also rebuffed. When the three try "to cover Orlando with their draperies" and muffle the trumpets (89), they are routed by the liberating force of androgyny. Purity is forced to return "to the hen roost"; Modesty retreats to some heavily-curtained nook; Chastity flees "to the still unravished heights of Surrey" (89). Orlando wakes, naked, and a woman. The biographer concludes with a prim parody of Jane Austen: "But let other pens treat of sex and sexuality; we quit such odious subjects as soon as we can" (91).

However many literary precedents there may be for Woolf's scene, surely the primary source is Plato. In this passage from *Orlando*—

> For Love, to which we may now return, has two faces; one white, the other black; two bodies, one smooth, the other hairy. It has two hands, two feet, two tails, two, indeed, of every member and each one is the exact opposite of the other. Yet so strictly are they joined together that you cannot separate them. (76)

the concept of love is analogous to the humorous and fantastical one offered by Aristophanes in the *Symposium*, when he postulated a composite human being with four arms and legs, four ears, and two faces. After Jupiter cut these circular beings in half, love became the force which drove the divided portions toward unity and restoration. Woolf's presentation of Orlando's quest for wholeness of personality through androgyny is a reflection of that Platonic wisdom which has Aristophanes assert: "The desire and the pursuit of integrity and union is that which we call love."[59]

After the trance from which Orlando wakes a woman, she writes blank verse poems in the "margins and blank spaces" (95) of *The Oak Tree* manuscript. A change of sex has in no way diminished her desire to write; it merely demonstrates that the "sleeping" multiplicities of her nature have now materialized: her feminine powers of intuition and feeling have at last awakened. The *literary* import of the sex change lies in its rejection of the realistic literary convention of *male* novelists as upheld by *male* critics. An overriding metaphor of transformation has been set up: personal change in Orlando is paralleled by change in literary styles. As Orlando becomes a woman, the heroic literature of the Elizabethan age and the rowdy masculinity of the Restoration become the elegant dignity of the Queen Anne period.

Orlando's first act as a woman is to ride off with the gipsy leader, Rustum. The gipsies soon come to resent her "English disease, a love of nature" (93), however. Nature poetry, according to Woolf and her father before her, expresses the essence of the English literary soul.[60] Because she prefers "a sunset to a flock of goats" (98), Orlando parts company with the gipsies and sets sail for England aboard the *Enamoured Lady*.

Even as a woman, Orlando is haunted by "that earliest, most persistent memory—the man with the big forehead . . . who sat writing" (107). She compares her image of the thoughtful poet's forehead to "the dome of a vast cathedral" (107) like St. Paul's, a metaphor very similar to the one used in *Jacob's Room*. The "great lines of Marlowe, Shakespeare, Ben Jonson, Milton" begin "booming and reverberating . . . in the cathedral tower which was her mind" (107). She works on *The Oak Tree*, worrying about too many present participles and the excessive sibilance of her poem, calling the offending phrases (sibilantly enough) "sinful reptiles in the first stanzas" (113). This slow development and perfecting of her craft is interrupted by the Archduchess Harriet, whose appearance is announced by an allusive recapitulation of her initial harpy theme: "This was the eyrie of that obscene vulture—this is the fatal fowl herself!" (116). Conveniently Harriet changes into the Archduke Harry.[61] A brilliantly witty episode follows, in which Harry doggedly courts an Orlando so indifferent and bored by this dullard that she drops "a small toad between his skin and his shirt" (120). Still the dense, unimaginative Harry perseveres, sending Orlando "a toad set in emeralds" (125). To rid herself of him, Orlando joins the fashionable society of the day, where her present gender is mandatory. That is to say, the eighteenth century requires Orlando to be a woman much as earlier eras necessitated masculinity. It is in feminine shape that Orlando can best frequent the literary salons, gossip demurely, and pour tea for the famous wits of the age.[62]

To Orlando the names of Addison, Dryden, and Pope seem "an incantation" (109), and she suffers "from the poison of three honeyed words" (129).[63] In an episode that would appear to be modeled upon Lytton Strachey's description of the Marquise's salon, Orlando visits that quintessential hostess, "old Madame du Deffand" (130). As Orlando finds the company "assembled in a semicircle around the fire" (129), so Strachey described the guests arranged in a circle around the fireplace.[64] Where Woolf alludes to Madame du Deffand's "famous 'mot de Saint Denis' " (130), Strachey mentions that "famous 'mot de Saint Denis,' so dear to the heart of Voltaire."[65] Woolf even borrows her allusive metaphor for Madame du Deffand from Strachey, calling her a "modern

Sibyl" (130) as Strachey had called her "an ancient Sybil."[66] The metaphor nicely captures du Deffand's ability as a hostess to be "a witch who
lays her guests under a spell" (130). Woolf is perhaps a shade more
skeptical than Strachey about just how constantly brilliant salon wit was,
however. The *mot de Saint Denis* aside, Madame "said no more than three
witty things in the course of fifty years" (130).[67] Rather, as Sibyl-witch
she cast a spell in which the *illusion* of wit prevailed. This illusion is
shattered by "a little gentleman" (131) who says three witty things in the
same evening, a demonstration of unleashed genius that "no society
could survive" (132). Woolf leaves a taunting blank space where the
man's devastating witticisms should stand quoted and adds the footnote,
"These sayings are too well known to require repetition, and besides,
they are all to be found in his published works" (132).

The omission is more than just arbitrary caprice or an allusion by
imitation to Sterne. It is an effective assertion of Woolf's thesis that
neither tea parties nor critics nor biographers reveal a writer—only his
words do that. Great writers are in fact great *only as writers* ("their wit is
all in their books," 138); as mere men they can be tedious and dull. In
person, Mr. Alexander Pope (the little gentleman, identified) causes
complete disillusionment:

> His lean and misshapen frame was shaken by a variety of emotions.
> Darts of malice, rage, triumph, wit and terror (he was shaking like a
> leaf) shot from his eyes. He looked like some squat reptile set with a
> burning topaz in its forehead. (132)

Divine intellect can lodge "in the most seedy of carcases" (139). But that
literary capacity through which a writer transcends his personal self must
be respected: "A poet is Atlantic and lion in one. While one drowns us the
other gnaws us. If we survive the teeth, we succumb to the waves. A man
who can destroy illusions is both beast and flood" (133).

In the grip of this paradox, Orlando feels that "life is a dream. 'Tis
waking that kills us" (133).[68] Any poet can be a disillusioning shadow of
that public self which shines in his works; Pope was both physically
deformed and "the greatest wit in her Majesty's dominions" (134),
throwing the paradox of genius and deficiency into the sharpest possible
relief. Because Pope is a genius, Orlando wants to believe in "how noble
his brow is," but she is forced to recognize that this epitome of an entire
age[69] is in fact a "wretched man, . . . ignoble, . . . despicable. . . . Deformed and weakly" (134). This ambivalence is conveyed by the alterations of light and darkness through which they ride home together in a
coach. Those alterations symbolize the Platonic contrast of illusion and
reality and suggest that light of genius, sometimes shadowed by dark
moments, which is Pope's.

Orlando pours tea not only for Pope but for Addison and Swift as well. In her association with this trinity of the most representative writers of the eighteenth century,[70] there are parallels to Sackville family history. As patroness of the arts, Orlando reflects the activities of Charles Sackville, sixth Earl of Dorset, who was patron of Matthew Prior, Pope, and Dryden. Orlando "put bank notes, which they took very kindly, beneath their plates at dinner" (138), directly echoing Charles Sackville's patronage of Dryden, who also "found a hundred-pound note hidden under his plate" (*Knole*, p. 149).[71] And like her historical counterpart, Orlando "accepted their dedications."[72]

Because a writer is his work, we are not given biographical gossip about how Pope, Addison, and Swift looked and behaved. We are given selections from their writings. Lines from Pope's *Rape of the Lock* are quoted (136), which stress typically feminine concerns: preservation of chastity, clothes, prayers, and masquerade balls. Next a passage by Addison is quoted (137), which speaks slightingly of "woman as a beautiful, romantic animal" to be indulged in luxuries like furs, jewels, and silks.[73] Both the Addison and Pope allusions are antifeminist.[74] The third and last passage (137–38), by Swift,[75] lists some sixteen types of unsatisfactory human beings and is a fine example of "the intense misanthropy"[76] that pervades *Gulliver*. The biographer-narrator reacts to it by crying out: "Stop your iron pelt of words, lest you flay us all alive" (138). With Swift as with Pope, all sides of complicated genius must be acknowledged: Swift "scorns the whole world, yet talks baby language to a girl, and will die, can we doubt it, in a madhouse" (138).[77] One more writer is quoted—Lord Chesterfield. His misogynous belief, shared by all men, is that " 'women are but children of a larger growth. . . . A man of sense only trifles with them, plays with them, humours and flatters them' " (139).[78]

Woolf does not deal in obscure writers or atypical passages while documenting her feminist thesis. She alludes to the truly representative writers of the eighteenth century, and she discovers in "the sneer of Mr. Pope, in the condescension of Mr. Addison, and in the secret of Lord Chesterfield" (143) a very low estimate of women.[79] As one last proof, Woolf shows us the result of Orlando's accidentally spilling some tea on Mr. Pope. He retaliates "with the rough draught of a certain famous line in the 'Characters of Women' " (140). The line is left unquoted, like those earlier three witty sayings by Pope, but we cannot doubt that it is the infamous remark from the *Moral Essays:* "Most women have no characters at all." This is the dark side of that brilliant feminist wit which Woolf directed against dull Harry, the hapless Archduke. Using allusions as "proof," Woolf has marshaled passages that convince readers of the lamentable truth of her larger thesis:

A woman knows very well that, though a wit sends her his poems, praises her judgment, solicits her criticism, and drinks her tea, this by no means signifies that he respects her opinions, admires her understanding, or will refuse, though the rapier is denied him, to run her through the body with his pen. (140)

Hereafter Orlando observes wits from afar, "watching three shadows on the blind drinking tea together" (145). The little shadow, "fidgeting . . . petulant, officious" is James Boswell; the "bent female shadow" is Mrs. Williams; "the Roman looking rolling shadow in the big arm chair" (145) is Samuel Johnson. Woolf captures the essence of that famous literary friendship in two quick strokes: one shows Boswell's reverential attitude ("But with what humility did he not abase himself before the great rolling shadow"), and the other embodies Dr. Johnson's monumental physical and literary *presence* in "the great rolling shadow, who now rose to its full height and rocking somewhat as he stood there rolled out the most magnificent phrases that have ever left human lips" (145–46).[80] After Johnson and his Boswell, there is nothing significant left to say of the eighteenth century. The clock strikes midnight, a dark cloud spreads over the sky until all London is black and "the nineteenth century had begun" (147).[81]

In earlier chapters the weather served to characterize the age and its literary products; in the fifth chapter occasional metaphors become full-fledged pathetic fallacies. Those "clear and uniform skies" (151) which expressed the lucid eighteenth century give way to a "bruised and sullen canopy" (148) of a sky; now "men felt the chill in their hearts; the damp in their minds" (149). Because damp permeates everything, through "subterfuge . . . Evasions and concealments" (149), people simulate warmth by denying the cold. Rampant plant life symbolizes rampant human fertility: the nineteenth century's "undistinguished fecundity" (150) covers all. A woman's life is one of early marriage and "a succession of childbirths" (149). This life-style is "antipathetic" to Orlando: "It took her and broke her" (159), for it is in direct conflict with her writing ambitions. The manuscript of *The Oak Tree* has become "a roll of paper, sea-stained, blood-stained, travel-stained" (154). Dated 1586 in her former "boyish hand" (154), it is a fitting talisman of Orlando's struggles to realize and perfect her poem against the prevailing unsympathetic age.[82] It is difficult going: her quill is dirty and the ink comes out in blots upon the page, blots that are monsters of Victorian Female Verse at its worst, "something between a bat and a wombat" (155). Orlando writes eight lines of a maudlin poem beginning "I am myself but a vile link / Amid life's weary chain" but quickly realizes that it is "the most insipid verse she had ever read in her life" (155). Her flowery effort at describing a woman's countenance ("She was so changed, the soft carnation cloud / Once mantling o'er her cheek like that which eve / Hangs o'er the sky. . .") is awful; she has to blot it "from human sight she hoped for ever" (156).

These "cascades of involuntary inspiration" (156) are the aesthetic equivalent of that same triumph of "undistinguished fecundity" that haunts the whole century. Orlando's verse is terrible; she is timid and fearful. Victorian morality demands marriage and motherhood. She feels forced to "yield completely and submissively to the spirit of the age, and take a husband" (159). Historically speaking, even ruling monarchs have changed for the worst. The Elizabethan era was virile; the Victorian is stuffy and maternal. The Virgin Queen who presided over a brilliant, vital age, who "had stood astride the fireplace with a flagon of beer in her hand" (153), has become Motherly Victoria, a monumental symbol of weighty crinolines, fussy bassinettes, and wedding cakes (151).

There is certainly little that is attractive about Woolf's version of the nineteenth century. She hated Victorian conventionality, sentimentality, domesticity, and prudery. In a work brimming with allusion, this chapter almost omits the great nineteenth-century writers. There are fewer than a half a dozen allusions in it. The scarcity is in keeping with the novel's implicit thesis that the Victorian era produced little literature worth quoting, but it is also a subtle distortion of literary history. Woolf has thrown out the baby of Romanticism with the murky bathwater of Victorianism. By rejecting the entire century, she has dismissed those first two decades in which Victoria was not on the throne, in which Wordsworth, Coleridge, Byron, Shelley, and Keats were writing anything but oppressed and stuffy poetry, and Jane Austen produced six novels.[83] Yet in *Orlando* the Romantic poets suffer the fate of neglect.[84]

Under psychological pressure from the antipathetic nineteenth century to marry, Orlando conveniently meets a man on horseback, "chivalrous, passionate, melancholy," to whom she is engaged "a few minutes later" (163). Marmaduke Bonthrop Shelmerdine is both epitome and parody of the romantic image of masculinity. He is a soldier and an adventurer who sails around Cape Horn; he owns a ruined "castle in the Hebrides" (164); he first appears charging out of the mists upon a great horse, like a parody of Charlotte Brontë's Rochester.[85] Shelmerdine is as androgynous as Orlando: " 'You're a woman, Shel!' she cried. 'You're a man, Orlando!' he cried" (164). Instead of reproducing the conversation between the lovers, the biographer resorts to the Sternesque device of a blank space "which must be taken to indicate that the space is filled to repletion" (165).

Shelmerdine knows all of Shelley by heart; he and the entire scene in which he appears are a parodic echo of Shelley. One suspects the whole impetuous lyric episode, with its emphasis on leaves blowing in the wind, is meant to evoke Shelley's *Ode to the West Wind*. His "wild West wind, thou breath of Autumn's being" (l. 1) is reproduced in *Orlando*'s setting of autumn, "the 26th of October" (170). Like Shelley's leaves, Orlando and Shelmerdine are quickened to "a new birth" (l. 64).[86] Shelley's "trumpet of a prophecy!" (l. 69) becomes in *Orlando* the bells rung to announce their wedding, which takes place in great "movement and confusion" (171) as the chapter ends.

In the final chapter Orlando realizes that "she had just managed, by some dexterous deference to the spirit of the age, by putting on a ring and finding a man on a moor, by loving nature . . . to pass its examination successfully" (174). At peace with history and still her own person, Orlando "could write, and write she did. She wrote. She wrote. She wrote" (174). At this stage readers are given the following four lines from Orlando's epic, *The Oak Tree:* "And then I came to a field where the springing grass / Was dulled by the hanging cups of fritillaries, / Sullen and foreign-looking, the snaky flower, / Scarfed in dull purple, like Egyptian girls—" (173). The lines are in fact from the "Spring" section of Vita Sackville-West's *The Land*. By offering unsuspecting readers a quotation masquerading as an original composition, Woolf reverses Sterne's allusive technique of offering "quotations" which he has in fact invented.

Orlando reads "her" lines with a coolly critical eye, evaluating phrases: "Grass . . . is all right; the hanging cups of fritillaries—admirable; the snaky flower—a thought strong from a lady's pen, perhaps, but Wordsworth, no doubt, sanctions it" (173). The allusion to Wordsworth epitomizes that preoccupation with nature which characterizes Orlando's poem, and it implies the literary ancestors of *The Land*, an ancestry which includes Virgil[87] and Thomson, to whose poem *The Seasons* Nick Greene later compares the work.

Orlando feels the urge to share her poetic vision with others: "As if it [the manuscript] were a living thing, . . . It wanted to be read. It must be read. It would die in her bosom if it were not read" (178). The poem is published, ironically enough, by the very Nick Greene who in Elizabethan times rejected and disparaged it. Orlando achieves "Fame! Seven editions. A prize. Photographs in the evening papers. . . . The Burdett Coutts' Memorial Prize" (204). She even hears the once-libelous Nick Greene "comparing her with Milton (save for his blindness)" (212). Orlando's prize for *The Oak Tree* is the equivalent of Vita Sackville-West's 1927 Hawthornden Prize for *The Land*. Woolf's added stroke of irony here is the reference to Baroness Angela Georgina Burdett-Coutts, a crucial figure in the social history of Victorian England, whose fifty years of philanthropy and art patronage led King Edward VIII to declare her, after Queen Victoria, "the most remarkable woman in the kingdom."[88] The prize represents to Orlando what prizes in general signified to Virginia Woolf: the world's shallow and irrelevant admiration.[89]

Transformed by publication, *The Oak Tree* is no longer a ragged manuscript but "a little square book bound in red cloth" (212). Orlando is seized by an impulse to bury the volume amid the tangled roots of her real oak tree "as a tribute, . . . a return to the land of what the land has given me" (212). Even though it is abandoned as sentimental, such a symbolic act celebrates the seriousness and significance of artistic creation. The litany twice repeats the title of the actual poem by Vita, linking tree to land, *Tree* to *Land*, fantasy to fact, novel to biography—all moments before Orlando has her final experience of unity and integration at the book's end. Orlando, the poem, and the actual tree have all grown "bigger, sturdier, and more knotted since . . . 1588, but it was still in the prime of life" (211) in the twentieth century. *The Oak Tree* has persisted through more than 300 years of personal and cultural history.[90] Its continuing presence means that, on one level, *Orlando* is aesthetic history—the tale of a poet writing his poem, a poem which survives even the most radical changes, sexual, social, cultural. Orlando never neglects to carry the "much-scored manuscript" (81) about with him, and fittingly so, for it is the embodiment of the analogous development of his selfhood and his literary skill. *The Oak Tree* is personal and aesthetic evolution going on simultaneously in historical time.

Against Orlando's artistic triumph in completing *The Oak Tree* and the insistent rhetoric of "She wrote. She wrote. She wrote," the chauvinist male biographer intercedes to paraphrase a male chauvinist poet: "Love, the poet has said, is woman's whole existence" (175). Not only is this smug Byronicism perfectly suited to the hidden feminist theme of *Orlando*, it is consistent with the ongoing references to Sackville family history. George John Frederick, fourth Duke of Dorset, had a brief schoolboy friendship with Byron at Harrow and was alluded to in *Hours of Idleness* (*Knole*, pp. 203–4).

A beautiful woman like Orlando, the biographer continues,

> will soon give over this pretence of writing and thinking and begin to think, at least of a gamekeeper (and as long as she thinks of a man, nobody objects to a woman thinking). And then she will write him a little note (and as long as she writes little notes nobody objects to a woman writing either) and make an assignation for Sunday dusk; and Sunday dusk will come; and the gamekeeper will whistle under the window—all of which is, of course, the very stuff of life and the only possible subject for fiction. (175–76)

This talk of assignations and gamekeepers sounds very like a travesty of *Lady Chatterley's Lover*. Certainly Woolf was scornful of D.H. Lawrence's emphasis on sexuality as the most important topic of fiction; she condemned his literary "display of self-conscious virility."[91] By invoking Byron and parodying Lawrence, Woolf makes her feminist point about "love—as the male novelists define it—and who, after all, speak with greater authority?" (176). Further on in the chapter there is another jab at literary chauvinists: "Hail, happiness! . . . and all fulfillment of natural desire, whether it is what the male novelist says it is" (192). Tellingly, it is "at this moment" (177) that Orlando finishes *The Oak Tree*. Her triumph is over male opposition as well as specific aesthetic problems.

Orlando next encounters a reincarnation of Nick Greene, "now risen in the world . . . he was a Knight; he was a Litt. D.; he was a Professor.[92] He was the author of a score of volumes. He was, in short, the most influential critic of the Victorian age" (181). By living almost as long as Orlando, Nick Greene becomes as prototypal as Orlando. He embodies a mock-history of literary criticism and serves as the vehicle of Woolf's burlesque of critics. Now the Victorian epitome of how Respectable literature can be, Sir Nicholas has not lost ironic echoes of his namesake. He is as proud of his titles and degrees as was Robert Greene, whose vanity caused him always to list his two Master's degrees on his title pages.[93] He is still as imitative as his namesake, only now Sir Nicholas is "the imitation of fine breeding" (181), where once he had aspired to imitate talent. And he continues to slander living authors while praising dead ones:

> "Ah! my dear Lady, the great days of literature are over. Marlowe, Shakespeare, Ben Jonson, those were the giants. Dryden, Pope, Addison—those were the heroes. All, all are dead now. And whom have they left us? Tennyson, Browning, Carlyle!"—he threw an immense amount of scorn into his voice. . . . "the great days are over. We live in degenerate times. We must cherish the past; honour those writers . . . who take antiquity for their model. . . . " (182)

Greene's opinion as to the "giants" is of course a complete reversal of his earlier (Elizabethan) opinion. Greek literature has given way to praise for Dryden, Pope, and Addison. He has replaced Shakespeare, Browne, and Marlowe with Browning, Tennyson, and Carlyle, the latest trinity to decry in the eternally "degenerate" times.[94] Now Greene writes articles on John Donne, the very "mountebank" whose style he had decreed would be out of fashion in a year. Those "precious conceits and wild experiments" of the Elizabethans, which the Greeks never would have tolerated, have now become conceits and experiments, "none of which the Elizabethans would have tolerated for an instant" (182).

Stately Cicero has given way to "Addison as one's model" (182). Where once he presumed to easy familiarity with Kit Marlowe and Ben Jonson, Sir Nicholas's current anecdotes are of his "dear friends" Pope and Addison.

However, Sir Nicholas now respects Orlando's writing efforts. His verdict on her *Oak Tree* is that it reminds him "of Addison's *Cato*. It compared favourably with Thomson's *Seasons*" (183). It does indeed compare with *The Seasons*, which has four parts ("Winter," "Summer," "Spring," and "Autumn") titled exactly like Vita Sackville-West's *The Land*. But Addison's *Cato* is not an especially apt analogy. Rather, what Sir Nicholas's allusion illustrates is an Addison bias that causes him to make off-center literary judgments.[95] He likens *The Oak Tree* to *Cato* because he wishes literature to have "no trace . . . of the modern spirit," no "unscrupulous eccentricity" (183).

Orlando struggles to comprehend "the noble art of prose composition" (186) by confronting those "innumerable little volumes, bright, identical, ephemeral" (185) which make up Victorian literature. She discovers that the blight of fertility is rampant everywhere: "Sentences swelled, adjectives multiplied, lyrics became epics, and little trifles that had been essays a column long were now encyclopedias in ten or twenty volumes" (150). *Her* taste is for "the little literature of the sixteenth, seventeenth, and eighteenth centuries" (189); she had seen Spenser's "little crabbed hand . . . Shakespeare's script and Milton's" (185). But the Victorian age is nothing if not massive. It has "vast piles of memoirs" (190) and "works about other works" (185). It prizes most the analytic temperament; becoming a critic seems to be the only way to "write the best English prose of my time" (187). Yet Orlando finds the practice of criticism supremely irrelevant: it is telling "little anecdotes . . . about what Tupper said about Smiles" (187). That Martin Farquhar Tupper and Samuel Smiles have to be explained to most readers is precisely the point. And that point is intensified by Woolf's presentation of Victorian literature as a long list of the obscure, "a mass of Alexander Smiths, Dixons, Blacks, Milmans, Buckles, Taines, Paynes, Tuppers, Jamesons—all vocal, clamorous, prominent, and requiring as much attention as anybody else" (190). These Victorians deliberately chosen for their mediocrity furnish comic proof that the era was as guilty of "undistinguished fecundity" in literature as in life.[96]

Orlando concludes that Victorian differs from earlier literatures in that "it would be impolitic in the extreme to wrap a ten-pound note around the sugar tongs when Miss Christina Rossetti came to tea" (190). That is to say, there is no longer any lordly patronizing of poets as in earlier times, and Rossetti is a prime example of a writer most impolitic to patronize, for she symbolized uncompromising art.[97]

Along with literature, life itself has changed. Purity, Modesty, and Chastity no longer come to the biographer's aid in telling "what now has to be told delicately" (191)—that Orlando has given birth to a son (193). The Victorian age passes into the Edwardian twentieth century. The sky is "no longer so thick, so watery, so prismatic. . . . The clouds had shrunk to a thin gauze. . . . It was a little alarming—this shrinkage" (194). The shrinkage gives the era a "definite and distinct" quality "which reminded her of the eighteenth century, except that there is a distraction, a desperation" (195). As the light gets brighter and the clock ticks louder, it becomes October 11, 1928, "the present moment" (195). Orlando recalls a centuries-long past and ponders how many multiple selves can in fact exist simultaneously in one human body. She concludes that "the true length of a person's life, whatever the *Dictionary of National Biography* may say, is always a matter of dispute" (200). Although the origins of *Orlando* rest in part in a prototype like the *DNB*, Woolf cannot resist a glancing blow at her father's opus, or more precisely, at the "masculine" notion that a life can be fully or objectively rendered by a reporter of chronological events.

Orlando has found "the Captain self, the Key self, which amalgamates and controls them all" (203). A fully lived life is not only integration of various selves, "some say [as many as] two thousand and fifty-two" (201), but of the various historical ages and eras present in one's consciousness. Orlando's relation to Sackville family history is reaffirmed through her final visit to her estate; the house "belonged to time now; to history" (208). It contains, if only in the captured images of paintings, Orlando's "old friends Dryden, Pope, Swift, Addison" (206), and when she sees the rows of armchairs, she fancies that they are "holding their arms out for . . . Shakespeare it might be" (208).[98] Winning the Memorial Prize for her *Oak Tree* represented artistic fulfillment; marriage and motherhood represent her fulfillment as a woman. She is "now one and entire, and presented, it may be, a larger surface to the shock of time" (209). Transcending clock-time, historical periods, even sexual roles, she is both herself and the literary tradition she inherits. Through her, life *and* literature go on—and at the moment that she realizes this, the quintessential image of "Sh—p—re!" (204) recurs. Like Orlando, he is a manifold, encompassing identity, spanning centuries, defeating time.

When Orlando sees Shakespeare "in the pool of the mind" (214), the allusive circle is complete. From the sixteen-year-old Elizabethan boy who caught a glimpse of a shabby poet writing at his desk, to a thirty-six-year-old, twentieth-century wife, mother, and poet—Shakespeare bridges all. It is "midnight, Thursday, the eleventh of October, Nineteen Hundred and Twenty-eight" (215). The precision of the date is not arbitrary whim. On that date the first edition of *Orlando* appeared; in

1928, like Orlando, Vita Sackville-West was thirty-six years old; in October of 1928 Virginia Woolf gave the lectures on "Women and Fiction" that were later expanded into *A Room of One's Own*, the feminist companion piece to *Orlando* (published one year later, *in October*). The stroke of midnight, the end of one day and the beginning of another, stresses the archetypal rebirth pattern: things end, to begin again.

As it had in the scene of Orlando's marriage to Shelmerdine, a Shelleyan wind comes up, and her husband descends from an airplane to join her. Shelmerdine is palpable evidence of Woolf's belief that "some collaboration has to take place in the mind between the woman and the man before the act of creation can be accomplished. Some marriage of opposites has to be consummated."[99] The fully developed human being and the artist are androgynous; Orlando's separate embodiments of maleness and femaleness, followed by integration with Shelmerdine, are Platonic, for Aristophanes postulated an androgynous third sex "common to male and female."[100]

Orlando's final perception of reality is embodied in the image of "a single wild bird. . . . The wild goose" (215), which springs up over Shelmerdine's head. After more than three centuries, the wild-goose chase has come to fruition, for Orlando and for her biographer. Love; friendship; truth; the meaning of life; liberation; rebirth phoenixlike from the ashes; the creative imagination soaring high and free—all are symbolized by the wild goose. Earlier Orlando confessed that she had been haunted by the wild bird's flight: "But the goose flies too fast . . . out to sea and always I fling after it words like nets" (205). The wild goose of artistic excellence is a persistent dream, pursued down through the centuries by all writers, including Orlando. And it will go on *after* Orlando as it has *in* Orlando.

Rebecca West's startling claim that *Orlando* is "the only successfully invented myth in English literature of our time" may be altogether right.[101] Like *Jacob's Room*, this work has been underrated. However readily conceded its obvious brilliance has been, the notion that something so brilliantly said, such a "joke," cannot also be profound or moving dies hard. One might defend Woolf's achievement in *Orlando* by quoting her: "Only the most profound masters of style can tell the truth" (169). *Orlando* is a dazzling work: brilliant, vivid and multifaceted, witty, original. It is indeed "a prime instance of the encyclopedic style fashioning an entire work of art."[102] The position that Virginia Woolf occupies as "an inheritor of and contributor to the magnificent tradition of English letters" is magnificently evident in *Orlando*.[103] In this work especially do the numerous allusions function as a "truly brilliant" vehicle for exploring her constant concern—the mingling of life and literature.[104]

five

The Waves

Perhaps the best "training" for reading as demandingly difficult and extraordinary a work as *The Waves* is to have read Virginia Woolf's earlier novels in chronological order. Such a procedure would reveal Woolf's oblique progress from the conventional (*The Voyage Out*) to the experimental (*Jacob's Room*), through sustained poetic exploration of consciousness (*Mrs. Dalloway*) and fantastic comedy (*Orlando*), to the primacy of abstract pattern in *The Waves*.

Every one of the previous novels has been concerned with the large issues of time and love and death, and *The Waves* is no exception. Rather the *form* in which it treats these topics is radically different from all other novels and from Woolf's other novels. *The Waves* is a realization of that wish for a novel about silence, about the things people do not say, first expressed by Terence Hewet in *The Voyage Out*. It takes the symbols of the horse and the wave, used by Woolf to represent the active power of the personality, to their ultimate expression. And it gives readers, in Percival, the most profound ramifications of that recurring hero figure, replete with horse and sword, which we first glimpsed, only partially and ironically, in Jacob and in Orlando. Jacob Flanders was bereft of the external trappings of characterization that a traditional novel would dutifully supply; he is the ancestor of the very abstract characters of *The Waves*. Ideas of multiple personality and androgyny, and fascination with the process of literary creation, so evident in *Orlando*, reappear in *The Waves*. And like *Orlando*, *The Waves* is a hybrid genre. Called a "play-poem" by its creator,[1] it offers the imagery and condensed symbolism of poetry, the psychological characterizations of the novel, and the soliloquy form from the drama. Finally, like *Orlando*, *The Waves* makes few concessions to conventional notions of reality. Indeed it might be argued that the liberation of Woolf's style, the freedom from delimiting concepts of "reality" displayed in *Orlando*, were necessary steps on the high road to *The Waves*.

There are several literary precedents for the imagery of the title itself. It has been suggested that *The Waves* expands upon Samuel Butler's image of life and death;[2] upon De Quincey's image of the sea;[3] upon the closing lines of Meredith's *Modern Love*;[4] upon the sea imagery in

Portrait of the Artist as a Young Man;[5] upon Henri Bergson's metaphor of mankind as a single immense wave.[6] No one can say with absolute certainty whether Woolf meant to allude to one, some, all, or none of these precedents, but the life-as-a-wave trope appears throughout her fiction and her literary essays as well.[7] What is most important is that her sea imagery exploits that archetypal symbolism which has a universal capacity to evoke powerful associations in readers.

The daring artistic ambition of *The Waves* is Joycean: it is nothing less than an attempt to explore man's place in the entire universe. As the furthest extension of her vision and technique, *The Waves* has been seen as "Virginia Woolf's *Finnegans Wake*,"[8] "a novel to end all novels."[9] As it probes the deepest layers of the human mind, it enters a region where the accepted conventions of the traditional novel cannot suffice, any more than they did for Joyce when he wrote *Ulysses* and *Finnegans Wake*. One critic has justly praised *The Waves* for encompassing "as much of fundamental meaning as the mind can hold. His incredible cleverness aside, not even Joyce pursues his reality more relentlessly than does Mrs. Woolf."[10]

The highly stylized form of *The Waves* alternates nine italicized interludes with nine long sequences in which the six characters variously "speak" their interior soliloquies. Readers who expect to apply ordinary notions of scene, character, and plot will find they have an invalid framework with which to encounter this demanding work. It must be read on its own terms, not scolded for being what it is. The setting, for example, is entirely symbolic; even specifically named places like India and Hampton Court function as do the more obviously symbolic locations (for example, childhood in the garden). The prose-poem interludes provide a physical setting that presents an objective, phenomenal world of tides, birds, a house alternately lit or shadowed by the sun. Even these natural events foreshadow the mental and physical states of the six characters, however. The sequence of events within the interludes follows the passage of a single day, but that day is resolutely cosmic, for concurrent with the passage of the sun across the sky is the passage of the seasons of the year and the maturation of the characters. The cycles, then, speak of time, nature, and human life. No human figure appears in these brief interchapters, and the narrative voice is one of abstracted omniscience; there are no allusions within these passages.[11]

The first interlude is Virginia Woolf's own story of Creation. Her imagery—primordial contrasts of light and darkness out of which individualized forms emerge—reproduces that found in countless primitive myths and in the Biblical account of Creation. "The sun had not yet risen. The sea was indistinguishable from the sky" (179)—so *The Waves* begins, echoing "and the earth was without form, and void; and darkness *was* upon the face of the deep" (Gen. 1:2). Woolf's sky whitens, dividing itself from the sea; so God "divided the light from the darkness" (Gen. 1:4) and the land from the water (Gen. 1:9). Six children, three male, the other three female, move about in "the garden" (179) in much the same way that "God planted a garden eastward in Eden; and there he put the man whom he had formed" (Gen. 2:8).

Since pattern is plot in *The Waves*, after this resonant Beginning, the cyclic pattern of nature in the interludes is supplemented by the psychological growth revealed in the soliloquies, which as one critic has recognized is "an almost exact structural parallel of the developmental process."[12] As the story of human life from birth to death, *The Waves* is *Bildungsroman*, but of course on a mythopoetic level that quite surpasses its conventional relatives.

Woolf tries to achieve universality by using a standardized diction and syntax for all six characters. Because each of the six voices abstracts and epitomizes basic elements of the human psyche, taken together they represent a single, universal human consciousness.[13] Despite their archetypal sameness, however, the six are distinctly different in sensibilities, actions, attitudes, and responses; they even have characteristic metaphors and allusions. In other words, they exist as universals *and* as individuals. In Woolf's presentation, the self is largely submerged in the unconscious and is expressed symbolically (this is consistent with psychoanalytic theory). Beneath the sextet's differences, which result from dissimilar life experiences and widely varying capacities to achieve the common objects of desire, there is a sameness of libido that allows Woolf to universalize them into the human condition. *The Waves*, then, deals with the profound symbolic realities of the psyche, and as such has been rightly called "a presentation of the purest psychological analysis in literature."[14] This symbolic approach to character portrayal is formalized in the series of interior monologues, where the emphasis is not on narrative but on self-revelation.

Following the *Genesis*-like introduction, we are formally introduced to six characters.[15] Little has been said of the naming of these characters (who lack surnames), but the given names seem to have mattered considerably to Woolf: the manuscript drafts show many name changes, especially for Bernard.[16] Bernard, who has the last word in this novel, also has the first. As a child, he sees a quivering ring in "a loop of light" (180). This image, appropriate to his Dantesque role as seer and explainer, capitalizes upon the archetypal significance of *light* as the revealer of transcendent reality, and of *the circle* as symbol of perfection, unity, and infinity. The English mystic poet Henry Vaughan began "The World" thus: "I saw eternity the other night / Like a great ring of pure and endless light," and of course Dante's *Paradiso* exploits light/sun imagery to convey the experience of knowledge and fulfillment. Virginia Woolf used Bernard's metaphor herself in her famous declaration that "life is a luminous halo."[17]

The images used by the other characters to establish their respective personalities are slabs of color (Susan); a globe (Neville); a crimson and gold tassel (Jinny); a chained beast stamping (Louis); and a bird chirping (Rhoda). After these initial perceptions are presented, the children play in the garden for a while, then go to bed. That is all that happens, yet the essential nature of each character has been given. Neville is a precise observer; the insecure Louis feels menaced by external forces; Jinny is a creature of physical sensation and immediacy; Susan is an elemental woman of elemental emotions; Rhoda is terrified of other people and the world; Bernard is an explorer and story-teller, "making phrases" (186). Cyclic truth pervades *The Waves:* in their beginnings, their endings can be found; in their endings, a recapitulation of their beginnings.

In the second interlude of morning and increasing light, the six young children go off to school. As they move past their communal childhood, life forces increasing individuation upon them. For one thing, school separates the boys from the girls. The three men develop intellectual and literary awareness; allusions are a major part of their psychic lives. Use of allusion by their three female counterparts is nearly nonexistent, except in the case of Rhoda.

Susan is an abstract of the elemental, natural life. She identifies with and finds fulfillment in nature's basic seasonal processes. Her role is confined to that of wife and mother, home and family; she lives in a nearly archaic, fundamental world of feminine instinct. This indisputable earth-mother quality makes her nonintellectual; her mind holds no literary knowledge or allusions.

Jinny is an unmitigated sensualist who looks for no kind of fulfillment other than the physical and sexual, which is her way of knowing self and world. But her repetitive sexual rituals trap her in a limited, personal immediacy that becomes a means of avoiding larger realities. Self-consciousness, the reflective life of the mind, is an impossibility: "When I read, a purple rim runs around the black edge of the textbook. Yet I cannot follow any word through its changes. I cannot follow any thought from present to past" (203). In her life of the body, like Susan, Jinny too is bereft of literary allusion.

104

Jinny is both foil and complement to Susan. Unlike Susan, who feels rooted to the earth and its meanings, restless Jinny refuses to "let myself be attached to one person only. I do not want to be fixed, to be pinioned" (212). For Susan love is permanent possession; for Jinny it is temporary ecstasy. As domestic wife and uninhibited mistress, they encompass the two sensual elements of the female psyche: maternal and sexual. If they can summon up a literary reality at all, it is never a consciously chosen allusion. It merely floats to the surface of their soliloquies as an undifferentiated part of their experience; for example, there is something Dantesque about Susan's "I see a crack in the earth and hot steam hisses up" (191–92). That reminder of the *Inferno* becomes in Jinny's thoughts: "I leap like one of those flames that run between the cracks of the earth" (203).

The last of the female characters is Rhoda. Hypersensitive and imaginative, she is also withdrawn, a dreamer fearful of life, finally suicidal. She is in sharp contrast to Jinny and Susan: where they live in the reality of the here and now, Rhoda is the essence of alienation— "Identity failed me" (219). Fearful of life where Jinny is brave, fragmented where Susan is whole, Rhoda can function neither as mistress nor mother. Because she dreads the life of the body, she also dreads individuality and any revelation of self: "I hate looking-glasses which show me my real face" (204).

Rhoda's lyric, breathless diction is out of Shelley. She cries out "Oh, but I sink, I fall!" (193) and "I faint, I fail" (214), echoing such Shelleyan exclamations as "I pant, I sink, I tremble, I expire!" (*Epipsychidion*, l. 591) and "I die! I faint! I fail!" (*The Indian Serenade*, l. 18).[18] These scattered echoes are made explicit in an episode in which Rhoda reads from a library book (significantly, she is not enough conscious of literature to *own* poetry books) "a poem about a hedge" (213). Jinny and Susan have also encountered a hedge, but to their realistic, antipoetic sensibilities, it is simply a shrub with a gap: Jinny observes "a hole in the hedge," and Susan calls it "the chink in the hedge" (183). To Rhoda's frail lyric imagination, it is "the warm hedge" in Shelley's *The Question* (l. 17).[19] Rhoda immediately internalizes the poem, making Shelley's language her own.[20] When she voices Shelley's question, she is expressing both her desire and her incapacity to enter into an intimate and binding relationship with others: "To whom shall I give all that now flows through me, from my warm, my porous body? I will gather my flowers and present them—Oh! to whom?" (214). The allusion links Rhoda's personal/sexual problems to imaginative/artistic problems: she cannot cope with love, nor can she give adequate formal embodiment to her vague lyric longings. The demanding realities of *relationships*—in life or in art—are too much for her fragmented consciousness. Thus her passionate allusive question is no mere rhetorical irrelevance, but a genuine revelation of character.

Rhoda's search for order, psychological and artistic, also consumes her male counterpart, Louis. They are both attenuated personalities; outsiders who have a pronounced taste for solitude and silence, which deepens into alienation; both self-conscious in a tortured way; both prone to mysticism; both concerned with what is real. Human racial memory, the collective unconscious, is expressed through Louis and his acute awareness of the repetitive nature of past time. He feels he has "lived many thousand years" (220). Even as a child in the garden, he had felt "my eyes are the lidless eyes of a stone figure in a desert by the Nile" (182). At school he continues to be conscious of "the long, long history that began in Egypt" (220). Because of his deep feelings of inadequacy ("I have no firm ground to which I go," 220), he needs the comfort of seeing himself as part of the vast community of man. By cultivating his sense of historical progression, Louis escapes chaos and fragmentation.

His need to compensate for his felt social inferiority, especially his Australian accent, sometimes results in grandiose fantasies of being "the friend of Richelieu, or the Duke of St. Simon holding out a snuff-box to the King himself" (210). That Louis shares his given name with the aristocratic Saint-Simon and several French kings only accents the irony of these allusions. Trying to belie his inferior class status, Louis imagines that he, like some Saint-Simon who wrote critically of bourgeois official-dom, might personally bring enlightenment to a world gone wrong. This is the same sort of naive *hubris* to which Jacob Flanders was subject. But Louis is not, of course, capable of bestowing reason upon a world that alternately ignores or threatens him, and he himself knows his efforts are too desperate to succeed: "I force myself to state, if only in one line of unwritten poetry, this moment; to mark this inch in the long, long history" (220).

The incessant stamping foot of the great chained beast—that charac-terizing image which he first uttered in the garden—is muted only by Louis's sense of historical continuity and tradition. He responds to Dr. Crane the schoolmaster by delighting in "his authority" (198). He has an altogether reverent appreciation of Crane handing out "Horace, Tenny-son, the complete works of Keats and Matthew Arnold suitably in-scribed,"[21] and he notes Crane's uplifting Biblical quotation: "He has bid us 'quit ourselves like men' " (214). Louis respects "the hand which gave" the inscribed volumes more than he seems to realize the individual worth of poets, whom he sees as a class—"some unhappy poets" whose names are inscribed on the walls, along with the names of statesmen and sol-diers (214). His need to achieve "some gigantic amalgamation" (211) prevents him from savoring the unique, unclassifiable significance of widely different poets like Horace and Keats. Yet he reads poets with what Bernard recognizes as "ferocious tenacity" (208), for reading relates Louis to the human community and frees him from inadequacy: "When darkness comes I put off this unenviable body . . . and inhabit space. I am then Virgil's companion, and Plato's" (210).

As Susan and Jinny resembled each other, Louis has a kinship with Neville. Like Louis, Neville is introverted, neat, and fastidious; a perfectionist with an intense desire for order. The intellectual Neville reveres absolute clarity; for him even passion must be "a passion that is never obscure or formless" (196). The traditions of school and church that roused Louis's admiration because they represented order need to be verbal traditions for Neville. His order is in language; he takes pleasure even in the small precisions of grammar: "Each tense . . . means differently. There is an order in this world; there are distinctions" (188). But like Louis's urge toward order, Neville's exactness is obsessive: through it he denies the complexity of human personality and reduces the world to falsely narrowed dimensions he can control. While both assume the role of Outsider in society, it is birth and class that ostracize Louis; Neville is a voluntary isolate whose arrogant intellectual snobbery protects him from Louis's sense of rejection. "I come, like a lord to his hall appointed" (196) Neville can say, without apparent irony.

Neville lives in a timeless literary culture. In his intellectual and aesthetic ecstasies, he refines himself out of contact with unstructured, *lived* experience. Still he feels a definite literature-versus-life conflict within himself: "It would be better to breed horses and live in one of those red villas than to run in and out of the skulls of Sophocles and Euripides like a maggot," but he knows that an attenuated life "will be my fate" (223). However much he may wonder whether he should "desert these form rooms and libraries, and the broad yellow page in which I read Catullus, for woods and fields," he realizes that he cannot respond to the "sublimities and vastitudes" of nature (210). He feels alienated from the natural physical world, which neither notices nor conforms to his predilections. And like his preference for Catullus over "too vegetable" (210) nature, his homosexuality is an apt symbol of his distance from nature's basic processes.

Neville's use of literature as compensation for his inability to confront life is reflected in such revealing remarks as: "Now I pretend to read. I raise my book, till it almost covers my eyes" (223). His bookish reality is the means by which he tries to prevent the world's intrusions, but his attempted (and sometimes *pretended*) disinterest is never whole: he is curiously *dependent* upon the mediocrity of the ordinary world ("Let me denounce this piffling, trifling, self-satisfied world," 223) from which he derives his own sense of superiority. Then too his denunciations have their roots in personal frustration rather than high moral principle—the world is detestable because it makes it "impossible for me always to read Catullus in a third-class railway carriage" (223).

Even as a schoolboy Neville had declared, "I shall explore the exactitudes of the Latin language, and step firmly upon the well-laid sentences, and pronounce the explicit, the sonorous hexameters of Virgil; of Lucretius; and chant . . . the loves of Catullus" (196).[22] His classicism is the complement of Louis's historical sense. In the precision of Roman literature Neville seeks the timeless perfection of beauty, structure, and harmony. He reads "Shakespeare and Catullus, lying in the long grass" (207).[23] In Catullus, whom he "adores" (235), Neville can find a scornful contempt for ordinary life, an inclination to unsparing ridicule, and deviances from heterosexual love in which male friends are addressed as lovers, much as he expresses his own love for Percival. Byron, whom Neville dislikes, called Catullus one of the "scholars" of the subject of love and noted with mock shock that "Catullus scarcely has a decent poem" (*Don Juan*, 1.42.331). Catullus supplies what Neville lacks: unrestrained sexuality of the indecent and obscene variety, and passionate abandonment of that fastidious perfectionism which prevents him from tasting pure freedom of feeling. Probably only vicariously, through Catullus, can Neville experience that "vulgarity" of living which he affects to despise in others. As the effete scholar William Pepper in Woolf's first novel "let himself go" in his passion for Petronius and Catullus, so Neville glories in the indecent intensity of Catullus's poems.

Neville's characteristic superiority pervades even his allusive thoughts. He copies other poets' styles with a tinge of smug arrogance: "Do I not know already how to rhyme, how to imitate Pope, Dryden, even Shakespeare?" (207).[24] Nevertheless he is not immune from becoming the target of his own intolerance for mediocrity. When he equates his "sense of self" with "my contempt" (224), we realize how much the prisoner of his inadequacies he is. In typical self-aggrandizement, he declares: "There is that in me which will consume them entirely" (223). This is a thinly disguised borrowing from Byron, a source that flatly *contradicts* Neville's sense of himself. He has scorned Bernard for taking Byron as his model and derided Bernard's Byronic role-playing by comparing his own "whole" behavior: "I am one person—myself. I do not impersonate Catullus" (235). That Neville should now unwittingly appropriate Byron's attitude is masterful irony, for it implies that all poets somehow contain something of Byron, or that Neville's self-awareness is riddled with blind spots, or both.

In this second chapter it is Bernard who announces their collective departure for school. Feeling the need to defend himself against the urgent, chaotic nature of the occasion by using his talent for story-telling, Bernard declares, "I must make phrases and phrases and so interpose something hard between myself and the stare of housemaids, the stare of clocks, staring faces, indifferent faces, or I shall cry" (195). At school his reaction to Dr. Crane is a wise amalgamation of Louis's blind reverence and Neville's hostile disdain: "I love tremendous and sonorous words. But his words are too hearty to be true. Yet by this time he is convinced of their truth" (196). Bernard's wit is not as nasty as Neville's, but it is as finely tuned; he says of Dr. Crane, "His departure leaves us not only with a sense of relief, but also with a sense of something removed, like a tooth" (208). Such *freedom from distorting extremes of response* enables him to function as the most reliable interpreter in the group. His interpretation of human character is keen, yet quite disinterested: "When I am grown up I shall carry a notebook—a fat book with many pages, methodically lettered. I shall enter my phrases" (199). He quite understands his own phrase-making compulsion, which he can express with vivid imagery: "The bubbles are rising like the silver bubbles from the floor of a saucepan; image on top of image. . . . I must open the little trap-door and let out these linked phrases" (208). When he declares: "I wish to add to my collection of valuable observations upon the true nature of human life" (221), his confidence does not smack of Louis's defensiveness or Neville's arrogance. It is achievement-oriented egotism, an honest appraisal of what he knows to be his "steady unquenchable thirst" (221) for words. He sees himself clearly (as nonreflective and requiring "the concrete in everything," 222) and he sees others clearly ("There is about both Neville and Louis a precision, an exactitude that I admire and shall never possess," 222).

We are given a paradigm of Bernard's story-telling ability when he invents a brief situation about Dr. and Mrs. Crane:

> [There is] a bridge of rosy light from the lamp at the bedside where Mrs. Crane lies with her hair on the pillow reading a French memoir. As she reads, she sweeps her hand with an abandoned and despairing gesture over her forehead and sighs, "Is this all?" comparing herself with some French duchess. Now, says the doctor, in two years I shall retire. I shall clip yew hedges in a west country garden. An admiral I might have been; or a judge; not a schoolmaster. What forces, he asks, . . . have brought me to this? What vast forces? (209)

Bernard's capacities as a novelist are in clear evidence here.[25] He already possesses the knack of detailed description, sympathetic insight into human emotions, and the broad perspective from which to ask philosophic questions about life. Most tellingly, he seems to be the projection of Woolf's own novelistic voice. Mrs. Crane's bedroom reading of a French memoir recalls Clarissa in *Mrs. Dalloway;* the despairing question "Is this all?" echoes Lady Charles in *Jacob's Room.* When Bernard admits he "cannot go on with this story" (209), the persistent problem of his life has been stated. Variations on that aesthetic theme—the limited ability of words to encompass life—reappear throughout *The Waves.*

Only once in this chapter does Bernard speak of his reading, and then it remains unspecified: "I need no longer smuggle in bits of candle ends and immoral literature" (215). Woolf is showing us not the voracious readers we have seen Louis and Neville to be, but the dynamic *process* of the literary imagination in Bernard, this humane, observant, social young man whose curiosity caused him to say as a child, "Let us inhabit the underworld. Let us take possession of our secret territory" (189).

In the *"growing light"* (226) of the third interlude, the scene is sharp with intimations of antagonism. Joy and fear are mingled in the birds' song (225), the wind is rising, and the waves are drumming against the shore (227). For the third time it is Bernard who speaks first, of "the complexity of things" (227) now that the near-adult characters are creating the permanent patterns of their lives.

True to her elemental nature, Susan lives on a country farm, so close to the natural cycles as almost to have lost her personal identity: "I am the seasons, . . . the mud, the mist, the dawn" (243). When she states "I sit with my sewing by the table" (244), we see her as a near-mythic figure, a female deity of Fate.

Jinny is involved in London social life, which she loves: "This is my world" (245). A totally sensual creature who is concerned only with the succession of men she attracts, she discovers "I do not care for anything in this world . . . save this man whose name I do not know" (246).

Rhoda is also part of the London social scene, but for her the experience is one of failure. The image of an opening door, which to Jinny means "risk, . . . adventure," is an image of terror for Rhoda: "The door opens; the tiger leaps[26] . . . terror upon terror, pursuing me" (247). Rhoda, who hates "this clumsy, this ill-fitting body" and "all details of the individual life," cries out in her pain: "What amulet is there against this disaster?" (248). Even as a youngster at school, she had asked for "amulets against disaster" (204). Woolf thought *Shelley* was "an amulet against disaster,"[27] and Rhoda's longings are certainly Shelleyan. When she seeks "a world immune from change" (249), Rhoda seeks the world of *Adonais,* where "the One remains" and Eternity is a "white radiance."

Louis has taken his place in the business world, but he is extremely unhappy there. To dispel his sense of isolation and inferiority, he continues to appropriate great figures of classical literature: "I, the companion of Plato, of Virgil" (240), the same brace of authors he read at school. In an effort to achieve inner peace, he imposes his sense of art-as-rigid-structure upon the disorder that surrounds him. He develops a coercive image of literature as a "binding power [that] ropes you in" and calls the book he is reading "this ramrod of beaten steel" (240). Such a notion of literature as forged steel is very different from the diaphanous freedom of Bernard's "words at once make smoke rings" (221). Louis's rather desperate need for structure and perfection is a need that is both personal and aesthetic, for perfect poetic form, if he were able to find it, would *fix* forever the mutability of life.

Neville and Bernard are at college, where a rather startling shift takes place in Neville's perspective: "In a world which contains the present moment, . . . why discriminate?" (231). He has moved from fastidious selectivity to an undiscriminating acceptance of all sensation, a move not entirely unconnected to his indiscriminate homosexual predilections: "All they [i.e., some "powerful young men" he is observing] do is beautiful" (231).

As with Neville's earlier, inadvertent allusion to Byron, Woolf plants a sly allusion that partly undermines Neville's credibility. He says: "Far away a bell tolls, but not for death" (231). Moments later he is saying "Yet how painful to . . . have one's self adulterated, mixed up, become part of another" (232). Such opinions[28] contradict the expressed creed of one of Woolf's favorite poets:

> No man is an island, entire of itself; every man is a piece of the continent, a part of the main; . . . any man's death diminishes me, because I am involved in mankind; and therefore never send to know for whom the bell tolls; it tolls for thee. . . . (Donne, *Devotions*, 17)

Measured against that which it invokes, Neville's denial of death and time, and his fear of being mixed up with others, seem futile and shallow.

Neville's high literary ambitions ("Surely I am a great poet," 231) bring with them certain artistic problems. He feels his inspiration "becomes artificial, insincere. . . . There is some flaw in me—some fatal hesitancy. . . . Am I too fast, too facile?" (232). Thus we see that as artist and as person, Neville is characterized by fear of self-surrender. This limiting incapacity causes him to mock its presence in Bernard.

Barnard begins this chapter with a situation reminiscent of *Orlando*: he is mocking what his future biographer will say of his androgynous nature. His search for identity is complicated by the fact that "I am not

111

one and simple, but complex and many" (227). Characteristically, he creates his multiple selves through language; he shapes his own personality by vicariously assuming the qualities of a series of literary figures. The first of his role models is the most important: "I feel that I am that dashing yet reflective man, that bold and deleterious figure, who, lightly throwing off his cloak, seizes his pen and at once flings off the following letter to the girl with whom he is passionately in love" (228). Bernard is playing "Byron of course" (229).

Bernard is Byronic in several crucial ways. He is as aware of his limitations as Byron, who put them to comic use: "I don't pretend that I quite understand / My own meaning when I would be *very* fine" (*Don Juan*, 4.5. 36–37). And like Byron, Bernard is troubled by identity problems; he is a "liar" poet who can "take all colours—like the hands of dyers" (*DJ*, 3.87. 792). Both detached and involved, he is the same impetuous, protean personality that Woolf imagined Byron to be.

Knowing how Woolf saw Byron helps readers understand Bernard's complexity better: Woolf found Byron simultaneously irritating and fascinating. She called *Childe Harold's Pilgrimage* a combination of "the weakest sentimental Mrs. Hemans combined with tremendous bare vigour."[29] She listed as aspects of Byron's personality a "manufactured" romantic posturing, a "vigorous rhetorical" quality, a deeply poetic quality, a satiric vein, and a "half-assumed, half genuine tragic note."[30] She found in his works

> much that is spurious, vapid, yet very changeable, and then rich and with greater range than the other poets, . . . [He sometimes sneered at things.] But then the sneer may have been a pose too. The truth may be that if you are charged at such high voltage you can't fit any of the ordinary human feelings; must pose; must rhapsodise; don't fit in. (*Writer's Diary*, p. 150)

Making the analogy to Bernard complete, she declared of Byron: "A novelist, he might have been."[31] Interestingly, these remarks on Byron were all made when Woolf was working on *The Waves*.

Assuming his Byronic stance, Bernard writes a love letter, which he wants to combine "speed and carelessness" with "some subtle suggestion of intimacy and respect" (228–29).[32] Deliberately calculating the devastating effect this impetuous yet reflective letter should have upon the young lady, Bernard aims for "the hot, molten effect, the lava flow of sentence into sentence" (229). How well this evokes the Byron who declared "I cannot stop to alter words once written" (*DJ*, 10.77. 612), the Byron who spoke of "hot haste" (*Childe Harold*, 3.25. 217) and referred to his passion as "a lava flood" (*The Giaour*, 1.1101).

This chapter contains an allusive confrontation between Neville and

Bernard, which sharply reveals their essential character differences.[33] It begins with Bernard holding "Gray's *Elegy* in one hand" (232).[34] Significantly, the theme of the *Elegy* reinforces certain thematic preoccupations in *The Waves*. As a cemetery full of obscure people prompted Gray's exquisitely melancholy meditations on man's inevitable end, so Bernard contemplates man's transient status in the world. He too composes his own kind of *Elegy* at the novel's close. And Neville, who earlier disavowed those Donne-like bells tolling time and death, is once again (allusively) faced with a sort of *memento mori*: a poet who declared that "the paths of glory lead but to the grave."

Neville perceives that Bernard has been "marking the passages [in *Don Juan*] that seem to approve of your own character. I find marks against all those sentences which seem to express a sardonic yet passionate nature" (234). Neville considers himself "one person—myself" (235), but we have seen how mistaken a boast this was—he unwittingly appropriated Byron even as he maintained that he did not impersonate literary figures. Apart from his self-blindness, Neville is expressing his very real need to be one discrete, highly ordered person; this need is counter to Bernard's complex multiplicity of selves and his "Byronic untidiness" (237).[35]

Neville mentions twice that Bernard is reading *Don Juan*, that masterpiece of vitality and humor in which Byron fully expressed his enormously complex personality.[36] It is especially pertinent to Bernard, for he shares Byron's self-conscious emphasis on language. Remarks about phrases, words, and stories abound in *Don Juan*; Byron's ambivalence about *words* is Bernard's,[37] and so is his acute awareness of *phrases* as such.[38] Even Byron's rhetorical stance reads like Bernard: "But let me to my story: I must own, / If I have any fault it is digression— / Leaving my people to proceed alone, / While I soliloquize beyond expression" (*DJ*, 3.96. 857–60).

When readers realize the depth of Bernard's similarity to Byron, they better understand Neville's hostility. Neville cannot cope with what he sees as Bernard's "innumerable perplexities" (208); added to Byron's, they overwhelm his precarious selfhood and his rigid sense of precision. He tries to diminish Bernard's diffusion by deriding his Byronic stance: "That is not Byron, that is you" (235), or "Yet Byron never made tea as you do" (234). Nor can Neville, in his insular arrogance, quite tolerate the thought that "we are all phrases in Bernard's story" (223). Although they both deal in language, words for Neville must be formal and precise. To Bernard words are dynamic and creative. Neville has a notebook in which he enters "curious uses of the past participle" (235), and the nearly comic narrowness of such a project forms a striking contrast to Bernard's phrase book.

On a higher symbolic level, Neville's intellectuality and Bernard's intuitiveness, his limited perfectionism contrasted to Bernard's expansive imagination, is the battle of form and feeling, Classicism and Romanticism.[39] For Virginia Woolf it also represented the conflict of the poet and the novelist. Shortly after *The Waves*, she wrote "A Letter to a Young Poet," in which the poet she addresses is strikingly like Neville,[40] and her prototypal novelist sounds like a virtual recapitulation of Bernard.[41] Her own assumption that the novelist enjoyed a wider range than the poet is reflected in Bernard's declaration: "My scope embraces what Neville never reaches" (237).[42]

Bernard acknowledges, "I am Bernard; I am Byron;[43] I am this, that and the other" (236). Neville says, "Once you were Tolstoi's young man; now you are Byron's young man; perhaps you will be Meredith's young man" (235). Bernard acknowledges the Meredith role (365), but Tolstoi is Neville's own erroneous attribution.[44] It appears (once again, through the use of allusion) that Neville's insight into Bernard is as flawed as his insight into himself.

In the fourth interlude and set of soliloquies, something rather different starts to happen. At the same time as the risen sun and thudding waves and vehement birds are singing in *"the pressure of the morning"* (250), the six characters come together at a restaurant to celebrate the departure for India of their childhood friend, Percival, who enters the novel only through the consciousness of the sextet. This deliberately shadowy figure is nonetheless their unifier. Not only does he bring them together physically at the dinner, but he is the cause of their emotional harmony, the catalyst through which they transcend their diversity and fragmentation to achieve self-completion and general unity. He is the common significance to which they can relate in order to redeem themselves from the isolation of individuality.

Neville says, "The reign of chaos is over. He has imposed order" (260); Jinny refers to "this globe whose walls are made of Percival, of youth and beauty, and something so deep sunk within us that we shall perhaps never make this moment out of one man again" (276); Bernard thinks of their assemblage as "a seven-sided flower . . . a whole flower" (263). Only Louis suffers so in his sense of separation that even Percival cannot release him from the grip of his personal concerns into community with others. As if the name of the particular poet did not matter to one who has such a timeless historical sense, Louis wonders about "my poet—is it Lucretius?" (264).[45] Such vagueness in allusive characterization prepares readers for Louis's movement toward anonymity, which culminates in a significant allusion discussed below.

The fifth section is both the high noon of nature and the exact structural center of the work. A bitter and despairing Neville speaks first: Percival has been thrown from his horse—he is dead. This is the end of unity, the triumph of random chance and meaninglessness in the world. Percival has left all his friends with a disabling sense of incompleteness, but it is Neville for whom the loss is most personally crushing. Traumatized by the absurdity of Percival's death—the horse was "tripped by mole-hills" (280)—Neville expresses his agony in diction like "Come, pain, feed on me. Bury your fangs in my flesh. Tear me asunder. I sob, I sob" (281). It has been described as childishly immature diction.[46] It is also strongly reminiscent of Shelley, as in "I fall upon the thorns of life! I bleed!" (*Ode to the West Wind*, 4.54). Because it is extravagant, Romantic diction, it is yet another ironic example of Neville's lack of self-knowledge.

For Rhoda the dead Percival is the lost phantom lover, "the figure that was robed in beauty" (285). His death has revealed "this terror, has left me to undergo this humiliation" (286).[47] Her imagery is unconsciously out of T.S. Eliot when she professes to see "envy, jealousy, hatred and spite scuttle like crabs over the sand" (286).[48] She returns to *The Question*, that poem we first saw her reading, to answer Shelley's query, "Oh!—to whom?," by making a garland of violets and flinging them into the sea, "my offering to Percival" (289).

Bernard is the only other character to appear in this section. He is clearly the vehicle of the enduring life force: "My son is born; Percival is dead" (281). In that blunt juxtaposition is the classic conflict of Eros and Thanatos. He mourns with a mature grief the loss of "a leader" (282) and prophetically vows to let this death lie buried, "hidden in the depths of my mind some day to fructify . . . in a moment of revelation" (284–85). In the midst of Rhoda's contempt and Neville's bitterness, Bernard is the rational, existential rebel against the absurdity of existence:

> I say, addressing what is abstract, facing me eyeless at the end of the avenue, in the sky, "Is this the utmost you can do?" "Then we have triumphed. You have done your utmost," I say, addressing that blank and brutal face . . . I am not going to lie down and weep away a life of care. (An entry to be made in my pocketbook; contempt for those who inflict meaningless death.) (282)

The contrast of attitudes toward Percival's death is thus made an allusive one. Rhoda translated Shelley's question and the garland in his poem into action. Neville unwittingly appropriated the more self-pitying bathos of Shelley's lyric mode. Bernard's "I am not going to lie down and weep away a life of care" derives from Shelley's *Stanzas Written in Dejection, Near Naples*, yet he has turned it into an explicit *denial* of passive pessimism.[49]

As his unique "funeral service" (284) for Percival, Bernard visits the National Gallery. There he contemplates painters and poets, calling the latter "scapegoats . . . chained to the rock" (284). When Bernard likens the poet to Prometheus, that titanic figure of creativity, suffering, and rebellion, it is clear that his concept of the artist is a Romantic, heroic one. Shelley wrote a great *Prometheus Unbound*, and Byron—who could encompass the cynicism of Don Juan and the defiance of the Titan—also wrote a *Prometheus*.[50] The breaking of the laws of the gods is represented by the birth of consciousness in many myths; *Prometheus* means *forethought* in Greek. He is therefore a superb allusive symbol of rebellion and consciousness, the ultimate values in Woolf's own work.

In the sixth episode decline sets in. The sun's light is oblique and slanted, fish are stranded upon the shore, there is *"darkness in mounds of unmoulded shape"* (290). It is the middle age of life, and the only episode in which Bernard does not appear. Instead the conventional world of Louis and Susan and the unorthodox world of Jinny and Neville are contrasted, as we are shown the inescapable limits of the career and domesticity and the varieties of sexual promiscuity.

Susan is "glutted with natural happiness. Yet more will come, more children; more cradles, more baskets in the kitchen" (295). Her total submergence in the biological roles of wife and mother is expressed in this image of restriction: "Steam has obscured the window" (294). Jinny has lost herself in the perpetual flow of existence: "The activity is endless. And tomorrow it begins again" (297). Because Jinny recognizes that "we who live in the body see with the body's imagination things in outline" (297), she does not read allusions, she *enacts* them, especially the myths of pursuit and seduction: "I am pursued through the forest. . . . Now I hear crash and rending of boughs and the crack of antlers as if the beasts of the forest were all hunting, all rearing high and plunging down among the thorns. One has pierced me. One is driven deep within me" (298). In this erotic imagery is the archetypal experience of Daphne fleeing from Apollo through the deep forest, the nymph Syrinx running from the god Pan, or Arethusa pursued by the river-god Alpheus.

Continuing to render sexual meaning through mythological allusions, Jinny says: "Now let us sing our love song—Come, come, come. . . . Jug, jug, jug, I sing like the nightingale whose melody is crowded in the too narrow passage of her throat" (298). This evocation of the nightingale in Eliot's *Waste Land* has been called a repudiation of Eliot's "sexual disgust."[51] It is true that sex is not disgusting to Jinny—

116

at least not consciously—and that Woolf did seem to be impatient with Eliot's need to reveal something disgusting behind the song's beauty.[52] Yet even in *Jacob's Room* it was an "obscene" nightingale, and here the reference to the nightingale's too narrow *throat* conjures up the allusion behind the allusion. Eliot's own source was the myth of Philomela, vividly told by Ovid (*Metamorphoses*, book 6): Philomela is raped by King Tereus, who brutally cuts out her tongue to keep her silent, then violates her a second time. She later changed into a nightingale, but the song has its origins in sexual violence and mutilation. And these allusive intimations of deformity and force should not be disregarded in interpreting Jinny's deepest, unconscious attitudes toward her manifestly brave promiscuity. If she sees herself as singing *like the nightingale*, she sees herself as wronged innocence raped by a violently lustful world.[53]

This set of soliloquies is begun by Louis, whose insecurity is still causing him to assume important identities from history: "Now a duke, now Plato, companion of Socrates" (291). Louis's worldly success does not truly compensate for his inferiority; rather it interferes with his genuine talents, which are intellectual and scholarly. He cannot merge his business, poetic, and scholarly lives into an integrated whole. Although he turns back "to finger what Plato said" (292), such efforts must take second place to the business world in which he pursues public success. "I have read my poet in an eating-house" (292), he informs us; he must give poetry such snatches of time as he can manage to spare from his world of "the typewriter and the telephone" (291). Only in his attic room—and we know the power of that symbol in Woolf—is he secure from the success that falsifies his true identity. There he reads and thinks of Percival: "Percival has died; (he died in Egypt; he died in Greece; all deaths are one death)" (293). This eloquent transformation of a single death into the archetypal human experience shows profound wisdom, the kind of Donne-like insight that Neville disavowed and that Bernard will reformulate at the close of the novel.

Neville's soliloquy reinforces the growing intensification of Percival's symbolic significance. By juxtaposing him to "Alcibiades, Ajax, Hector" (301), Neville transforms Percival into a recurring archetype of male beauty and leadership. He worships in Percival the masculinity he does not have: "I lack bodily grace and the courage that comes with it" (264). But because Neville's reconstruction of a perfectly idealized hero is neither undercut nor mitigated by the slightest doubt or irony, Neville is destined to seek–perpetually and in vain – the mere illusion of perfection. In his many homosexual partners, he searches for an embodiment of the impossible myth of Percival he has created in his own mind. And although he knows his search for the human being to reflect and replace Percival is futile, Neville's compulsions are stronger than his grasp on reality: "After unspeakable anguish, I shall then—for there is no end to the folly of the human heart—seek another, find another" (301). In what has been called his "desperate homosexuality"[54] and his continued denial of time and death ("let us abolish the ticking of time's clock with one blow. Come closer," 301), Neville is doomed to failure. He and Jinny do not transcend time or loneliness through sexual promiscuity; their brief moments of variety and intensity end in a deeper isolation, which mocks their struggles to deny it.

A poet-lover in conflict with himself, Neville compromises *both* his visionary and realistic ambitions, to end in an unworthy adjustment. Now in middle age, when he commands, "Let us read writers of Roman severity and virtue" (300), he is using the classics as means, not end; as bait to impress and attract his latest sexual partner: "But I love to slip the virtue and severity of the noble Romans under the grey light of your eyes, and . . . of naked cabin boys" (301).[55] Louis's attic room houses his conflicted psyche; Neville's room of homosexual assignations is a room hermetically sealed against the undeniable realities of procreation, time, and death.

In the seventh interlude the sun has sunk and all is shrouded in "*uncertainty and ambiguity*" (303). An uneasy Susan wonders "what shock can loosen my laboriously gathered, relentlessly pressed-down life?" (308). It was she whom Percival loved, for both were close to primary realities, he through the life of action, she through her basic instincts. Jinny is in a London Tube station, and her reactions to the scene are singularly Dantesque. "Millions descend these stairs in a terrible descent" (310), she thinks. She is fearful of "the soundless flight of upright bodies down the moving stairs like the pinioned and terrible descent of some army of the dead downwards" (310). True to her unreflecting nature, she does not consciously liken the scene to the *Inferno*. Rather, she lives this allusive reality vividly enough to suggest the submerged allusion.[56] When Jinny's soliloquy ends with "let the silent army of the dead descend. I march forward" (312), we move past her surface bravery to her unconscious identification of herself as a damned sinner. Indeed, as with the reference to the nightingale Philomela, the only indication readers have of Jinny's unconscious guilt about her promiscuity is rendered via allusion.

Neville is now a spiritually impoverished sensationalist who tries to make life bearable by surrendering to direct, immediate experience: "Throw caution to the winds and when the door opens accept absolutely" (314). His shift from fastidiousness to a "unanimous, indiscriminate, uncounted" (312) attitude is reflected in his approach to literature, which is much less sharp and demanding now than in the past. He speaks of reading "half a page of anything" (313), or he reads Shakespeare methodically: "Here's the fool, here's the villain, here in a car comes Cleopatra, burning on her barge" (312).[57] His defeatism is further reflected in his effort to make ordinary speech qualify as poetry. He began by assuming that magnificent language could order the world; finding that assumption insufficient to keep chaos at bay, he now accommodates to the disorderly world by redefining poetry as overheard ordinary dialogue.

Bernard (who once again opens this episode) is also feeling the effects of time and lost youth. Ironically enough, he is in Rome, the eternal city, taking stock of his limitations: "I am not so gifted as at one time seemed likely. Certain things lie beyond my scope. I shall never understand the harder problems of philosophy. . . . Nor shall I learn Russian or read the Vedas" (305).[58] This latter reference adds a spiritual dimension to Bernard's character, underscoring his curiosity about man's relation to the cosmos as it reiterates his interest in the seers' vision of truth and reality. In the Upanishads, part of the Vedic writings, one can see many of the crucial preoccupations of Woolf in *The Waves*. For example, in the first of the ten principal Upanishads, man is admonished to do precisely what Bernard is doing: "Meditate on the eternal spirit; remember past deeds." The second Upanishad anticipates the conclusion of *The Waves* in its assertion that "revelation is the conquest of death," as does the Upanishad that asserts: "The dreaming mind enjoys its greatness. What it has seen it sees again; what it has heard it hears again." The fifth Upanishad talks of precisely that "impersonal Self" which Bernard seeks; the tenth asks, "What is he who has no desire? . . . He does not die like others; he is of Spirit, he becomes Spirit"—an extraordinary correlation to Bernard's search for the reality of a world seen without a self. Indeed in the last Upanishad one may read a foreshadowing of the conclusion of *The Waves*:

> As the skin of a snake is peeled off and lies dead on an ant-hill, so this body falls and lies on the ground; but the Self is bodiless, immortal, full of light; he is of Spirit, he becomes Spirit. . . . He, whose Self lying in this mysterious uncertain body is awakened, becomes Spirit. *He becomes the maker of the world, the maker of everything. His is the world, he is the world itself.*[59]

Moreover, the allusion to the Vedas is in keeping with Bernard's constant quest for the *logos*, for the Word itself. In the enigmatic Vedas Bernard might find what he seeks through his Byronic preoccupation with words and in his notebook full of phrases—*the* Word, the sacred *Ôm* that represents the completed Self and the creative principle. That special word, according to the third Upanishad, "is the ultimate foundation. Who finds it is adored among the saints." Bernard *does* find a supreme word of sorts—yet another literary allusion—and its use puts him in contact with an ultimate reality principle of profound, cyclic significance. By suggesting Bernard's desire to read the Vedas, Woolf keeps us in constant touch with his (and her own) perpetual quest, through literature, for the all-encompassing "true story, *the one story* to which all these phrases refer" (306, italics mine).

Rhoda, who cannot tolerate physical love, has broken off her affair with Louis because she "feared embraces" (318). Her soliloquy is a cry of Shelleyan anguish: "I have been stained by you and corrupted" (317) she says of life, in an obvious approximation of Shelley's phrase about "the contagion of the world's slow stain" (*Adonais*, 40.356). She reintroduces the images from the Shelley poem that first revealed her sensibility: "Who then comes with me? Flowers only, the cowbind and the moonlight coloured may. Gathering them loosely in a sheaf I made of them a garland and gave them—Oh, to whom?" (319).

Louis engages in his daily business life carrying a gold-handled cane, which betokens authority and his need for respect: "I like to fancy that Richelieu walked with such a cane" (314).[60] Pondering the discrepancy between the scope of history and his own meager role in it, he offers a series of negative images: soot-stained roofs, "slinking cats and attic windows . . . broken glass, . . . blistered tiles, . . . vile and famished faces" (316), all strongly reminiscent of Eliot's images in *Prufock* and *The Hollow Men*.[61] Louis finally selects an allusion that demonstrates both his conviction that "a vast inheritance of experience is packed in me" (291) and his "desire above all things to be taken to the arms with love" (240). Woolf takes several pages to develop this allusion, one of the most significant in the novel.

The episode begins with Louis thinking "one poem is enough" (315). Clearly he is searching for some transcendent truth, for the total human experience unified into a single poem. One wonders what poem could meet such requirements, and what such a poem would take as its theme. We are first given only the phrase "O western wind" (315), which is juxtaposed to Louis's revelation that he has taken a vulgar Cockney actress as his mistress. To that phrase, "when wilt thou blow" is added, and the line is repeated (315), while Louis thinks of Rhoda and Percival. Then a second line is added, "That the small rain down can rain?," as Louis dares to think he might "make reason of it all—one poem on a page, and then die" (316). The two lines are repeated again (317), with Louis once again thinking of Percival and Rhoda. At last the full poem is given:

O western wind, when wilt thou blow,
That the small rain down can rain?
Christ! that my love were in my arms,
And I in my bed again! (317)

Louis's ultimate poem has unmistakable simplicity, strength, and passion; Woolf herself quoted it to illustrate that abstract, impersonal truth of poetry which expresses an "intense and generalized" mood and has a "hard and direct" impact.[62] It was Louis who recognized that all deaths and Percival's are one; fittingly, his sense of historical perspective dictates this selection of an anonymous poet. But the allusion moves outward, going beyond its characterizing function to illustrate the hidden hypothesis of *The Waves*—that all poets are one poet (therefore nameless) and all poems express one universal theme: love and the pain of loss. Louis has given us, in effect, *the* archetypal poet and poem. Second only to the final allusion of the novel, given by Bernard, this moves us as close to the human condition as words can.

The eighth interlude takes place in *"the evening sun"* (321). The waves sound *"like a wall falling,"* the wind has come up, a bird sings in loneliness, a sun-bleached bone lies on the moor (320). Bernard (again the first to speak) announces that the six characters have all assembled for a second time, at Hampton Court (321). The solidarity and optimism that prevailed at the first dinner have been abolished by Percival's death; now there is loss of unity and discord. Neville captures the dominant mood in his feeling that all is "distasteful, forced and fatiguing" (338).

The conflict of this episode is between him and Susan. Disturbed by her eyes, "full of turnips and cornfields," Neville feels he must "find my credentials—what I carry to prove my superiority" (323). Her "maternal splendour" threatens him; he knows she sees "the narrow limits of my life and the line it cannot pass" (324). He seeks to justify himself partly in literary terms: "Beneath my eyes opens—a book; I see to the bottom; I see to the depths" (324). Against his narrow intellectual depth, Susan marshals her natural fulfillment: "My body has been used daily, rightly. . . . Seen through your pale and yielding flesh, even apples and bunches of fruit must have a filmed look . . . you see one inch of flesh only . . . but nothing entire" (325). These are the basic modes of apprehension; the narrow, deep vision versus the substantial, comprehensive vision, and each has its attendant advantages and limitations.

Louis's mental landscapes are composed largely of gloomy images out of T.S. Eliot—"cats scraping their mangy sides upon the blistered chimney stacks; broken windows, and the hoarse clangour of bells from the steeple" (328–29). When he adds, "Over broken tiles and splinters of glass I pick my way" (328), he truly sounds like one of Eliot's hollow men.

For Bernard it is a time of recollection and self-assessment. He recalls "feeling a sudden conviction of immortality" that prompted him to say, " 'I too know what Shakespeare knew.' But that has gone" (334). Nevertheless his conditioned response to life is still to invent stories: "A girl sits at a cottage door; she is waiting; for whom? Seduced, or not seduced? The headmaster's . . . wife, drawing her fingers through the waves of her still abundant hair reflects—et cetera" (327). By now the Byronic stance is reflex action to Bernard: his slighty bored "et cetera" is Byron's own ironically bored beginning to Canto 3 of *Don Juan*: "Hail, Muse! *et cetera.*" Yet his is the last word in the sequence, for beyond Bernard's recurring hesitations is something indomitable: "I rise; 'Fight,' I cry, 'fight!' " (333).[63]

In the ninth and last section "*sky and sea were indistinguishable*" (340), as in the first interlude. There are "*vast curtains of darkness*" and the leaves seem to "*await dissolution*" (340). The final burden of explication is assumed by the only character in the novel equal to the task: " 'Now to sum up,' said Bernard. 'Now to explain to you the meaning of my life' " (341). The one who distrusts "neat designs of life" (341), the humane skeptic, is the most qualified to discourse upon his own life and the lives of the others. Earlier Bernard had anticipated being "called upon to provide, some winter's night, a meaning for all my observations . . . a summing up that completes" (255). The time has arrived.

Bernard's recapitulation is characteristically mitigated by his awareness of the outer limits of verbal expression. He retains to the end his skepticism about the ability of literature to render life fully: "Life is not susceptible perhaps to the treatment we give it when we try to tell it" (362).[64] It is the recognition of this inherent aesthetic problem that made Bernard "fail" while Neville succeeded as a writer. He sees what Neville ignores: that the structure of a subjective work of art may be totally false to reality, for life itself, limitless, open-ended, is "imperfect, an unfinished phrase" (373). Or as his most significant role-model put it: "It would strike you blind / Could I do justice to the full detail; / So, luckily for both, my phrases fail" (*Don Juan*, 5.97. 774–76).

Being acutely aware of the existential facts (like love and death) that seem to lie beyond literature, Bernard feels the need of "some little language such as lovers use, broken words, inarticulate words" (342).[65] He uses images that reach toward the primal confrontations of *King Lear*, calling up a vast cosmic scene in which man is pitted against physical nature. He speaks of "lying in a ditch on a stormy day, . . . tattered clouds, . . . the confusion, the height, the indifference and the fury . . . something sulphurous . . . helter-skelter; towering, trailing, broken off, lost" (342),[66] and he speaks of a time "when the storm crosses the marsh and sweeps over me where I lie in the ditch unregarded" (382). His feeling that "I need a howl; a cry" (381) is directly analogous to Lear's own "howl, howl, howl, howl!" (5.3.257).

Bernard knows how he differed from the others: "Louis was disgusted by the nature of human flesh; Rhoda by our cruelty; Susan could not share; Neville wanted order; Jinny love. . . . Yet I was preserved from these excesses" (344). He did not denigrate their life-styles ("All had their rapture," 361); rather, he kept himself sufficiently detached to observe truly and "made notes for stories" (344). He has felt Rhoda's frightening sense of disconnection; Neville's sense of intensely concentrated, discrete experience; Jinny's fleeting feelings of ecstasy; Susan's biological time and Louis's historical time. He has synthesized the passional world of Neville and Jinny, the historical-cultural world of Louis, the domestic, instinctive realm of Susan, and the detached, abstract world that is Rhoda's. He incorporates Louis's historical memory, which seems sometimes to be an expression of a Jungian collective unconscious, and Neville's civilized intellect of exactitude and wit. He has reconciled the others' disparities and assimilated their sensibilities.

In combining the qualities of the other five, Bernard displays that androgynous psyche Virginia Woolf thought so necessary: "Nor do I always know if I am man or woman, Bernard or Neville, Louis, Susan, Jinny or Rhoda" (372). Moreover, he has gone one step further than the others, who could never sacrifice their separateness and recognize their unity with others, or refrain from imposing upon the world an order that was only an extension of their private desires. They tend to *reduce* the world to their own psychic size; Bernard struggles to *expand into it*. He tries to direct his attention "to that which is beyond and outside our own predicament; to that which is symbolic, and thus perhaps permanent" (349).

Paradoxically enough, Bernard's individual identity is the result of his absorption of several extrinsic literary identities: "I changed and changed, was Hamlet, was Shelley, was the hero, whose name I now forget, of a novel by Dostoevsky . . . but was Byron chiefly" (349). Like Shelley, Bernard has the soul of a lyric poet and idealist; like Hamlet, he is visited by intellectual doubts, hesitations, moody questionings, and occasional satiety with "words, words, words." Bernard does not single out a particular hero from Dostoevsky's gallery of introspective, tormented, and complex characters,[67] but his understanding of what Woolf termed the "strange contradictions and anomalies which make a man at once divine and bestial"[68] means Dostoevsky is a logical choice for Bernard, who is a man wise enough to see that "the old brute, too, the savage, . . . squats in me" (377–78).

In addition to the parallels already explored, Bernard shares several other personality traits with Byron. There is his tendency to digress ("So on I ramble, now and then narrating," *DJ*, 9.42. 329); his commonsense intellectual integrity ("I mean to show things really as they are, / Not as they ought to be," *DJ*, 12.40. 314–15); his sense of psychological maturation ("But time strips our illusions of their hue," *DJ*, 5.21. 166); his novelistic impulse to describe ("description is my forte," *DJ*, 5.52. 409); his acknowledgment of how complex life is ("I leave the thing a problem, like all things," *DJ*, 17.13. 97); his awareness of the complexity of human nature ("If people contradict themselves, can I / Help contradicting them, and everybody, / Even my veracious self?," *DJ*, 15.88. 697–99); his Hamlet-like metaphysical doubts (" 'To be, or not to be?'—Ere I decide, / I should be glad to know that which *is being*," *DJ*, 9.16. 121–22); his encompassing skepticism ("So little do we know what we're about in / This world, I doubt if doubt itself be doubting," *DJ*, 9.17. 135–36). Even Bernard's feeling that "life is a dream surely" (367) is paralleled by Byron's "*What*, after all, are *all* things—but a *show?*" (*DJ*, 7.2. 16).

When Bernard reiterates his allusive identities a short time later, he adds Meredith. His feeling that he was "Meredith's young man" (365) reflects that interest in the clash between illusion and reality, that respect for complexity, and that admixture of poet and novelist which he shares not only with Meredith but with Terence Hewet, the first of Meredith's young men in *The Voyage Out*. Having assimilated the identities of his actual friends and the identities of his various literary models,[69] Bernard can lay claim to being the most protean character. His experiential scope far exceeds that of the other characters.

It is given to Bernard to reveal that Rhoda has committed suicide (371). His is the final comment upon her essence, and he sees her as a configuration of images taken from the Romantic poets. He twice calls her "the nymph of the fountain" (356, 367), and because the myth of Arethusa is a tale of flight from sex ending in a watery fate, it is an apt analogue to Rhoda's own flight from Louis and her suicide by drowning. Moreover, Arethusa is the subject of a poem by Shelley, Rhoda's characterizing poet, which makes the allusive web a very complex pattern of interlocking references.

After describing Rhoda in Shelleyan terms, Bernard describes the world in which she moved in singularly Keatsian language. "The willow as she saw it grew on the verge of a grey desert where no bird sang. The leaves shrivelled as she looked at them" (351) uses images and phrases out of *La Belle Dame Sans Merci*,[70] and the garland in Keats's poem provides a connecting link to Rhoda's earlier garland out of Shelley's poem.

The fundamental conflict of life and death is embodied in Rhoda and Bernard. Pervical's death generated suicidal despair in Rhoda and renewed existence in Bernard. Rhoda found the immunity from change for which she searched in the timeless transcendence of death—the search and the solution being typically Shelleyan. Bernard looks past change to find a deeper pattern of permanence. Rhoda was defeated by her perception of life's meaninglessness; Bernard struggles to formulate meaning.

Bernard's "absorbing pursuit" is to strive to capture human and physical nature in a phrase, to retrieve them "from formlessness with words" (364).[71] He feels he is part of mankind's continuity: "The whole of life, its adventurers then appeared in long ranks of magnificent human beings behind me; and I was the inheritor; I, the continuer; I, the person miraculously appointed to carry it on" (352). When Bernard speaks of " 'figures without features robed in beauty, doomed yet eternal' " (365), he is expressing what one critic has called "the Keatsian Grecian Urn concept of art."[72]

Prerequisite to a search for ultimate truth, in life or art, is an understanding of how various and complicated "truth" is. Of all the characters, Bernard best realized that "it is a mistake, this extreme precision, this orderly and military progress; a convenience, a lie. There is always deep below it . . . a rushing stream of broken dreams, nursery rhymes, street cries, half-finished sentences and sights" (353–54). He is aware of verbal incongruities and absurdities, of the fact that "one may be humming any nonsense under one's breath . . . 'Hark, hark, the dogs do bark,' 'Come away, come away, death.' 'Let me not to the marriage of true minds,' and so on" (356).[73] Bernard has mingled an unexalted (but prototypal because anonymous) nursery rhyme with two Shakespearean quotations. Taken together they are vivid examples of that mixture of "nonsense and poetry" which is "floating in the stream [of consciousness]" (373). In their larger thematic functions, these allusions are equivalent to Louis's allusion to the anonymous "O western wind." Woolf is seeking the outer boundaries of poetry where the universal poem will express universal human truth. Along with anonymous poets (and anonymous rhymes) down through the ages, Shakespeare in particular has achieved that impersonal, archetypal truth in which individual personality is transcended. First Louis, now Bernard expresses *The Waves*' thesis that all poets are one great timeless poet who sings the one great timeless song of love and loss.

To that trinity of allusions Bernard adds still more lines: "Pillicock sat on Pillicock's Hill" and "The world's great age begins anew" (373). The latter line opens the last chorus in Shelley's *Hellas* and makes explicit the rebirth theme crucial to both Woolf's novel and Shelley's lyric drama. Shelley's *Notes* to the chorus from which Bernard has taken his line stress that the most difficult task of the poet is "to anticipate however darkly a period of regeneration."

"Pillicock sat on Pillicock's Hill" is from the crucial scene on the heath in *Lear*; disguised as a madman, Edgar chants, "Pillicock sat on Pillicock-hill: / Halloo, halloo, loo, loo!" This allusion is possibly *the* most striking blend of poetry and nonsense offered. As an epitome of nonsense approaching madness, it underscores Bernard's determination to confront the utmost verbal extremes of human consciousness. The pattern of Bernard's realization, in its own less titanic way, is as intricate as Lear's. His confrontations, like Lear's, are with the fundamental mysteries of self and the primordial vastness of nature. His existential task, like Lear's, is to become fully human.

As none of the others did, Bernard sees that self-realization is a paradox—genuine selfhood requires the loss of a constricted ego. He has developed what one critic has called the "almost agapeistic sympathy that is real self-enlargement"[74]—a fact made clear by his "here on my brow is the blow I got when Percival fell. Here on the nape of my neck is the kiss Jinny gave Louis. My eyes fill with Susan's tears. I . . . feel the rush of the wind of her flight when she [Rhoda] leapt" (377).

The mind of the artist must be both all-embracing and impersonal. As Bernard phrases the aesthetic problem, it is how to "describe the world seen without a self" (376). Artistic truth, as the allusions have been hinting, resides in the anonymity of the archetype and is best expressed by an impartial artist who has cleansed himself of distracting subjectivities in order to present an all-embracing timeless vision. The perfect novelist would combine the impersonality of the Greek tragedies Woolf revered with the Platonic quest that takes one past the many colors of apparent reality to a Shelleyan "white radiance of eternity."[75]

One final and very important aspect of Bernard's character needs to be considered in detail: his attitude toward Percival. It is a complex attitude, which partakes of both reverence and caution over sentimentalizing his death, and it is allusively expressed. Bernard feels that Percival "would have done justice. . . . No lullaby has ever occurred to me capable of singing him to rest" (345). This diction makes Bernard a Horatio who cannot put into words his ineffable loss, who must be content with "flights of angels" to sing his noble friend "to thy rest!" And when he discusses Percival with Jinny, he recalls what "had been said by others; 'the lily of the day is fairer far in May'; we compared Percival to a lily" (360). Bernard realizes that "covered with lilies" though Percival literally may be, verbally the lilies are gilding: "Let us commit any blasphemy of laughter and criticism rather than exude this lily-sweet glue and cover him with phrases" (360).

What *can* Bernard say, then? What can he make of mysterious Percival, the mute and invisible presence in this novel? What has Woolf's novel *already* made of Percival up to the point at which we now find Bernard?

Percival is in fact the vehicle of an intricate network of meanings, which establishes points of contact in every direction. To the paradox-prone Bernard, "He is conventional; he is a hero" (260), for even the ordinary life has symbolic dimension.[76] In his perfect adjustment to day-to-day living, Percival is the natural being, the ideal well-rounded person. A young man of such wholeness and simplicity lives the life of action and is akin to the athletic Greek hero-figures Neville invoked when he idealized Percival as Ajax or Hector. That was the beginning of the legend of Percival as classic hero.

When his friends assembled to mourn their lost hero, Percival further intensified in referential importance, becoming a *godlike* hero. Bernard visualized Percival in India, treated by the multitudes "as if he were—what indeed he is—a God" (269). Symbolic in life, Percival became a mythic figure after his death. It is his *name* that confers archetypal status, for it makes manifest the high symbolic value and the recurrence essential to any prototypal pattern.[77]

Percival's name must bear what is, even in Woolf's allusive fiction, an unprecedented weight; it must and does surpass even a name like Orlando in the scope of its literary manifestations. Since its rhetorical success is dependent upon its "rightness," it must, in one word, immediately suggest an entire mythic background. Calling up as it does images of the knights of Grail legends, the name *Percival* has universal significance. Yet critics have not explored the rich ambiguities of its presence. Perhaps most of them have felt with William York Tindall that the connections between Woolf's Percival and literary legend are too baffling and obscure.[78] They are really neither; they are merely—if such an adverb may be applied to *The Waves*—as intricately structured and complexly wrought as the rest of the novel. Louis remarks that Percival "inspires poetry" (202) and notes that his "magnificence is that of some mediaeval commander" (200).[79] Such observations only begin to suggest the brilliant referential aptness of Woolf's naming.

In fact the Grail legend has formed a kind of oblique background for *The Waves* from the very beginning. The central action of the novel is itself a variation on the archetypal quest situation, and the quests of the six individual characters are succinctly symbolized in Percival. The garden in which the children first play is called Elvedon,[80] which bears a curious phonetic resemblance to Avalon, "the Celtic Elysium."[81] Bernard calls it "an unknown land" and notes its "rotten oak apples" (186). Neville is haunted by an image of "death among the apple trees" (191)— Avalon was the Isle of Apples.[82]

Quests and apple gardens are not the only accumulating echoes of the Perceval legend. The several symbols of that Grail for which Percival quested appear throughout *The Waves*. For example, Rhoda describes Percival as "a stone fallen into a pond round which minnows swarm . . . conscious of the presence of a great stone" (269–70). In the German *Parzival* the Grail is symbolized by a precious *stone*.[83] Then there is the sun, whose progress in the interludes of *The Waves* complements the waxing and waning of Percival's life. He is himself a sun—the others' source of illumination. As God can be symbolized by the sun, so the Grail was represented by the presence of light.[84] Indeed Louis notes that there seems to be "a wake of light" (200) behind Percival, and Rhoda feels "these lights, from Percival" (272). Neville (300) and Bernard (269) both mention Percival's "sun-helmet," evoking the helmeted Knights of the Round Table.[85] The cup or dish, another Grail symbol,[86] and the lance or sword, Perceval's knightly talisman,[87] also appear in the Percival sections of *The Waves*.

The six characters celebrate Percival at a dinner table that is both Arthur's Round Table and the table of the Last Supper. They experience a sense of spiritual wholeness in Percival's magical presence: "Comfort steals over us . . . the heart beats in serenity, in confidence, in some trance of well-being, in some rapture of benignity" (270). They use religiously tinged words like *communion* (262), *festival* (259), and *penance* (331). Louis makes the sacramental tone explicit when he speaks of "coming together, like separated parts of one body and soul" (270). The eucharistic meanings of the Hampton Court ceremonial feast are apparent in the mention of penance, bread, wine, and a cup (331). At the earlier dinner party as well, Jinny had noticed "the chair, the cup, the table—nothing remains unlit" (272).

Finally the description of Percival as rider reiterates his allusive role. Bernard's observation that Percival "rides a flea-bitten mare" (269) may at first lure readers into the belief that Woolf is ironically undercutting the hero image. She is in fact presenting an accurately transcribed version of the legendary Perceval, who first rode out to Arthur's court[88] on a "bony, piebald horse, with his uncouth trappings."[89] He cut a slightly ridiculous figure as a rustic simpleton, which only made his subsequent assumption of the hero role that much more effective: the Great Fool transformed becomes the renowned Quest-hero.

Moreover, attention to these allusive analogues puts the death of Woolf's Percival into proper perspective. His premature demise is another instance of Woolf's familiar theme of the absent hero,[90] but it does not necessarily signify that he has failed in a final, absolute sense. The legendary Perceval also "failed" in some accounts.[91] Indeed, in Malory and Tennyson, he is entirely replaced by Galahad, who finally achieves the Grail vision. These extenuating circumstances make the legendary Perceval a *modified* hero perhaps, but they do not make him (or Woolf's reincarnation) *mock* heroic. Given the radical relativism of *The Waves*, its insistence upon uncertainty and provisional conclusions, the choice of a "flawed" hero as the paradigm is much more *appropriate* than *pessimistic*. That the Percival of *The Waves* possesses no subtlety of intellect does not disqualify him either.[92] Like the medieval Perceval who fails to question the mysteries he observes, Woolf's Percival is neither reflective nor questioning, and rightly so.[93] This, then, is the accumulated weight and significance of Percival up to the last pages of *The Waves*.

Bernard has shed the confines of selfhood and absorbed many varieties of human nature, real and literary. He is ready to confront the ultimate mystery: "What does the central shadow hold?" (379). As he has outgrown his older, limited self, so he must discard its illusory emblem: "My book, stuffed with phrases, has dropped to the floor. It lies under the table to be swept up by the charwoman" (381). In harmony with Bernard's readiness, there is "a kindling in the sky" (382). Bernard perceives dawn not only as a "whitening" (382), with all of the Shelleyan connotations accruing to that color, but as "another general awakening: . . . Yes, this is the eternal renewal, the incessant rise and fall and rise again" (382–83). This growing light—which is also spiritual illumination and the imminence of a vision—symbolizes nothing less than the Grail-like quest for truth and reality that pervades the novel.

Carrying the entire burden of the novel as it does, Bernard's vision must be climactically synoptic, overcoming the widespread singularity of all of the divergent specifics explored above. This is the vision upon which *The Waves* closes:

> And in me too the wave rises. It swells; it arches its back. I am aware once more of a new desire, something rising beneath me like the proud horse whose rider first spurs and then pulls him back. What enemy do we now perceive advancing against us, you whom I ride now, as we stand pawing this stretch of pavement? It is death. Death is the enemy. It is death against whom I ride with my spear couched and my hair flying back like a young man's, like Percival's

when he galloped in India. I strike spurs into my horse. Against you I will fling myself, unvanquished and unyielding, O Death!
The waves broke on the shore. (383)

The arching wave now symbolizes the rhythm of Bernard's effort. Struggle is indeed the theme, as Woolf explained: "The theme effort, effort, dominates, not the waves: and personality: and defiance."[94] Here Bernard likens life to a proud horse; as far back as *Jacob's Room* it was "something that the courageous mount and ride out to sea on—the hair blown back" (153). Riding into battle, Bernard discovers that his enemy is death, the ultimate separation, the final human tragedy; most significantly, the obliteration of creative consciousness. Bernard will not, in his own defiant words, "submit to the stupidity of nature" (363). This defiance is not one man's ego, but the voice of humanity asserting itself against the indifference of the universe; thus the passage has a genuinely heroic ring. Because all men are riders against death, Bernard is mankind. But if he is all men in general, he is also the creative artist in particular, for man's only triumph over death is in his consciousness of rebellion against it, and in his ability to *record* his rebellion.

The other characters now exist only in Bernard's mind. He uses images that have belonged to them; he reports the physical world as given in the novel's interludes—thus his inclusive consciousness is equivalent to that of an omniscient narrator.[95] Nowhere does he justify more convincingly the burden of understanding and explication that his authorial position demands than in his visionary invocation of Percival. Earlier Bernard had deemed Percival "a ridiculous name" (282). Now his task as spokesman is to reveal the significance of that cipher, to "create" Percival by unifying the heretofore scattered ramifications of the symbol of the questing Grail-hero.

However, the attainment of any Grail (be it salvation, enlightenment, wisdom through suffering, eternal life, self-knowledge, or psychic wholeness) cannot be brought to fruition by an unquestioning hero. As the legendary Perceval gave way to a more worthy knight of active consciousness such as Galahad, the Percival of *The Waves* gives way to Bernard. Bernard has a voice where Percival was dumb. In the closing lines Bernard assumes his most important literary identity yet, and *becomes the allusion he has invoked.*

The transformation of Bernard into Quest Hero is neither arbitrary nor vague. Earlier images have been preparing for it: the omniscient interludes held *"turbaned warriors"* bearing *"assegais"* (227). Images of horses and lances appeared in the fourth interlude (250). In the interlude preceding Percival's death, the waves were compared to *"great horses"* (280). Percival's flea-bitten mare is now Bernard's proud horse pawing the pavement. Bernard rides into battle bearing a spear, that legendary accoutrement which is both "pagan weapon" and "Christian relic."[96]

Bernard meets the heroic requirements established by the various Perceval legends. The Grail quest involves "surrender of the ego to the mystery of 'grace' "[97]—Bernard has endeavored to see the world without a self. The successful Grail hero "beholds the vision . . . shares in the secrets"[98]—Bernard has had his epiphany, which has its formal implementation in an allusion. The task of the Grail hero is to develop a consciousness that symbolizes the collective coming-to-awareness of mankind—in the closing lines of *The Waves*, Bernard has *total* consciousness. His defiance of death is made in the context of knowledge of self, of friends, of Percival, and of nature. Finally the worthy beholder of the Grail vision is an intermediary between present and hereafter. Bernard has certainly linked present to *past*; via Percival, he has articulated a recurring truth in the consciousness of all men, closing the gap between time and eternity. As for connecting present to future, Bernard accomplishes that because he is a creative artist. Language, the instrument of Bernard's defiance, will survive him, to be taken up by some future novelist who will repeat Bernard's task. That future storyteller will take the isolated, mortal phenomenon of Percival's life—Percival who is all men, for the ordinary man is a hero, life is a quest, and the final enemy is death—and immortalize it in an enduring conceptualization known as *art*. The Bernards of the past and future create and recreate mankind, condensing all human aspiration under some particularly significant name like Percival. It is as Shelley said in the drama from which Bernard took the line about the world's great age: "A new Ulysses leaves once more." Having discovered the pattern of truth, Bernard has discovered his true story, retold eternally yet eternally new and illuminating. Art *is* immortal in the way that Keats suggested, for literature is the universal memory of mankind. And so Bernard—novelist and knight in quest of the truths of art and life—defeats the enemy death.[99]

"The last enemy *that* shall be destroyed *is* death" (1 Cor. 15:26).

The last, italicized sentence of the novel does not signify Bernard's defeat by the natural universe. It is rather the final demonstration of Bernard's total consciousness, for absolute awareness must include a perception of that external, physical world which is eternally present. The conjunction of fact and vision, implicit in the structure of this work from the very beginning, is the basis of the revelation in the final line. There is the *simultaneity* of man and nature, death and the waves. This reality of conflicting truths simply exists. It does not admit of "solution." It *is* and it must be accepted.

The human and natural worlds are irreconcilable. One critic has said, "The elements themselves have the final word,"[100] but that is precisely why they cannot be said to have "won." Nature has no words; man is articulate. Man is the only creature who *knows* death is the enemy against whom he rides. He is the only creature who can write novels, paint pictures, or compose symphonies against that inevitable doom. Nature is another order outside of man. The profound significance of the final italicized line of *The Waves* is that it is "simply and sublimely irrelevant to Bernard, as Bernard to it, and therein lies its enormous power."[101]

As the creative consciousness of mankind, Bernard must create whatever victory and affirmation there is. Nature is as unmoved by human optimism as by defeatism; man generates his own values. Virginia Woolf's designation of the theme as defiance ("effort, effort dominates, *not the waves,*" she said) stresses the primacy of *human* values, which are beyond nature's capacity to defeat or endorse. Blind, dumb, indifferent nature goes on, in cycles of stupidity, breaking and reassembling its waves upon the shore. Human consciousness goes on, perceiving the external world and recreating itself in an infinite succession of Percivals and Bernards. Such is man's true story. The quest for the Grail of reality ends (to begin again) *in the mind of the artist.*

The Waves is not Virginia Woolf's last novel, but it is by general consensus the consummation of her poetic method. It has been called "one of the books which comes nearest to stating the mystery of life, and so, in a sense nearest to solving it."[102] With tenacious courage Woolf worked her way through seven large manuscript notebooks before *The Waves* was bodied forth in its final form. Journeying through these notebooks on this voyage out with Woolf, one reaches a final scrawled page—a little more illegible than her usually illegible handwriting—on which she and Bernard triumphantly achieved the Grail at the end of their difficult quest. In her *Diary* she recorded the sensations thus: "I wrote the words O Death fifteen minutes ago, having reeled across the last ten pages with . . . intensity and intoxication . . . it is done; and I have been sitting these 15 minutes in a state of glory, and calm, and some tears."[103]

Along with her androgynous phrase-maker, Woolf absorbed the literary tradition available to her in *The Waves* as never before. She made herself the receiver and continuer of that inheritance. No longer exterior to it, employing its riches as an aspect of her style, she *became* the great literary tradition behind her, much as Bernard became the allusions he invoked. *Orlando* was comic demonstration that every poet recapitulates the poets of the past; *The Waves* is the most poetic, intense, and profound proof Woolf ever offered. "Think of yourself," she once advised the poet, as "a poet in whom live all the poets of the past, from whom all poets in time to come will spring . . . you are an immensely ancient, complex, and continuous character."[104]

The Quest is aesthetic; the Grail is literary excellence; the Way is allusive. We have traveled Bernard's "illuminated and everlasting road"[105] and joined "the innumerable congregations of past time" and come to know the full force of Virginia Woolf's conviction:

Great poets do not die; they are continuing presences.

Allusions in the Novels

Allusions are listed alphabetically, exactly as given by Woolf, whether in the form of quotation, author's name, or title of work. Unless the author appears with a first name, Woolf has used only the surname as her allusion. Verbatim quotes are alphabetized separately, except when the author's name or work(s) have also been alluded to; in such cases, the quotation will be found under the author's name. Characters' names, where deemed allusive, are noted, as are historical or philosophical allusions that have a quasiliterary status (for example, Gibbon and Plato). I have included classical images basic to Western literature, such as sirens and harpies, as well mythological references. Any foreign-language allusions appear at the end of each list. Works already discussed within the text or in footnotes are here annotated briefly or not at all. Pagination refers to the most widely available paperback editions, which are cited in the text and Bibliography. No pages are given for allusively named characters.

Allusions in *The Voyage Out*

Addison   171

Anabasis   227 "very much as school boys translate an easy passage from the Anabasis." Xenophon's *The Anabasis, or Expedition of Cyrus* is in seven books.

the *Antigone*   45

Arnold, Matthew   44

> What a set! What a set!   (44) Arnold twice makes this exclamation in his essay "Shelley," in *Essays in Criticism: Second Series.* He writes that Shelley's life is "a sore trial for our love of Shelley. What a set! what a world!" And again: "Godwin's house of sordid horror, . . . and the green-spectacled Mrs. Godwin, . . . and Hunt . . . and, to go up higher, Sir Timothy Shelley, . . . and Lord Byron with his deep grain of coarseness and commonness, his affectation, his brutal selfishness—what a set!"

tone is stressed; for example, the ship is "sad" and "gives a melancholy moan" (16). Even its symbolic quality as ship-of-life is tinged with this irony: the Euphrosyne is "an emblem of the loneliness of human life" (87). It is possible that Woolf's choice of name was a Bloomsbury in-joke: in 1905 a collection of anonymous verse entitled *Euphrosyne* was privately published; its contributors included Clive Bell, Lytton Strachey, Saxon Sydney-Turner, and Leonard Woolf.

Euphues   253
Fielding's grave   39

and let loose a small bird . . . because one hates to think of anything in a cage (39–40). In *Tom Jones*, book 4, chapter 3, Master Blifil lets loose Sophia's pet bird and afterwards explains to Mr. Allworthy: "Thinking the poor creature languished for liberty, I own I could not forbear giving it what it desired." Thanks to Blifil's pious interference, Tom falls in the canal, and the bird is carried off by a hawk.

Gibbon   110; 154; 163; 171–75; 196; 200–3; 212; 306

Decline and Fall of the Roman Empire 200 The title is variously rendered, sometimes as *History of the Decline and Fall of Rome* (106), sometimes as *History of the Roman Empire* (171).

His generals, in the early part of his reign, . . . barbarians who despised life when it was separated from freedom (174–75). A long paragraph, the beginning and end of which are given here, is quoted as Rachel's reading. It is from Gibbon's *Decline and Fall*, vol. 1, chapter 1, third paragraph.

Good, then, is indefinable; and yet, so far as I know, there is only one ethical writer, Prof. Henry Sidwick, who has clearly recognized and stated this fact (74). G.E. Moore, *Principia Ethica*, chapter 1, n. 14. There is an earlier reference to the *Principia*, this one describing "a sentence about the Reality of Matter, or the Nature of Good" (33).

Hardy, Thomas   54;110

I speak as one who plumbs
  Life's dim profound,
One who at length can sound
  Clear views and certain.
But—after love what comes?
  A scene that lours,
A few sad vacant hours,
  And then, the Curtain
(110). Hardy's 1883 poem,
"He Abjures Love," from *Time's Laughingstocks*, last stanza.

Homer   46
Ibsen   123; 223
Icelandic Sagas   19

In shrinking trepidation
His shame he seems to hide
While to the king his relation
He brings the corpse-like Bride.
Seems it so senseless what I say?   35 Wagner's *Tristan and Isolde*, Act 1, Scene 2. Because Rachel is reading these translated lines from the libretto, the opera has become a quasiliterary phenomenon. Phrases like "the corpse-like Bride" forecast Rachel's destiny, even though she answers an irreverent yes

to the question that ends the quotation. This is perhaps what Fleishman had in mind when he observed that "Woolf manages to scorn the *Liebestod* motif and affirm it, too" (*Critical Reading*, p. 16).

Johnson, Samuel   56;171

Here lies the duck that Samuel Johnson sat on. 56 In the first chapter of *Samuel Johnson* by Sir Leslie Stephen, Woolf's father reproduced the epitaph Johnson was said to have written at the tender age of three: "Here lies good master duck / Whom Samuel Johnson trod on; / If it had lived, it had been good luck, / For then we had had an odd one."

Jorrocks   171 The ommission of italics is misleading; John Jorrocks is the fictional character, created by Robert Smith Surtees, whose name appears as part of the title of Surtees's 1838 work, *Jorrocks' Jaunts and Jollities*. The slight, topical humor of *Jorrocks* prompted Ridley Ambrose's remark in the Later TS: " 'I'm idiotic enough to like Jorrocks.' "

Keats   65; 171

Kingsley, Mr.   201

Be good, sweet maid 201 "Be good, sweet maid, and let who can be clever," the beginning of the last stanza of Kingsley's 1856 poem, "A Farewell."

They wrestled up, they wrestled down,
    They wrestled sore and still:
The fiend who blinds the eyes of men,
    That night he had his will.
Like stags full spent, among the bent
    They dropped awhile to rest—   350 From "A New Forest Ballad," lines 45–50.

Lars Porsena of Clusium
By the nine Gods he swore—
That the Great House of Tarquin
Should suffer wrong no more   10–11 Macaulay, *Lays of Ancient Rome*, "Horatius," stanza 1. The Holograph draft of the novel (MS I, March 29, 1912) contains these four lines from "Horatius"; the Earlier TS does not.

Man and Superman   223

Marlowe   171

Maternity by Michael Jessop   371 Hughling Elliot, the Oxford don, volunteers this guess as the identity of a novel Miss Allan is reading. Aside from some faint satiric point about popular fiction and levels of taste, the effect is mitigated by the distinct possibility that this author's novel simply does not exist. The Earlier TS has Elliot offering a different (and equally untraceable) guess: " '*Marraige* [sic] by Michael Farren, I presume.' "

Maupassant   124

Meredith   124; 179

Diana of the Crossways 124 Heroine in the novel of the same title by George Meredith.

Love in the Valley   296

Modern Love   110

Milton   326

Peor and Baalim
Forsake their Temples dim,
    With that twice batter'd God of Palestine
And mooned Astaroth—   351 Milton, "On the Morning of Christ's Nativity," the Hymn, stanza 22, lines 197–200.

Sabrina fair,
   Listen where thou art sitting
Under the glassy, cool translucent wave,
   In twisted braids of lilies knitting
The loose train of thy amber dropping hair,
Listen for dear honour's sake,
   Goddess of the silver lake,
   Listen and save!   327 Milton, *Comus*, Song, lines 859–66. Three lines (861–63) are repeated as Rachel later tries "to remember how the lines went" (329), and then Woolf's text, a few sentences later, uses Milton's phrase about the glassy, cool translucent wave without quotation marks.
There is a gentle Nymph not far from hence,
That with moist curb sways the smooth Severn stream.
Sabrina is her name, a virgin pure;
Whilom she was the daughter of Locrine,
That had the sceptre from his father Brute   326 *Comus*, lines 824–28.

Miss Appleby's Adventure   104 The title appears to be Woolf's invention, but it achieves just the right tonal balance between genteel good taste and faint intimations of adventure. Real or invented, the allusion captures the ambiance of its genre, which includes such specimens as Mrs. Clara Louise Burnham's 1897 effort, *Miss Archer Archer* [sic], and the 1912 plays of one Evelyn Glover, "Miss Appleyard's Awakening" and "A Chat with Mrs. Chicky." Thackeray's daughter, Lady Anne Isabella Ritchie, also wrote a novel of this sort, entitled *Miss Angel.*

Odysseus   19

Pascal   52

Petronius   25

Pindar   24; 152; 168; 170; 224

Plato   46; 171

   Symposium   199 When Mrs. Thornbury asks, " 'Where would you be if it weren't for the women!' " Ridley's answer is " 'Read the *Symposium*.' " Which is to say men without women would be at all-male drinking parties— a symposium, literally—talking about the nature of love, and even perhaps deciding that spiritual, homosexually tinged friendships are the highest form of relationship.

Pope   164; 171 The Oxford don, Hughling Elliot's response to Miss Allan's comment that she must "despatch Alexander Pope" (164) for her *Primer* is, " 'Who reads Pope, I should like to know? And as for reading about him— No, not you, Miss Allan; be persuaded you will benefit the world much more by dancing than by writing' " (164). In his chauvinistic assignment of charming and insignificant tasks like dancing to women, Elliot is not unlike the very poet he abruptly dismisses, who wrote the infamous line "most women have no characters at all," a line that irritated the feminist Woolf in *A Room of One's Own* and is hinted at, darkly, in *Orlando* (see below).

rats who followed the piper   152 The arrival of musicians hired to play at a dance is described thus: "The father, the daughter, and the son-in-law who played the horn flourished with one accord. Like the rats who followed the piper, heads instantly appeared in the doorway." This allusion to the story of the Pied Piper of Hamelin functions as a striking simile in which Woolf's party-goers are not very flatteringly presented.

St. John [St. John Hirst]   Omitted from the published text is an Earlier TS remark of Helen's that St. John is "the name of a character in Thackeray whom I particularly detest." Woolf must have had in mind *Henry Esmond*, in which the following description occurs: "Incomparably more brilliant, more splendid, eloquent, accomplished than his rival, the great St. John could be as selfish as Oxford was, and could act the double part . . . notoriously of no religion, he toasted church and queen as boldly as the stupid Sacheverel, whom he used and laughed at" (book 3, chapter 10).

Sappho   230; 237; 238   Cf. the *Swinburne* note below.

Shakespeare   54; 154; 202; 268

Full fathom five thy father lies   54 Ariel's Song in *The Tempest*, 1.2.396ff. The song involves Ferdinand's memories of his drowned father; the lines "nothing of him that doth fade, / But doth suffer a sea change / Into something rich and strange" were inscribed on Shelley's gravestone after *he* drowned. This seemingly trivial "watery" allusion anticipates the circumstances of Rachel's own allusive and watery death.

Hamlet   54

Henry the Fifth   54

Lear's speeches   227

the sonnets   54

Shelley   44; 58; 65; 98; 171

Adonais   44 See footnote 8.

Siren   246

Sophocles   171

spinning the thread of fate   208 In epic accounts, three female deities, Clotho, Lachesis, and Atropos, spin out the life of man.

Swift   171

Swinburne   230; 316 Hirst identifies "the first line of a Greek poem" with "the translation opposite" as "Sappho . . . The one Swinburne did." This is followed by omniscient narration, which calls it "the Ode to Aphrodite" (230). It is difficult to determine precisely which work Woolf had in mind. She could mean Swinburne's "On the Cliffs," which begins with a Greek line from Sappho and renders some of her fragments within its own verbose meditations. Or she could have meant to refer to "Anactoria," which is also prefaced by a Greek quote from Sappho and contains Swinburne's renderings of fragments. Perhaps she meant to allude to "Sapphics," a metric *tour de force* in which the title designates the verse form. This poem specifically mentions Aphrodite.

Terence [Terence Hewet]   The name of the classic Roman poet-dramatist whom Meredith cites several times in his *Idea of Comedy and of the Uses of the Comic Spirit*. Terence Hewet is a would-be novelist who admires Meredith, who wrote about Terence. Meredith also wrote novels, and the plays of Terence contain what Edith Hamilton has called "the germ of the novel."

Thackeray   216

Webster   172 John Webster, the dramatist.

Wedekind   172 The German playwright's first play, "Spring's Awakening" (1891), was a candid and for its time shocking account of the inner torment and ultimate suicide of adolescents in the grip of the elemental power of the sex drive. Subsequent expressionistic plays, "Earth Spirit" (1895) and "Pandora's Box" (1903), are character studies of the amoral Lulu.

Whoever you are holding me now in your hand,

Without one thing all will be useless   267 Walt Whitman, *Calamus*, book 5,

Leaves of Grass. Woolf has misquoted slightly, adding the word *your* to the first line.

Willoughby [Willoughby Vinrace]   Rachel's father shares his given name with Sir Willoughby Patterne in Meredith's *The Egoist.* In that novel is a character, Vernon Whitford, inspired by yet another father—Virginia Woolf's own. Willoughby's own daughter Rachel (to compound the interrelationships) reads Meredith.

Wordsworth   103; 143; 171 There is also a reference to "W.W." 179
　　The Prelude   103 *The Prelude; Or, Growth of a Poet's Mind: An Autobiographical Poem.*

πολλὰ τὰ δεινά, κουδὲν αν-
θρώπου δεινότερον πέλει.
τοῦτο καὶ πολιοῦ πέραν
πόντου χειμερίῳ νότῳ
χωρεῖ, περιβρυχίοισι
περῶν ὑπ' ο'ίδμασι.   45 In the Sir Richard Jebb translation (*The Tragedies of Sophocles* [Cambridge: Cambridge University Press, 1904]), this passage is the second choral song, strophe 1: "Wonders are many, and none is more wonderful than man; the power that crosses the white sea, driven by the stormy south-wind, making a path under surges that threaten to engulf him" (p. 138).

Allusions in *Jacob's Room*

Achilles   167; 168
Aeschylus   75; 76
Aristophanes   70
Austen, Jane   39
Balzac   145
Barfoot, Captain   Lame in one leg, Barfoot may be an ironically oblique version of Oedipus, whose Greek name of "swollen foot" reflects the *bar* driven through his feet. Another possibility is *Captain* Blifil, whose epitaph closes chapter 9, book 2, of *Tom Jones.*
Barrett, Miss   Cf. Miss Elizabeth Barrett (Browning)
Betty Flanders   Possibly a play on Defoe's Moll (a variant form of Betty/Elizabeth) Flanders.
Bennett, Mr.   Cf. Arnold Bennett
a Brontë   106   Charlotte, Emily, or Anne Brontë.
bulls of Bashan   102   Ps. 22, lines 12–13: "Strong bulls of Bashan have beset me round. They gaped upon me with their mouths, as a ravening and a roaring lion."
Byron   22; 36; 93; 173
Carlyle   39
Catullus   41
Chloe   Edwin Mallet, suitor of Clara Durrant, addresses verses to her in a stock, mock-Pope mode: "And read their doom in Chloe's eyes" (84) is one sample.
Clutterbuck, Mr.   Surname of the red-haired poetess in Thackeray's *Book of Snobs* and of the imaginary editor of "the Abbot" in Scott's 1822 novel, *The Fortunes of Nigel.*

Congreve, Lady   Cf. William Congreve

Cowper   93 Cf. the reference to Cowper's *Letters* in *The Voyage Out*.

Crawley   The surname has an impressive literary lineage: Dickens's *Pickwick Papers*, Trollope's *Framley Parsonage*, and two of Thackeray's novels—Sir Pit in *Vanity Fair* and Sir Wilmot in *Henry Esmond*.

Dickens   39 There are also minor characters named Mr. and Mrs. Dickens.

Donne   160; 161; 169

Dumas   121 Again the problem of the imprecise allusion: *père* or *fils*?

an Eliot   106 George Eliot.

Erasmus Cowan   Cf. Desiderius Erasmus, the Renaissance scholar.

Euripides   138

Everard   A soldier in Scott's 1826 novel, *Woodstock*.

Faery Queen   39

Fanny Elmer   Like Florinda (below), Fanny has a literary given name with ironic overtones. It is the first name of Joseph's pure and virginal sweetheart in Fielding's *Joseph Andrews*, though her destiny with regard to Jacob does not parallel her namesake's bliss with Joseph: "Joseph remains blessed with his Fanny, whom he dotes on with the utmost tenderness. . . . The happiness of this couple is a perpetual fountain of pleasure" (final paragraph, *Joseph Andrews*). Then too, Fanny reads Fielding; *Tom Jones* is Jacob's recommendation.

Fielding, Henry   122

Tom Jones   122; 123; 124

Finlay's *Byzantine Empire*   66 George Finlay's *History of the Byzantine Empire from DCCXVI to MLVII*. The allusion reiterates Jacob's preoccupation with the Greeks, for Finlay went to Greece shortly before Byron.

Florinda   Florinda is "without a surname," thereby focusing attention on the given name, one which several poets bestowed upon very virginal heroines. In Southey's *Roderick, the Last of the Goths*, Florinda is the victim of "violation." In Scott's "The Vision of Don Roderick," there is talk of "fair Florinda's plundered charms" (stanza 4, line 34). In *Jacob's Room* her name "had been bestowed upon her by a painter who had wished it to signify that the flower of her maidenhood was still unplucked." Her dubious virginity is a mock issue in the novel: she has an affair with Jacob and becomes pregnant by Nick Bramham.

Fraser   Tutor to the titular hero of George Eliot's *Daniel Deronda*. In *Jacob's Room* he is one of the eccentrics in the British Museum Reading Room, "a pale, spotted irritable" atheist writing anti-Christian pamphlets.

Gibbon   108; 136

Julian the Apostate   45; 46

Hey diddle diddle, the cat and the fiddle   126 Called "probably the best-known nonsense verse in the language" by the *Oxford Dictionary of Nursery Rhymes*.

Homer   35

the *Inferno*   77

Jacob   The etymology of the Biblical form means "he will over-reach" (*The Interpreter's Dictionary of the Bible*, 1962 edition, vol. 2, 783). Hafley (168) notes that *Jacob* means *supplanter*. The Biblical story of Jacob, from birth (25:26) to burial (49:33) comprises nearly half of the book of *Genesis*. The Esau-Jacob rivalry culminates in Jacob's flight from Esau's murderous hatred (27:41–28:5). Esau sells Jacob his birthright for "bread and pottage of lentils" (25:33–34). Jacob is finally raised to the status of father of his country when his sons become the heads of the twelve tribes of Israel.

Keats   43; 44; 51

Kempis, Thomas à   68

Lothair   113

Louÿs, Pierre   127 Louÿs treated the subject of lesbianism is his *Les Chansons de Bilitis*. His other works include a novel of courtesan life in Alexandria, *Aphrodite*, and *La Femme et la Pantin*, a sordid tale of sadomasochistic love, which traces the emotional disintegration of a man who becomes the victim of a worthless woman.

Lucretius   69

Macaulay   105; 106; 108

Magdalen   110; 111 Woolf's reference to "the splendid Magdalen, brown, warm, voluminous, . . . with her sandalled feet" is perhaps a sly allusion to the Biblical Mary Magdalene.

Mangin   111; 112; 123 "Mangin, the poet" could be Woolf's variant spelling of the nineteenth-century Irish poet James Clarence Mangan. One of his best-known poems was a tragic ballad, "The Nameless One," which is ironically relevant to Woolf's theme of anonymous death-in-battle.

Marlowe   106; 107; 108; 122 Christopher Marlowe

Masefield, Mr.   107 John Masefield

Molière   169

    Alceste 169

New Testament   133

Norris's novels, Mr.   31 See above, p. 33 and note 18.

Papworth   Cf. Sir Miles Papworth in Meredith's *Ordeal of Richard Feverel*.

Plato   107; 108; 109; 110; 149

    the *Phaedrus* 109; 110

Ruck, Bertha   A tombstone inscription reads "I am Bertha Ruck" (133), yet the English novelist Berta Ruck was very much alive when Woolf consigned her to a hasty grave. Quentin Bell notes that Berta was "inclined to be litigious on the subject of her literary extinction" (2:91).

Scott   33; 121

    Waverley 33

Shakespeare   35; 47; 48; 70; 78; 79; 86; 105; 107; 108; 109; 122; 126; 138; 161

    Hamlet utters his soliloquy   109

    Hang there like fruit my soul   126 *Cymbeline*, 5.5. 264–65.

    The devil damn you black, you cream-faced loon!   126 *Macbeth*, 5.3.11.

    Who is Silvia? what is she?

    That all our swains commend her?   88 *Two Gentlemen of Verona*, "Song," 4.2. 39–40. Woolf follows this with lines 11–15 of the Song:

    Then to Silvia let us sing,
        That Silvia is excelling;
    She excels each mortal thing
        Upon the dull earth dwelling.
    To her let us garlands bring . . .

Shaw   35; 36

Shelley   78

    Adonais   78; 79, not italicized

Sophocles   69; 75; 76; 107

Springett   A Kipling surname in *Rewards and Fairies* (1910).

Tchekov   141; 144
Tennyson   72
Ulysses   170
Virgil   41; 42; 64; 69; 121; 135
 Arms, bees, or even the plough 41 A rather learnedly specific allusion to Virgil's subject matter. References to *arms* are frequent throughout Virgil, occurring in various Books of the *Georgics* and even in the *Aeneid*. The plough figures prominently in "Of Husbandry" (book 1, *Georgics*) and "Of Trees" (*Georgics*, 2).
 Virgil's bees 135 Book 4 of the *Georgics* is entitled "Of Bees."
Walpole   68
Wells   35; 36
Wentworth A captain in Austen's *Persuasion* and a colonel in Meredith's *Ordeal of Richard Feverel*.
Wycherley   69
Xenophon   138

Allusions in *Mrs. Dalloway*

Addison   192
Aeschylus   134
Brierly The name of Woolf's professor who lectures on Milton may harken back to Conrad's *Lord Jim*, where a character named Brierly commits suicide. The allusive presence of Conrad is further manifest in comments about horror; see the "horror, horror!" entry below.
Brontë, Emily 285
Ceres   129
Clarissa A character in Pope's *Rape of the Lock* and Richardson's famous heroine, Clarissa Harlowe, in *Clarissa: or the History of a Young Lady*. There are a few points of similarity (and many nonparallels) between the two Clarissas. However, an August 3, 1924, entry in her *Writer's Diary* makes it clear that Woolf had not read Richardson's novel. That she had a sense of the general literary weight of the name seems certain, however; she spoke of fictional women who "have burnt like beacons in all of the works of . . . the prose writers: Millamant, Clarissa, Becky Sharp" (*A Room of One's Own*).
Dante   133; 134
 the *Inferno* 133
harpy   135
Herrick   159
Horror! horror! she wanted to cry 39 This exclamation of one Maisie Johnson, upon observing a distraught Septimus, and Clarissa's " 'Oh this horror!' she said to herself" (53) may be echoes of Conrad. Cf. Kurtz's dying exclamation " 'The horror! The horror!' " in *Heart of Darkness* (chapter 3).
Jorrocks' *Jaunts and Jollities* 13 *Jorrocks' Jaunts and Jollities*, the 1843 work by Robert Smith Surtees. Cf. *Jorrocks* in *The Voyage Out*.
Keats   128
look in my eyes with thy sweet eyes intently, . . .
give me your hand and let me press it gently . . .

and if some one should see, what matter they?   124 The line "and if some one should see, what matter they?" is twice repeated on 125. The entire passage is from the mysterious song of the old beggar woman, who invites mythological interpretation as an earth-mother fertility figure, mourning her dead lover—symbolic of the cycle of the seasons, eternally regenerative nature. Since the ripe corn spirit was frequently personified as an old woman, Woolf's beggar also echoes the Ceres allusion. The lines have been identified by J.H. Miller ("Virginia Woolf's All Soul's Day: The Omniscient Narrator in *Mrs. Dalloway*," in *The Shaken Realist: Essays in Modern Literature*, ed. Melvin J. Friedman and John B. Vickery [Baton Rouge: Louisiana State University Press, 1970]). They are taken from a song by Richard Strauss with words by Hermann von Gilm (Miller, pp. 114–15).

Lovelace   159

Baron Marbot's *Memoirs*   46; 47; 205 *Mémoires du général baron de Marbot*, a late nineteenth-century work by Jean Baptiste Antoine Marcellin de Marbot.

Milton   267; 268; 269

Morris, William   49

Mrs. Asquith's *Memoirs*   13 This exact title seems not to have existed as such prior to 1925. Lady Asquith's *Diaries: 1915–1918* were known to friends of Woolf's (Desmond MacCarthy, Vita Sackville-West) and perhaps to her.

Plato   49

Pope   9; 192

Septimus [Septimus Warren Smith]   In addition to the *seventh* meaning I have proposed in the text, the name of Septimus has been linked to three literary characters by a recent critic. Katherine K. Blunt in "Jay and Hawk: Their Song, and Echoes in *Mrs. Dalloway*," *Virginia Woolf Quarterly* 2 nos. 3–4 (Summer and Fall 1976), proposes "Septimus Harding, gentle cleric and hero of Anthony Trollope's *The Warden*, 1855, first of the Barchester series; Septimus Crisparkle, minor canon in *The Mystery of Edwin Drood*, unfinished fragment Dickens was working on at the time of his death in 1870; and Septimus Ajax Dix, quixotic hero of William J. Locke's *Septimus*, 1909" (334, "Postscript"). Blunt admits that "none of the three Septimuses set up reverberations that relate to Mrs. Dalloway or Septimus Smith in the way that Hawthorne's Septimus Felton, his character, and his story do for me" (335), and offers an interesting analysis of the correlations between Woolf's character and Hawthorne's grotesque creation in the 1872 novel *Septimus Felton*. Although she mentions the connection of a recipe from the Borgias to Woolf's choice of the name Lucrezia (Rezia) for Septimus' wife (317), she does not mention a more immediate coincidence—Hawthorne's setting of Smithell Hall (cf. Septimus *Smith*). She is probably quite right to suppose, however, that some or all of these literary echoes were known to Woolf, a voracious reader.

Shakespeare   51; 102; 113; 128; 129; 133; 134; 135; 138; 212; 213; 222; 224; 274

Antony and Cleopatra   128; 133; 138

Fear no more the heat o' the sun
   Nor the furious winter's rages   13 *Cymbeline*, "Song," 4.2. 258–59. On 44 and 59, Woolf repeats just the first line. On 211 just the phrase "fear no more" is used, and in its final appearance, on 283, the entire first line is used.

If it were now to die, 'twere now to be most happy   51; 281 *Othello*, 2.1.
191—92.
Othello   51 the character.
Shakespeare's plays   130
Shakespeare's sonnets   113
this isle of men, this dear dear land   274 Cf. John of Gaunt's speech in
King Richard II (2.1.40ff). "This dear, dear land" is a direct quotation (l. 57),
while "this isle of men" is Lady Bruton's approximation of phrases like "this
scepter'd isle" and "this happy breed of men."
Shaw, Bernard   129
Shelley   49
sirens   86
Soapy Sponge   13 *Mr. Sponge's Sporting Tour* by Robert Smith Surtees, author of
the other book, *Jorrocks' Jaunts and Jollities*, in the shop window.
songs without words, always the best   291 "Songs without words are best,"
from George du Maurier's 1891 novel, *Peter Ibbetson*.
still it is better to have loved   292 " 'Tis better to have loved and lost / Than
never to have loved at all," Tennyson, *In Memoriam*, 27. 15–16.
Wickham   From Austen's *Pride and Prejudice*.

Allusions in *Orlando*

Note: Readers should consult Orlando's Preface for marginal allusions not included below. I have entered only those literary figures "standard" enough to
appear in such reference works as the *Penguin Companion to English Literature*,
Twentieth Century Writing: A Reader's Guide to Contemporary Literature, or the
Oxford Companion to English Literature.

Addison   109; 129; 136; 137; 138; 143; 182; 183; 186; 206
Cato   183
I consider woman as a beautiful, romantic animal . . . All this, I shall
indulge them in, but as for the petticoat I have been speaking of, I neither
can nor will allow it.   137 Identified in the narrative as a "passage from
the Spectator" (137).
the *Spectator*   136; 137
Aethelbert   9 A subject from legendary British history: Ethelbert, King of
Kent, is mentioned in *Historia Regum Britanniae*. In his capacity as editor of
the *DNB*, also alluded to in *Orlando*, Woolf's father quarreled with a pedantic
professor who wanted to preserve the Anglo-Saxon spelling of Aethelbert.
Noel Gilroy Annan reports in *Leslie Stephen* (Cambridge: Harvard University
Press, 1952) that "the diphthongs so seared Stephen's eyeballs that he was
prepared to risk a breach with the professor rather than let unnatural orthography prevail" (77–78). Virginia Woolf here lets the unnatural orthography
prevail. Cf. Thomas Hardy's Ethelberta, in *The Hand of Ethelberta*, who
writes an epic poem, thus living up to her heroic name.
Ajax   49 "The Death of Ajax," one of Orlando's early works. Along with
Achilles, Ajax was the most famous hero of the Trojan War. He stabbed
himself to death. Sophocles' tragedy *Ajax* presents him as a madman who

fancies a flock of sheep to be sons of Atreus. This sort of mad behavior is strikingly echoed by Ariosto's mad Orlando.

And then I came to a field where the springing grass
Was dulled by the hanging cups of fritillaries,
Sullen and foreign-looking, the snaky flower,
Scarfed in dull purple, like Egyptian girls— 173 Represented as Orlando's composition, but in fact from the "Spring" section of Vita Sackville-West's *The Land*.

Archduchess Harriet Griselda If Shelmerdine suggests Shelley, the Archduchess suggests Shelley's ill-fated first wife, the Harriet of several of his short poems. Griselda's literary lineage includes Boccaccio and Petrarch and several Renaissance versions in English and French. "Patient Griselda" was the model of simple-minded constancy and obedience, a far (and markedly ironic) cry from Woolf's formidable Archduchess, who is anything but a long-suffering, self-effacing, dutiful female: she turns into the Archduke Harry.

Bedivere, Sir 161 "Sir Bedivere flung the sword of Arthur," a reference to Bedivere's flinging of Excalibur into the Lake at the dying King Arthur's command.

Black, William 190 In 1883 Black wrote *Judith Shakespeare*, a novel about Shakespeare's daughter; cf. Woolf's "imaginary" character of Shakespeare's gifted sister Judith in *A Room of One's Own*.

Boswell, Mr. 145

Brontë, Emily 5

Browne, Sir Thomas 5; 46; 47; 49; 52; 57; 114

Browning, Robert 182

Buckle 190 Henry Thomas Buckle, historian who completed only two volumes of his projected work on English civilization before his death.

But let other pens treat of sex and sexuality; we quit such odious subjects as soon as we can 91 A parody of the first sentence of the last chapter of Jane Austen's *Mansfield Park*: "Let other pens dwell on guilt and misery. I quit such odious subjects as soon as I can."

Carlyle 182; 190

Chesterfield, Lord 139; 143; 189
Women are but children of a larger growth. . . . A man of sense only trifles with them, plays with them, humours and flatters them. 139 This is the "women are *only* children" passage from Chesterfield's London, September 5, 1784 letter to his son; italics are mine. Interestingly, Chesterfield's chauvinistic witticism is actually an altered allusion: in *All for Love*, Dryden's Dolabella says, "*Men* are but children of a larger growth" (4,1, italics mine).

Chloris Chloris/Flora, the classical deity of fertility, flowers, and plants. William Smith's sonnet cycle *Chloris* was written during this time period.

Cicero 58; 61; 67; 182

Clorinda Heroine of yet another Italian epic-romance in the *Orlando* vein, *Gerusalemme liberata*, by Tasso. Andrew Marvell wrote a short lyric, "Clorinda and Damon."

Daphne 72; 112; 208 This mythic personage is pictured on Orlando's tapestry-curtains, in flight from hunters (Apollo).

Deffand, Madame du 130

Defoe 5

Delia One of Virgil's shepherdesses; the lady love of the Roman elegiac poet Tibullus; a general poetic term of address for a female sweetheart. Like other Elizabethan sonnet cycles addressed to Diana, Clorinda, et al., there is Samuel Daniel's *Delia* and *Delia and Rosamond*.

De Quincey   5

Diana   Diana/Artemis from mythology; cf. Henry Constable's sonnet cycle *Diana*. As with the ladies of the other sonnets, Woolf's choice of allusive names echoes the literary practice of the time—sonnets written to real or imaginary mistresses.

Dixon   190 Richard Watson Dixon, poet who started a magazine with Edward Burne-Jones and William Morris.

Donne, John   57; 186; 188

Dryden   109; 129; 182; 206; 208

Eliot, Mr. and Mrs. T.S.   6

Euphrosyne   One of the Three Graces; cf. *The Voyage Out* allusion. Here Euphrosyne is Orlando's representation of the Lady Margaret O'Brien O'Dare O'Reilly Tyrconnel, and Orlando is banished from court when he refuses to marry her.

Eusebius Chubb   Chubb owes his given name to a theologian, known as the father of ecclesiastical history, who wrote a ten-volume work on the Christian church. Eusebius reappears in chapter 5 as a writer of memoirs.

Fates, the   77 In Greek mythology, three women spinning one's destiny or lot in life: Clotho, Lachesis, and Atropos. Cf. the "spinning the thread of fate" allusion in *The Voyage Out*.

Fletcher, Tom   A particularly apt surname for the Elizabethan era, which produced the famous dramatist John Fletcher of Beaumont and Fletcher; Giles Fletcher the elder, who wrote sonnet sequences; Giles Fletcher the younger, another poet; Phineas Fletcher, an imitator of Spenser.

Forster, Mr. E.M.   6

Gawain, Sir   A famous Arthurian knight, perhaps the original hero of the Grail quest. Note how intricate the allusive network of even minor names is: Arthur, Gawain, Bedivere. In her next work of fiction, Woolf was to exploit with utmost brilliance these first, small reverberations of the Grail legend. (See *Waves* listing, *Percival* entry, below.)

Graces, the   135 Three Greek goddesses, including Euphrosyne or Joy.

Greene, Nicholas   Cf. Robert Greene.

Hall, the falconer   Perhaps a sly invocation of Joseph Hall, the author of *Characters of Virtues and Vices*, an early seventeenth-century work.

harpy, the   76 In Greek mythology, women with wings. Cf. the sirens, which were birds with women's heads.

Hercules   61; 62 "The Death of Hercules," one of Orlando's early plays. Hercules died in agony after putting on the fatal gift of the poisoned shirt from Nessus, the centaur.

Hippolytus   49 "The Death of Hippolytus," another of Orlando's plays. He was thrown from his chariot and dragged to his death.

Iphigenia   49 Orlando's play "Iphigenia in Aulis." Iphigenia, subject of the Greek tragedians (and others, such as Racine), was Agamemnon's daughter, whom he proposed to sacrifice to the goddess Artemis. She was sent to Aulis, a harbor where the Greek fleet assembled before sailing to Troy.

Jameson   190 Anna Brownell Jameson, the only woman in Woolf's list of the illustrious obscure in Victorian literature. Her works include *Sacred and Legendary Art* and a somber death poem entitled "Take Me, Mother Earth."

Payne   190 John Payne, Victorian poet and scholar who wrote archaic prose.
Pope   109; 129; 132–40; 142; 143; 179; 182; 183; 206; 209
    a certain famous line in "The Characters of Women"   140 "Most Women
have no characters at all," the second line in *Moral Essays*, Epistle 2, "To A
Lady," subtitled "Of the Characters of Women."
    The Rape of the Lock   136; 137 Pope indirectly alludes to Ariosto's *Furioso*:
there Orlando's wits are stored in a vessel kept on the moon; Pope writes of
that "lunar sphere" where "heroes' wits are kept in pond'rous vases" (5.115).
    Whether the Nymph shall break Diana's Law,
    Or some frail China Jar receive a Flaw,
    Or stain her Honour, or her new Brocade,
    Forget her pray'rs,—or miss a Masquerade,
    Or lose her heart, or Necklace, at a Ball   136 From *The Rape of the Lock*,
2.105–9.
Princess Marousha Stanilovska Dagmar Natasha Iliana Romanovitch   A veritable compendium of Russian names, which Orlando reduces to Sasha. His
vision of her as "soft as snow, but with teeth of steel" may have been
suggested by a "Song" of Charles Sackville's, addressed to a "Sacharissa"
who had a faithless, cruel heart "in a frame so soft and white" (see
Chalmers, vol. 8, 346). Vita Sackville-West uses the name in a line from the
"Summer" section of *The Land*.
Pyramus   49 "The Birth of Pyramus," one of Orlando's early works. The
ill-fated Pyramus killed himself after mistakenly supposing his love Thisbe
was dead. What Woolf meant by directing Orlando's attention to the *birth* of
Pyramus is difficult to fathom. In the two most famous works dealing with
the legend, Ovid's *Metamorphoses* (book 4) and Shakespeare's travesty of the
story in *A Midsummer Night's Dream* (5.1), nothing is mentioned about the
birth or infancy of Pyramus.
Rattigan Glumphoboo   185; 186 These senseless words, which Orlando includes in her "cypher language" telegram to her husband to describe "a very
complicated spiritual state" (185), are in fact a sly parody of Joycean puzzle
language, out of *Finnegans Wake*. "*Rattigan's* corner" appears in the 1945
Viking edition of *Finnegans Wake* (p. 426, line 35, italics mine), and Woolf's
glumphoboo is a conglomerate of several words found in Joyce's work: *glume*
in "a spathe of calyptrous glume" (*Wake*, 613, line 17); *oboboes* in "his bay-
winds oboboes shall wail him rockbound" (*Wake*, 6, lines 36–37); and *boo* in
the following Joycean renderings—"Boo, you're through!" (247, line 12);
"Did you boo moiety lowd?" (232, line 22); "he made his boo to the public"
(423, line 22); "boof for a booby, boo" (333, lines 15–16).
Rossetti, Christina   190
Rustum   A mythical hero, son of a king of India and hero of the Persian epic,
the *Shah Namah*. Clive Bell called Eastern culture "illustrious" in part because of writers like Firdousi (author of the *Shah Namah*) and demanded,
"What do we know of either?" (*Civilization*, p. 54). Woolf appears to have
named her Gypsy accordingly. Cf. also Matthew Arnold's "Sohrab and
Rustum."
satyrs   12 A race a goatlike men who lived in the woodlands. See the *ogres*
entry above.
Scott, Sir Walter   5
Shakespeare   57; 58; 68; 107; 113; 182; 185; 204; 208; 214

Hamlet   59
Lear   59
Methinks it should be now a huge eclipse
Of sun and moon, and that the affrighted globe
Should yawn—   36 From *Othello*, 5.2.99–101.
Moor, the   35; 36 On 71, a further reference is made to "a Moor in Venice."
Othello   59
Shelley   170
sibyl   130 A female prophetess.
siren   121 See *harpy* entry above.
Sitwell, Mr. Osbert   6
Smiles   187 Samuel Smiles, one of Woolf's obscure Victorians; a Scot who wrote popular biographies of industrial leaders and something called *Self-Help*.
Smith, Alexander   190 Journalist, poet, essayist, and novelist whose works include *Edwin of Deira*, which uses a knightly theme involving King Ethelbert. His *Summer in Skye* visualizes Johnson and Boswell in the Hebrides, with Johnson Latinate as ever, calling mountains "protuberances."
Spenser   185
Sterne   5
Strachey, Mr. Lytton   6
Stubbs, the gardener   Philip Stubbs or Stubbes was a Puritan writer who denounced the evils of his time in *The Anatomie of Abuses*, in turn answered by the Elizabethan Thomas Nashe in *The Anatomie of Absurdities* (1589). Stubbs is a surname out of Thackeray and the name of Jorrocks's Yorkshire friend in *Jorrocks' Jaunts and Jollities*.
Swift   136; 137; 206; 209
Gulliver's Travels   136; 137
I enjoyed perfect Health of Body . . . Gamesters, Politicians, Wits, splenetick tedious Talkers. . . .   137–38 A long passage from *Gulliver*, part 4, opening paragraph of chapter 10 on the voyage to the Houyhnhnms.
Taine 190   Hippolyte Taine, French literary critic who emphasized deterministic influences in his *Histoire de la Littérature Anglaise*.
Tennyson, Lord   135; 182
Thomson's *Seasons*   183 James Thomson's eighteenth-century work, *The Seasons*.
Tupper   187; 190 Martin Farquhar Tupper, a popular versifier who attained some vogue during the Victorian period with works like *Proverbial Philosophy* (1838).
Williams, Mrs.   145 Anna Williams was the constant companion of Dr. Johnson and duly noted in Boswell's *Life*. Mrs. Williams was blind, wrote both poetry and prose, and did some translations. It is to the legend of their drinking tea together every night that Woolf's passage refers.
Winchilsea, Lady   While her life spans the seventeenth and eighteenth centuries, she is usually thought of as a minor eighteenth-century writer, friend of Pope, and author of poems on the pleasures of the country. Woolf saw her as a poet of "indignation against the position of women"; and she figures prominently in *A Room of One's Own*, the factual companion piece to *Orlando*.
Wordsworth   173

Allusions in *The Waves*

acquainted with grief   360 "a man of sorrows, and acquainted with grief" (Is. 53.3). Bernard uses this Old Testament diction to describe the paintings he saw at the National Gallery, which were "still as on the first day of creation, but acquainted with grief" (359–60).

Alcibiades   301 A charismatic leader famed for his sexual escapades and his friendship with his teacher, Socrates.

Ajax   301 An unfortunate hero who did not receive his just reward—the armor of Achilles.

Arnold, Matthew   214

Bernard   Bernard's name means *strong warrior* (Hafley, p. 168) and it has considerable religious and literary connotations, being the name of the patron saint of mountain climbers who lose their way, and of Saint Bernard of Clairvaux. In Spanish literature, Bernardo is a heroic figure, a favorite subject of Lope de Vega plays. And, in a provocative remembrance of *Orlando*, Bernardo is the man who defeats Orlando at Roncesvalles. In *Hamlet*, itself alluded to by Bernard in *The Waves*, Bernardo is an inveterate storyteller: "Sit down awhile; / And let us once again assail your ears" (1.1.30–31). Most revealingly, it was Bernard of Clairvaux who led Dante to his ultimate vision in the *Paradiso*. He was the contemplative spirit who saw truth plain and could guide others to it. At the climax of the *Paradiso*, St. Bernard explains the ranking placement of the blessed souls in Heaven (canto 32); Bernard's explicative function in *The Waves* is strikingly similar. St. Bernard's final orison (*Paradiso*, canto 33) is echoed by Bernard's final summing up, and Dante's glimpse of the great mystery of universal form (that is, the trinity) is paralleled by Bernard's vision of universal aesthetic truth or form.

Byron   229; 232; 234; 235; 236; 238; 349; 352; 355; 365 The phrase "Byronic untidiness" is used on 237.

Don Juan   235

Byron's tree, lachrymose, down-showering, lamenting   232 Fleishman identifies this as "Byron's tree at Cambridge" (*A Critical Reading*, p. 168).

there is that in me which will consume them entirely   223 Neville's assertion is most Byronic: cf. "But there is that within me which shall tire / Torture and Time, and breathe when I expire" (*Childe Harold's Pilgrimage*, 4.137.1228–29).

Catullus   196; 207; 210; 223; 235; 346

Dostoevsky   349; 352; 365

Dryden   207

Euripides   223

Gray's *Elegy*   232 Thomas Gray's famous *Elegy Written in a Country Churchyard*.

hark, hark, the dogs do bark   356; 373 From the anonymous nursery rhyme: "Hark, hark / The dogs do bark, / The beggars are coming to town; / Some in rags, / And some in jags, / And one in a velvet gown." The *Oxford Dictionary of Nursery Rhymes* reveals that the beggars in this rhyme, according to popular tradition, "were the Dutchmen in the train of William III" and that "one in a velvet gown" may refer to William himself. This bears an intriguing relation to Woolf's passing references to "King William" (369) and "King William mounts his horse wearing a wig" (334).

Hector   301 The last in the trinity of names Neville invokes for his homosexual partner: "Alcibiades, Ajax, Hector and Percival are also you," he says as he attempts to idealize them into the classic image of the hero. Hector was the bravest Trojan champion; he came to a noble end and was something of a cult hero as well.

Horace   214; 346 Roman poet of satires and odes; contemporary of Virgil (also alluded to in *The Waves*). Horace had a pervasive influence on English poetry and poets (for example, Pope, another *Waves* allusion).

Jug, jug, jug, I sing like the nightingale   298 Cf. "yet there the nightingale / Filled all the desert with inviolable voice / And still she cried, and still the world pursues, / 'Jug Jug' to dirty ears" (T.S. Eliot, *The Waste Land*, 2.100–103).

Keats   214

the lily of the day is fairer far in May   360 "A Lillie of a Day, / Is fairer farre, in May, / Although it fall, and die that night; / It was the plant, and flowre of light" (Ben Jonson, "To the Immortall Memorie and Friendship of That Noble Paire, Sir Lucious Cary and Sir H. Morison," lines 69–72).

Lucretius   196; 264; 346

Meredith   235; 365

nymph of the fountain   256; 356; 367 Bernard's description of Rhoda, linking her to Arethusa, the woodland nymph who was transformed into a fountain in order to escape Alpheus the river-god.

O western wind, when wilt thou blow,

That the small rain down can rain?

Christ! that my love were in my arms,

And I in my bed again!   317 Anonymous; sixteenth century. For Woolf's slow revelation of phrases and lines, see pages 120–21 above.

Percival   Medieval Arthurian legend is a veritable jungle of sources spanning centuries of time, different languages, poetry and prose, Christian and non-Christian approaches to Percival, Perceval, Parsifal, Percivale, et al. Sir Thomas Malory's *Le Mort Darthur* was the first important English text; it inspired numerous later treatments, perhaps the most well-known being Tennyson's *Idylls of the King*. The earliest Grail romances involving Perceval are Chrétien de Troyes's *Le Conte del Graal*, also known as *Perceval*, and Robert de Boron's *Joseph*, written in the last quarter of the twelfth century. In Chrétien's account, Perceval departs for Arthur's Court to become a knight; in *Joseph* the quest is Christian, and the Grail is the vessel of grace involved in the Last Supper. A third origin of Grail legends, in myths and rituals of the slain god and vegetation spirit, is the source used by Eliot in *The Waste Land*. There is a Middle English metrical romance, *Sir Perceval of Galles*; a thirteenth-century Welsh tale, *Peredur*; Wolfram von Eschenbach's German version, *Parzival*; a brief romance known as the *Didot Perceval*, which tries to synthesize the chivalric and sacramental elements; a French prose romance of the Grail called *Perlesvaus*; and four Continuations of Chrétien's *Perceval*, left uncompleted at the time of his death, two of them anonymous, one by Manessier, and the other by Gerbert. Such magnitude of reference demonstrates the universality Woolf wanted to capture by using this resonant name.

Plato   210; 240; 291; 292; 300

Pope   207

quit ourselves like men   214 "Watch ye, stand fast in the faith, quit you like men, be strong" (1 Cor. 16:13).

Shakespeare   207; 300; 312; 334; 366
  Cleopatra, burning on her barge   312 "The barge she sat in, like a bur-nish'd throne, / Burn'd on the water" (*Antony and Cleopatra*, 2.2.196–97). Neville's dulled paraphrase of that dazzling sight, which caused Enobarbus to say "It beggar'd all description" (2.2.203), is an example of his self-ful-filling prophecy, "We have lost our glory" (312). It is also reminiscent of how "shrivelled" the "intoxication of language" in *Antony and Cleopatra* came to be for Septimus Smith (*Mrs. Dalloway*, 133).
  Come away, come away death   356; 373 The opening line of the Song in *Twelfth Night* (2.4.52–67). Orsino wanted it sung because it expressed the essence of true love.
  Hamlet   349; 354
  Let me not to the marriage of true minds   356 Sonnet 116, first line. The sonnet reiterates *The Waves'* theme of permanence and change: love is "an ever-fixed mark," which survives unaltered, "even to the edge of doom." Pillicock sat on Pillicock's Hill   373 *King Lear*, 3.4.78.
  Shakespeare's sonnets   236; 322
Shelley   349; 352
  lie down and weep away a life of care   282 "I could lie down like a tired child, / And weep away the life of care / Which I have borne and yet must bear" (*Stanzas Written in Dejection, Near Naples*, lines 30–32).
  present them—Oh! to whom?   213; 214 "Present it!—oh! to whom?" (*The Question*, line 40). See footnotes 19 and 20 for further correspondences.
  the world's great age begins anew   373 From *Hellas*, opening line (1060) of the last Chorus.
Sophocles   223
Tennyson   214
Tolstoi   235
Vedas, the   305 References to Eastern literature are rare in Woolf. This allu-sion to the four sacred books of Knowledge, written in Sanskrit, suggests the background presence of T.S. Eliot: he alludes to the Upanishads in the closing section of *The Waste Land*. According to Andrew Lang (in *Myth, Ritual and Religion* (1906; rpt. 1968; New York: Arms Press, 2 vols.), the Vedas express the views of "sacred poets on their way to becoming a sacred caste" (1: 215).
Virgil   196; 210; 240

Notes

Work's appearing in the Bibliography are cited by author and title only.

Preface

1. Since this preface was originally written, Avrom Fleishman has proved to be the most conspicuous exception to the rule. His *Virginia Woolf: A Critical Reading* points out particular allusions from various novels and recognizes that allusiveness is "in the very tissue of her mind" (p. x). He also relates Woolf's deliberate aesthetic tactic, her "encyclopedic style," to "the dominant mode in modern British literature" (p. xi). "Virginia Woolf: Tradition and Modernity," an essay of Fleishman's appearing in *Forms of Modern British Fiction*, reiterates the same valuable points. His observation in both works (*A Critical Reading*, p. xi, and "Tradition and Modernity," p. 135) that the task of discovering the sources and relevance of Woolf's many references "has been left largely undone" seemed to be calling for the very sort of study I began in my 1974 Ph.D. dissertation.

1. *The Voyage Out*

1. Schaefer, *The Three-Fold Nature of Reality in the Novels of Virginia Woolf*, p. 46. Schaefer's contention that the allusive technique is superficial is weakened by her own inability to register the results of the "simple" method: she informs us that "Mr. Ambrose edited Horace" (p. 49). Ridley Ambrose's task is the editing of Pindar; that "tag" is associated with him throughout the novel (24, 152, 168, 170, 224). (Note: the page numbers following quotations, for this and the four subsequent texts, refer to editions cited in the Bibliography.) No reference to Horace is made by any character in the novel.

2. Schaefer comments on Evelyn's propensity toward overstrained hero-worship: "Her hatred of formality is equalled by her admiration for the heroism of men like Garibaldi" (p. 41). Schaefer here seems to be acknowledging a concept whose efficacy she disavowed when discussing Ridley Ambrose: that those figures, political or literary, who are admired by a given character *do* suggest the personality of the admirer.

3. Woolf specifies the Fifth Book of the *Prelude*, in the margins of which Miss Allan is penciling careful notes. In the Earlier TS version of this scene (Berg Collection, New York Public Library), lines from book 1 of the *Prelude* (464–66; 645–46) are quoted. Miss Allan finds them "very noble," but they do not prevent her from dozing off.

4. Miss Allan may be up to the middle of the eighteenth century, but her *Euphues*, which somewhat misleadingly lacks italicization, is the work of that Elizabethan novelist and playwright John Lyly. Lyly's marked influence on subsequent prose style is presumably what Miss Allan means by her juxtaposition " 'Euphues. The germ of the English novel.' "

5. Fielding's hillside grave in Lisbon "fell into a grievous state of neglect" because his countrymen were "scandalously neglectful," according to F. Holmes Dudden in *Henry Fielding: His Life, Works, and Times* (Oxford: Clarendon Press, 1952, 2:1054). In 1830, after the intervention of some concerned British citizens, a huge marble monument was erected, which occasioned ringing patriotism in British hearts: "They [Englishmen] may well be excused, if they kiss the cold tomb, as I did, of the author of *Amelia*" (Dudden, pp. 1055–56, citing George Borrow's *The Bible in Spain*). Clarissa's chauvinism therefore is in keeping with the facts.

6. Kelley, *The Novels of Virginia Woolf: Fact and Vision*, is quite correct in supposing that no one who recognizes this allusion to *Tom Jones* "can fail to catch the negative note in this element of Clarissa's character" (p. 14).

7. Joan Bennett links it to Woolf's general indifference to facts; the inaccuracy "is due to the essential feminineness of her mind" (*Virginia Woolf: Her Art as a Novelist*, p. 79). The Berg Collection material shows some confusion. In the undated Final TS, Clarissa speaks of having seen *Agamemnon*, which would then match her observation about Clytemnestras. But the Greek quoted by Pepper, inserted by hand into the TS, is from *Antigone*, as in the published text.

8. Clarissa has garbled stanza 40 from *Adonais*, making the stanza's third line follow the fifth line. As she recites her version of the third and fourth lines, they make little sense. Her thoughtful "Um-m-m" only serves to mock the omniscient "she went on quoting," for in rendering her "unrest which men miscall delight" line, she has gone *back*, not on, to restore the missing line. Even here the first two words of the line ("And that") have been omitted. The Final TS also has Clarissa misplacing the "unrest" line as she quotes. Shelley was a poet whose works Woolf knew extremely well, and intentionality would seem to be likely in this case. Fleishman thinks the *Adonais* quotation spotlights Clarissa's conflict of rejecting or accepting Shelley's values and notes that this dilemma of "social engagement" versus "chaste isolation" (*Critical Reading*, p. 16) appears later in Woolf's treatment of Clarissa in *Mrs. Dalloway*. In "Tradition and Modernity," Fleishman notes Clarissa's recitation of the *Adonais* lines without comment upon their garbled inaccuracy (p. 138), although elsewhere (p. 142) he catches Hewet's slight error in quoting Whitman.

9. All quotations are from "Jane Austen," rpt. in *Collected Essays*, ed. Leonard Woolf, 1:152.

10. *A Room of One's Own*, p. 130.

11. Matthew Arnold, "Shelley," in *Essays in Criticism: Second Series* (London: Macmillan, 1915), p. 243.

12. Ibid., p. 252.

13. Holtby, *Virginia Woolf*, p. 12.

14. Virginia Woolf's father, the model for the character of Ridley, wrote: "No reader of Macaulay's works will be surprised at the manliness which is stamped . . . upon them" (Leslie Stephen, *Hours in a Library* [New York: Putnam, 1904], 3:228). He had high praise for the *Lays of Ancient Rome*, their "swing and fire," their "strong rhetorical instinct" (ibid., 263).

15. None of the holograph or TSS versions contains the Bluebeard allusion. It appears to have been a last-minute addition.

16. Woolf characterized Dr. Bentley, another scholar, in much the same way: "For that man . . . knows Homer by heart; *reads Pindar* as we read the *Times*; and spends his life . . . wholly in the company of the Greeks" ("Outlines," *Collected Essays*, 4:106, italics mine).

17. The Earlier TS has Ridley advising Rachel to read "Homer, Shakespeare, Boswell."

18. An interesting variation on authors too terrible for young ladies to read occurs in the Later TS, in which Ridley thinks "*Swift*—no, that's too horrible" (italics mine).

19. Cf. Stephen, who said of Balzac: "He has some of the sinister power which makes him a fit guide to the horrors of our modern Inferno" (*Hours in a Library*, 1:288). In the Later TS, Rachel protests that she is "old enough" to read *La Cousine Bette*.

20. Fleishman also sees the irony of the unquoted end of the choral passage, and points out that the allusion serves to universalize the novel's action as a voyage of human enterprise (p. 18).

21. *Anatomy of Criticism*, p. 265.

22. Cf. Woolf, who once referred to "a decadence that was beyond the decadence of Swinburne himself" (quoted in Quentin Bell, *Virginia Woolf: A Biography*, 1:206).

23. Hirst's taste certainly cannot be attributed to Woolf, for she loved the sparse power of the Greek language, "so clear, so hard, so intense" ("On Not Knowing Greek," *Collected Essays*, 1:11). Swinburne's frequent flights into purple prose qualify him as one of the poets least able to render Sappho's simple and direct style.

24. Woolf took considerable pains reworking the Hewet-Hirst allusive debate, which centers around Hirst's chapel reading of Swinburne. The persistence of the allusive material through all versions, holograph and TSS, makes it clear how steadfastly Woolf believed that literary preferences reveal character.

25. In an Earlier TS remark, subsequently deleted from the published text, Hewet tells Hirst that he has "no feeling for literature" if he cannot see that Meredith was a great writer, despite his flaws.

26. Herbert Marder found Woolf "not altogether convincing" in attributing to Hewet her own interest in the daily experiences of women (*Feminism and Art: A Study of Virginia Woolf*, p. 68), perhaps because he neglects the allusive precedent that Meredith sets for Hewet.

27. Fleishman remarks that "the Hardian bitterness of abjuration comes readily" to Hewet ("Tradition and Modernity," p. 141), and points to earlier (unquoted) lines from Hardy's poem that relate it to Woolf's plot in two ways: by anticipating Hewet's own "desolation" and "Rachel's death by fever" (p. 141).

28. For example, Whitman's poem continues: 'The way is suspicious, the result uncertain, perhaps destructive." Only a few pages after Whitman is invoked, Woolf's lovers are "lost." Hewet had seemed "certain of his way, but as they walked he became doubtful," and Rachel finds she is following him blindly, "ignorant of the way" (272). Whitman's "stealth in some wood for trial," "sailing at sea," his "quiet island," being with one's love "on a high hill," the lovers' kiss—all are paralleled in Woolf's own plot action (270–72). And the "mermaid" incident between Rachel and Hewet (298) anticipates Whitman's "I will certainly elude you, / Even while you should think you had unquestionably caught me, behold! / Already you see I have escaped from you." Such detailed parallelisms are perhaps what Fleishman had in mind when he noted (*Critical Reading*, p. 19) that the "range of reference" of Whitman's poem is matched to Woolf's novel.

29. Hewet as novelist believes he is " 'good second-rate; about as good as Thackeray, I should say' " (216). Thackeray is here symbolic of those orthodox approaches to the novel that Hewet seeks to shed, as did his creator, who wrote: "Still, if you think of it, what answers [about people and life] do Arnold Bennett or Thackeray, for instance, suggest? Happy ones—satisfactory solutions—answers one would accept if one had the least respect for one's soul?" (*A Writer's Diary*, ed. Leonard Woolf, p. 21).

30. Peel, "Virginia Woolf," p. 81.

31. Sir Leslie Stephen said Defoe "had the most marvellous power ever known of giving verisimilitude to his fictions" (*Hours in a Library*, 1:4). His daughter called Defoe one of "the great plain writers, whose work is founded upon a knowledge of what is most persistent, though not most seductive, in human nature" (rpt. in *Collected Essays*, 1:68).

32. Leaska, for example, in "Virginia Woolf's *The Voyage Out*: Character Deduction and the Function of Ambiguity," builds an interpretation of Helen Ambrose as "an incompatibly riven personality" (p. 23), citing instances of her "veiled and controlled aggressiveness" (p. 19), and her "desperate, unconscious effort to cloud the atmosphere with irrationality and gloom and death" (p. 23).

33. Leaska sees Helen's "offhand decision about something so important" (p. 22) as an illustration of her "managerial" (p. 21) advice-giving. If, however, the allusive material allows us to see Helen as a fate figure, her offhand advice has the ring of the indifference of a turn of fate, that force which does not understand man's attributions of importance to himself and his life. Moreover, as Leaska himself notes, "Hirst asks Helen" (p. 22), thus imposing fate's whimsy upon himself by seeking so important a decision outside of his own judgment.

34. Schaefer observes that Helen "is compared to the Fates, spinning the threads of human life" (p. 47), but maintains that this allusive symbolism is too obscurely realized. She notes that Helen's role "requires wisdom and the large vision" (p. 46), but ignores the Moore allusion, which suggests just this philosophic awareness. She calls the embroidery an activity whereby "women, unlike men, relate themselves to a world of physical and not theoretical reality" (p. 24). But by reading *Principia Ethica*, Helen is assuredly relating herself to a theoretical world, just as Woolf is building a structure of symbolic import for Helen.

35. The evidence suggests that Woolf deliberately sharpened the Cowper reference. While the Later TS mentions the "spirit of poor old William Cowper," the Final TS is amended to "poor old Cowper, there at Olney." To enter into Cowper's spirit *during the Olney period* is to enter into a spirit of isolation, dejection, and despair. Cowper protested his nearly two decades at Olney in letter after letter, bemoaning the culturally deprived atmosphere and the total lack of intellectual stimulation.

36. The facts of Cowper's life—mental derangements, suicide attempts, and confinement in an asylum—have pointed similarity to Woolf's own. She was extremely fond of Cowper, whom she read "when I was 15" (*A Writer's Diary*, p. 237). She wrote of him in the *Second Common Reader* and deemed him one of the superior androgynous writers in *A Room of One's Own*.

37. Newton, *Virginia Woolf*, p. 21.

38. Woolf was impressed by Meredith's attempts to portray women beyond the context of their relationships with men, especially their friendships with other women. She cited Diana as an admirable attempt at the latter (*A Room of One's Own*, p. 143) and commented upon the "large and beautiful conception of womanhood in Diana" ("On Re-Reading Meredith," *Collected Essays*, 1:236–37).

Notes

39. Brewster, *Virginia Woolf*, pp. 89–90. Elsewhere she notes that life and death are offered as mysteries unsusceptible to solution (pp. 63, 66).

40. Newton, p. 21. Carole O. Brown in her article, "The Art of the Novel: Virginia Woolf's *The Voyage Out*" (*Virginia Woolf Quarterly* 3, nos. 1–2 [Winter and Spring 1977]: 67–84) refers to "the abrupt and apparently pointless sacrifice of Rachel" (p. 71). Holtby calls it "an interruption, an irrelevance" (p. 63). Jean Guiguet (*Virginia Woolf and Her Works*) finds it "pointless and unnecessary" (p. 198). Sean O'Faolain, *The Vanishing Hero: Studies in Novelists of the Twenties* (London: Eyre and Spottiswode, 1956), states that with Rachel's death the reader "is cruelly and wantonly smacked in the face" (p. 205). Marder believes that Rachel's death reflects Woolf's "inability to come to grips with the heroine's dilemma" (p. 21). William Troy, in "Virginia Woolf: The Novel of Sensibility," rpt. in *Virginia Woolf: A Collection of Critical Essays*, ed. Clair Sprague, asserts that Rachel's death "supplies a termination which might not otherwise be reached since none is inherent in the plan" (p. 30). Daiches, *Virginia Woolf*, asserts that Rachel "is sent to her death because for the moment Virginia Woolf can see no more of the quality of life by meditating on her further" (p. 12). R.B. Johnson, *Some Contemporary Novelists: Women* (1920; rpt. Freeport, N.Y.: Books for Libraries Press, 1967), claims that the death "is out of focus; and seems introduced with a kind of jerk" (p. 157) as the result of Woolf's "weakness . . . [for] the prevailing taste for tragedy" (p. 156). Edwin Burgum, *The Novel and the World's Dilemma* (New York: Oxford University Press, 1947), asserts that "the accident of sudden death was invoked to create a meretricious sympathy for her [Rachel] and a meretricious solution of her problem" (p. 125).

41. Guiguet, p. 198; Holtby, p. 77; E.M. Forster, *Abinger Harvest* (New York: Harcourt, Brace, 1936), p. 107; Thakur, *The Symbolism of Virginia Woolf*, p. 38.

42. Guiguet, p. 203; Thakur, p. 38; John K. Johnstone, *The Bloomsbury Group: A Study of E.M. Forster, Lytton Strachey, Virginia Woolf and Their Circle* (New York: Noonday Press, 1954), p. 325; Monique Nathan, *Virginia Woolf*, trans. Herma Briffault (New York: Grove Press, 1961), p. 100; Love, *Worlds in Consciousness: Mythopoetic Thought in the Novels of Virginia Woolf*, p. 79.

43. Brewster, p. 99; Marder, p. 25; Jones, "E.M. Forster and Virginia Woolf," p. 282; Schaefer, p. 44; Blackstone, *Virginia Woolf: A Commentary*, p. 210; James Gindin, *Harvest of a Quiet Eye: The Novel of Compassion* (Bloomington: Indiana University Press, 1971), p. 187.

44. *The Glass Roof: Virginia Woolf as Novelist*, p. 17, italics mine.

45. Schaefer, p. 46.

46. Frye, p. 291.

47. There is a startling parallel in Woolf's own voice: "Literature is open to everybody. . . . Lock up your libraries if you like; but there is no gate, no lock, no bolt that you can set upon *the freedom of my mind*" (*A Room of One's Own*, p. 131, italics mine).

48. Leaska assumes Sabrina's death "at the hand of her jealous step-mother" (p. 39) when arguing that Helen Ambrose's symbolic significance is in her approximation of Gwendolyn. The implication of Milton's lines, however, exonerates Gwendolyn from murder: Sabrina jumps into the river herself (see *Comus*, ll. 829–31). Thus Helen Ambrose is not a villainous counterpart of the "overpowering step-mother" (Leaska, p. 34). More importantly, if Sabrina's death is not murder by Gwendolyn but self-inflicted drowning, the symbolic analogy to Rachel's own semisuicidal death is that much more convincing.

49. As one critic remarked: "It is not coincidence that the 'saving' of Rachel consists of being released through her own death from her coming marriage to Terence Hewet" (Richter, *Virginia Woolf: The Inward Voyage*, p. 124).

50. The name of Milton's "Severn stream" is itself a corruption of Sabren-Habren-Sabrina's name. See Geoffrey of Monmouth, *Historia Regum Britanniae*, vols. 2 and 5.

51. Another example: in the essay on Shelley to which Richard Dalloway alluded, Matthew Arnold notes that during the reading of his grandfather's will, Shelley, unconcerned about the material things of this world, "remained outside the door and read *Comus*" (233).

52. Richter, p. 125, italics mine. Fleishman likens Rachel to Sabrina ("Tradition and Modernity," p. 143), but disagrees with Richter's view of Sabrina as death-wish (*Critical Reading*, p. 20). I think the problem here is that Rachel is, at different points, comparable to *both* Sabrina and the enchanted Lady. For example, like Milton's Lady, Rachel must triumph over sexuality through the strength of her virtue. The virgin Sabrina is the *Rescuer* of "insnared chastity" (l. 909). She becomes the agent of Rachel's redemption, as she was for Milton's Lady. The limitation of Fleishman's discussion of the *Comus* allusion is that he does not deal with the psychosexual meanings.

53. The MS and TSS versions show how painstakingly but persistently Woolf developed the organic relevance of *Comus* to her own novel. The Earlier TS does not include the allusion: both the Later TS and the March 29, 1912, holograph contain the lines which appear in the published text.

54. Brewster, citing Maitland's *Life* of Leslie Stephen, records that Woolf's father "always recited Milton's *Ode on the Nativity* on Christmas night" (p. 92). Woolf appears to have decided to use this specific poem at the last minute. In the MS and Earlier TS, Ridley does not recite any poetry, and in the Later TS he murmurs "a few lines of poetry."

55. In *Paradise Lost* Milton would describe Astoreth/Astarte as one "to whose bright image nightly by the moon / Sidonian virgins paid their vows and songs" (1.440–41). This makes Astarte inversely analogous to Sabrina; both are revered and invoked by supplicants, but Astarte represented hope of fertility, while Sabrina symbolizes protection of chastity.

56. Cf. Woolf's use of these two Miltonic quotations with her father's comment: "If we were able to exchange all the prose pamphlets for another *Comus* or a Christmas Hymn, the modern world would certainly be the gainer." *Studies of a Biographer* (New York: Putnam, 1907), 4:90.

57. Stanza 23. 211, "On the Morning of Christ's Nativity," italics mine. Clearly the word *brute* has links to *Comus* and to Woolf's development of the disturbing meaning of that word for Rachel.

58. For this reason I do not find that the lines from the *Nativity* occur "at a singularly unconvincing moment" (Fleishman, "Tradition and Modernity," p. 143). Precisely because they are offered at the point of Rachel's dissolution, with no transcendent resurrection in sight, they reinforce the oblique psychological "moral" of Woolf's plot and the price Rachel has had to pay for her escape.

2. *Jacob's Room*

1. Holtby, p. 117.
2. Quentin Bell, 2:88.

3. For example, Woolf's line "and ride out to sea on—the hair blown back" (153) is strikingly like Eliot's image of "the white hair of the waves blown back" (*Prufrock*, l. 133). The reference to "Prince Hamlet" in *Prufrock* is matched by the narrator of *Jacob's Room*, who mentions Hamlet uttering his soliloquy (109). The crab young Jacob sees crawling "on weakly legs on the sandy bottom" (9) recalls the *Prufrock* lines: "I should have been a pair of ragged claws / Scuttling across the floors of silent seas" (l. 79–80). The subtle, despairing "Why? Why? Why?" of Lady Charles (68) echoes the disturbing questions of *Prufrock*: "Do I dare / Disturb the universe?" (l. 51–52), or "So how should I presume?" (l. 60), or "And how should I begin?" (l. 75). And in the narrator's mini-essay on letters, the diction, the entire ambiance, is hauntingly out of Eliot: "A doubt insinuates itself; is this the way to spend our days? . . . for as we lift the cup, shake the hand, express the hope, something whispers, Is this all? Can I never know, share, be certain? Am I doomed all my days to write letters, send voices, which fall upon the tea table, fade upon the passage, making appointments, while life dwindles, to come and dine?" (93).

4. *Collected Essays*, 2:108–9, italics mine.

5. McLaurin, *Virginia Woolf: The Echoes Enslaved*, p. 167. Similarly, E.M. Forster commented that the style of *Jacob's Room*, with its "unanchored proper names," might seem at first "to be going nowhere. Yet the goal comes, the method and the matter prove to have been one" (p. 110).

6. In the holograph MS, Part I, April 15–November 24, 1920 (Berg Collection), Bonamy's last name was Teton.

7. For example, "Jacob have I loved, but Esau have I hated" (Rom. 9:13); "the excellency of Jacob whom He loved" (Ps. 47:4); "the Lord hath chosen Jacob unto himself . . . for his peculiar treasure" (Ps. 135:4). Unlike the Lord, however, Woolf seems to prefer "all the dwellings of Jacob" to "the gates of Zion" (Ps. 87:2).

8. A.D. Moody has been sensitive to "the relevance and deep irony of the allusion to the story of Jacob in *Genesis*," noting that Jacob's life "is characterized not by the fruitful abundance of human gifts, but by a piercing sense of waste and ultimate loss; the sheep's jaw he picks up on the beach is set against the Biblical flocks" (*Virginia Woolf*, p. 17).

9. The Biblical Jacob was often symbolized by the vineyard or by grapevines. Jacob's ladder (Gen. 28:12) links earthly and spiritual realms. In the Bible and in subsequent literature, it is frequently associated with the tragic, questing hero who exists halfway between mundane concerns and something greater or "higher."

10. See Holtby, p. 128, and Thakur, who proposes an elaborate framework in which the scene is symbolic of "their unexpressed desires, and vague, still unconscious, longing for children of their own. One bunch of white grapes and two of purple, lying curled warm in the basket, suggest an innocent babe and two hearts aflame with desire" (p. 44).

11. In an October 9, 1922, letter to Virginia Woolf, Strachey declared: "I am such a Bonamy" (*Virginia Woolf and Lytton Strachey: Letters*, ed. Leonard Woolf and James Strachey, p. 144).

12. Shakespeare had first been proposed in the holograph MS, Part II, then crossed out for Keats, a better choice, which implies the theme of early, tragic death.

13. In Part I of the holograph MS, Woolf had attempted to enumerate: "~~Mallarme~~, Baudelaire, Mallarme."

14. Holtby calls this congruence an "exercise of piety" and a unity "obtained by a trick of reference" (p. 143). Quentin Bell also notes the double appearance of the Damien reference, adding that in 1909 Virginia Woolf had observed "one Mrs. Campbell, an elderly body who had turned the life of Father Damien into verse" (1:143).

15. Cf. the ironic use to which Woolf put that other quest symbol, Jacob's ladder. Here as well, the stairway leads not to better or higher things, but to doubt and dissatisfaction.

16. In Part I of the holograph MS, Woolf hesitated over the degree of specificity she wanted: "lines in ~~Dante~~, The Inferno."

17. Woolf listed "the four famous names" (*A Room of One's Own*, p. 69) as Jane Austen, Charlotte and Emily Brontë, and George Eliot. She frequently mentions the Brontë sisters in her feminist works. In her essay "George Eliot," she speaks of the "dogged determination" in Eliot's "advance upon the citadel of culture," calling it "a deep-seated and noble ambition" (*Collected Essays*, 1:198–99). Woolf concludes that for Eliot "the burden and the complexity of womanhood were not enough; she must reach beyond the sanctuary and pluck for herself the strange bright fruits of art and knowledge" (ibid., 204).

18. Before *Jacob's Room* was published, Woolf had done two reviews of two different novels by W.E. Norris, the popular and prolific writer. In "Mr. Norris's Method" (a March 4, 1920, review of *The Triumphs of Sara*, rpt. in *Contemporary Writers*, pp. 128–30), Woolf characterizes Norris as a safe, competent writer who never risked anything beyond "his own neat strip of indisputable territory" (p. 129). In "Mr. Norris's Standard," a February 10, 1921, review of Norris's *Tony the Exceptional* (rpt. in *Contemporary Writers*, pp. 131–34), Woolf makes much the same point as in her earlier review, then adds an intriguing intimation of *Jacob's Room*-to-come: Norris's modest achievements as a novelist are such that "we would as soon read *Mr. Norris on a railway journey* as a good French novelist" (p. 134, italics mine).

19. "It" would seem to be *Adonais* that Florinda finds boring, for the narrator shortly thereafter refers to "Shakespeare and Adonais, Mozart and Bishop Berkeley" (79).

20. The holograph MS, Part II, shows Woolf contemplating Shakespeare's plays as possible reading matter for Fanny, who was first given "one of Jane Austen's novels." A margin note substitutes "Shelley's poems." As for the literature accompanying Fanny's chocolates, it was [Thomas Love] Peacock who originally bored her.

21. Woolf was undoubtedly aware of George Eliot's story "Brother Jacob," in which the titular hero is literally an idiot: "Jacob, you understand, was not an intense idiot, but within a certain limited range knew how to choose the good and reject the evil" ("Brother Jacob," in *Miscellaneous Essays* [New York: Doubleday, Page and Co., 1901], p. 480). Cf. the narrator's mock issue of whether Jacob was "a mere bumpkin" or "a stupid fellow" (154).

22. Nancy Topping Bazin, in *Virginia Woolf and the Androgynous Vision* (New Brunswick: Rutgers University Press, 1973), suggests that Clara, like Clarissa Dalloway, lives the gracious, polite, trivial life of the perfect hostess, and shares with Clarissa a fear of intimacy (p. 105). Hafley has noted that the symbolic meanings of their names are the same (p. 168).

23. Cf. Woolf's own characterization of Chloe as one of the past's "venerable if obscure figures" (*Three Guineas*, p. 122).

24. In *The Voyage Out*, Meredith was Woolf's vehicle for the Diana allusion.

Interestingly, two critics (Holtby, p. 128, and Thakur, p. 44) have called Clara Durrant, like Rachel Vinrace before her, "a Meredithian heroine."

25. E.B.C. Jones, p. 283.

26. Woolf found Walpole "witty, malicious, observant, detached, the liveliest of gossips" ("Horace Walpole," *Collected Essays*, 3:106). Cf. her father's view of Walpole as "the quintessence of contemporary gossip" (*Hours in a Library*, 2:104).

27. Cf. Woolf's comment "we do know . . . what Keats was going through when he tried to write poetry against the coming of death and the indifference of the world" (*A Room of One's Own*, 53–54).

28. Cf. *The Voyage Out*, in which schoolboys were learning to translate easy passages in (Xenophon's) *Anabasis*.

29. In the holograph MS, Woolf included the following jibe: "[not that Mr. Plumer admired Scott.] But there are more complete sets of the classics in the suburbs of Cambridge than in the whole of Europe put together."

30. Leslie Stephen was rather severe about Lothair: "Lothair reduces himself so completely to a mere 'passive bucket' to be pumped into by every variety of teacher, that he is unpleasantly like a fool" (*Hours in a Library*, 2:295). His interpretation would suggest that Jacob-as-bumpkin is very nearly a parody of Disraeli's hero.

31. For example, Brewster, p. 105, and Blackstone, p. 64.

32. The judgments in *Jacob's Room* anticipate critical statements Woolf made sometime later. She never said much in print about Masefield, who was not made Laureate until 1930; her most revealing comments about Arnold Bennett were to be made in the famous essay "Mr. Bennett and Mrs. Brown."

33. Fleishman finds that "this vision of the British Museum as a personified sum of human thought and creative energy bears some resemblance to Hardy's vision of a cosmic brain in *The Dynasts*" (*A Critical Reading*, p. 59). I would find a more likely resemblance in Carlyle, himself a key allusion in *Jacob's Room*. His "Hero as Man of Letters" essay (Lecture 5, *Heroes and Hero Worship*) contains this passage: "This London City, with all its houses, palaces, steam engines, cathedrals, and huge immeasurable traffic and tumult, what is it but a Thought, but millions of Thoughts made into One:—a huge immeasurable Spirit of a THOUGHT, embodied in brick, in iron, smoke, dust, Palaces, Parliaments, Hackney Coaches, Katherine Docks, and the rest of it! Not a brick was made but some man had to *think* of the making of that brick.—The thing we call 'bits of paper with traces of black ink,' is the *purest* embodiment a Thought of man can have. No wonder it is, in all ways, the activest and noblest."

34. Thakur, p. 46.

35. Ibid., p. 54. Byron appears to have been constant in Woolf's mind; the holograph MS, Part I, shows no alteration of choice.

36. Thakur, p. 43. Though not enclosed in quotation marks, the comment about "rather stupid or uneducated women unable to stand up to him" is verbatim from *A Writer's Diary* (p. 14).

37. From a letter to *The Nation*, rpt. in *Collected Essays*, 1:195.

38. From a 1924 letter to Lytton Strachey (*Letters*, p. 149).

39. *A Writer's Diary*, p. 15.

40. Stephen, *History of English Thought in the Eighteenth Century*, 2:320.

41. Love, p. 64.

42. The difference in the literary contents of Jacob's Cambridge room, from holograph to published text, is the addition of Carlyle and "all the Elizabethans."

43. "The Elizabethan Lumber Room," *Collected Essays*, 1:49–50.

44. Cf. the narrator's remark: "But then any one who's worth anything reads just what he likes" (39).

45. Woolf believed that Dickens had "to perfection the virtues conventionally ascribed to the male; he is self-assertive, self-reliant, self-assured, energetic in the extreme" ("David Copperfield," *Collected Essays*, 1:192). In the *Writer's Diary*, she said he was "all bold and coloured. Rather monotonous; yet so abundant, so creative: . . . rapid and attractive" (p. 289).

46. "The Character-mongers and Comedians" is one of the subtitles of her 1929 essay "Phases of Fiction" (*Collected Essays*, 2:71).

47. John Holloway, *The Victorian Sage: Studies in Argument* (New York: Norton, 1965), p. 87.

48. David Daiches, ed., *Penguin Companion to English Literature*, p. 90. Hereafter cited as *PCEL*.

49. Thakur, p. 53. Interestingly, when Thakur lists (p. 43) the works in Jacob's room, he omits the crucial reference to Carlyle.

50. The Strachey essay is printed in *The Really Interesting Question and Other Papers*, ed. Paul Levy (New York: Coward, McCann and Geoghegan, 1973).

51. So Bertrand Russell records in his *Autobiography: 1872–1914* (London: George Allen & Unwin, 1967), 1:73.

52. *De Rerum Natura*, 1, cited in *Western World Literature*, ed. Robbins and Coleman, p. 222, italics mine.

53. The holograph MS, Part I, reads: "The *effeminacy* of modern life was repudiated" (italics mine). The selection of William Wycherley as the target for expurgation is an especially happy choice: that lusty period of English literature is a congenial era for Jacob, and Wycherley, like Aristophanes (whom Jacob also cites), was highly critical of society. The plot of Wycherley's *The Plain Dealer* is taken from Molière's *Le Misanthrope*, an allusion we have seen applied to Jacob. Shakespeare, cited along with Aristophanes, was himself expurgated in Thomas Bowdler's edition, which established the precedent for the bowdlerizing in which Professor Bulteel now indulges. Once again, even Woolf's more "casual" allusions make intricate, interlocking sense.

54. Cf. Woolf's own furious reaction, in a February 1922 letter to Lytton Strachey, to "Morley's edition [of *Tristram Shandy*] with every tenth page cut out" (*Letters*, p. 140).

55. In the holograph MS, Part I, Jacob reads Milton after Florinda leaves. The line "Milton bored him" is crossed out, then Jacob finds "no comfort in the classics," thanks to Florinda's proximity.

56. *De Rerum Natura*, 3, quoted in Robbins and Coleman, p. 225.

57. Cf. Woolf: "It is this that draws us back and back to the Greeks; the stable, the permanent, the original human being is to be found there" ("On Not Knowing Greek," *Collected Essays*, 1:4).

58. "On Not Knowing Greek," *Collected Essays*, 1:7.

59. Ibid., 8: "It is Plato, of course, who reveals the life indoors."

60. "No one," Woolf declared, "however weak, can fail, even if he does not learn more from Plato, to love knowledge better" ("On Not Knowing Greek," *Collected Essays*, 1:8).

61. E.M. Forster noted this, remarking that Woolf succeeded in conveying "the actual working of a brain . . . there are passages in *Jacob's Room* where the process becomes as physical as the raising of a hand" (p. 112).

62. Cf. Woolf: "I have spotted the best lines in the play—almost in any play I should think—Imogen says—Think that you are upon a rock, & now throw me

again! & Posthumus answers—Hang there like fruit, my soul, till the tree die! Now if that doesn't send a shiver down your spine, . . . you are no true Shakespearean!" (quoted in Quentin Bell, 1:69).

63. "Notes on an Elizabethan Play," *Collected Essays*, 1:61.

64. *A Writer's Diary*, p. 52.

65. From William Gifford's 1818 review, "Keats's *Endymion*," rpt. in *Moulton's Library of Literary Criticism*, ed. Martin Tucker (New York: Frederick Ungar, 1966), 2:537.

66. In her essay "Horace Walpole," Woolf commented: "He would, in short, be nothing save what it pleased him to be. On the whole it pleased him best to be *a gentleman*" (*Collected Essays*, 3:106, italics mine).

67. Daiches, *PCEL*, p. 150, italics mine.

68. From Spenser's letter to Walter Raleigh, in which he expounded "his whole intention in the course of this worke," *The Faery Queen*.

69. Nearly twenty years later, in *Between the Acts*, Woolf characterized a "country gentleman's library" as containing, among other works, a manual by "Hibbert on the Diseases of the Horse."

70. McLaurin, p. 127.

71. Cf. the holograph MS, Part 2: "Books, so people say, are ~~provide~~ an infallible guide to character. Thus we might be worse occupied ~~in~~ than in examining the works."

3. *Mrs. Dalloway*

1. Sprague, p. 9.

2. The Dalloway-related story sequence has recently been published as *Mrs. Dalloway's Party*, ed. McNichol. Missing from this edition is "The Prime Minister," a TS story featuring Clarissa and Septimus (undated, Berg Collection).

3. Somewhat inexplicably, Blackstone complains that "a loss in expansiveness and allusion" (p. 97) has occurred since *Jacob's Room*. It is true that quantitatively there are fewer allusions in *Mrs. Dalloway*, but surely the Dante and Shakespeare allusions "expand" this novel beyond what is encountered in *Jacob's Room*. Daiches has compared the allusiveness of Joyce's *Ulysses* to *Mrs. Dalloway*, only to declare that Woolf has avoided "all such elaborate analogies. . . . Joyce analogizes to compensate for lack of selection, but Virginia Woolf, who selects and refines as she writes, has no need of such a device" (*Virginia Woolf*, p. 71). But allusiveness and selective refinement are not mutually exclusive. *Mrs. Dalloway*, more "discriminating" than Joyce's sprawling, monumental work, may be more discriminatingly allusive, but allusive it assuredly is.

4. Benjamin, "Towards an Understanding of the Meaning of Virginia Woolf's *Mrs. Dalloway*," p. 215. Yet another critic has devoted an article to the Dalloway allusions: see Wyatt, "*Mrs. Dalloway*: Literary Allusion as Structural Metaphor."

5. Brower, "Something Central Which Permeated: Virginia Woolf and *Mrs. Dalloway*," in *The Fields of Light* (New York: Oxford University Press, 1951), rpt. in Sprague, p. 61.

6. For example, Kenneth J. Ames, having written an article on mock-

heroic elements in the novel, cites the passage Brower dislikes, deeming it successful ("Elements of Mock-Heroic in Virginia Woolf's *Mrs. Dalloway*," p. 368).

7. Ames sees this as a depiction of Kilman in "mock-heroic terms" (p. 371).

8. Mollach, "Thematic and Structural Unity in *Mrs. Dalloway*." Mollach observes that the satyr image communicates the fundamental, hidden drives "of the psyche—sex, pain, death" (p. 70).

9. Cf. what A.D. Moody calls "the unmasking of Clarissa Dalloway" in his article of the same name.

10. Only one critic appears to have recognized that the horrors of war bear directly upon the fate of Septimus Smith and are conveyed in "the irony of the allusion to Ceres" (McLaurin, p. 156). Wyatt takes the somewhat circuitous route of linking Septimus' image of himself as a drowned sailor on a rock to the drowned sailor in Eliot's *Waste Land* (1.47), then observing that the fertility god was thrown into the sea to secure rain for the crops (p. 444). Once the Ceres allusion is noted, however, the connection is much more direct and easily substantiated.

11. In holograph corrections of November 22, 1924, Woolf had crossed out the crucial phrase ("Miss Isabel Pole ~~in a green dress~~ walking in a square"), but it reappears in the published version.

12. Frazer, *The New Golden Bough*, p. 360.

13. Ibid., p. 363.

14. Ibid., p. 407.

15. *Prolegomena to the Study of Greek Religion* (Cambridge: Cambridge University Press, 1908), p. 80.

16. In "On Not Knowing Greek," Woolf speaks of the "out-of-doors manner" of the Greek and Italian peoples, noting the "laughing nimbleness of wit and tongue peculiar to the Southern races, which has nothing in common with the slow reserve, the low half-tones, the brooding introspective melancholy of people [i.e., the English] accustomed to live more than half the year indoors" (*Collected Essays*, 1:2).

17. Wyatt notes the allusions to Pope and Addison only insofar as they relate *negatively* to Peter's character; she observes that despite admiring these two writers, Peter becomes a "prey to blinding sentimentality" (p. 43).

18. Doner, "Virginia Woolf: The Service of Style," p. 11.

19. "Addison," *Collected Essays*, 1:90.

20. Wyatt, p. 446. Cf. the text, in which Clarissa calls Peter's habit "his *silly unconventionality*, his weakness" (69, italics mine).

21. Woolf's own phrase in "Addison," *Collected Essays*, 1:87.

22. Stephen, *Pope*, p. 40. We should not forget that *The Rape of the Lock* discloses the shallowness of social life, much as *Mrs. Dalloway* does. Moreover, there is a Clarissa in Pope's poem.

23. Cf. Rosamond Lehmann's comment on Virginia Woolf: "There was something about her that made one think of William Morris and the New Age and the Emancipation of Women" (*Recollections of Virginia Woolf*, ed. Joan Russell Noble, p. 62).

24. Wyatt, p. 440.

25. Rosenberg, "The Match in the Crocus: Obtrusive Art in Virginia Woolf's *Mrs. Dalloway*," p. 214.

26. Ibid., p. 213.

27. Ames, the critic who sees mock-heroic parallels of Pope's *Rape of the Lock* to *Mrs. Dalloway*, calls proportion a neoclassic value, which "mirrors the eigh-

teenth century ideal of balance" (p. 370). The neoclassic ideal, however, is derived; Greek models constitute the original source for both Pope and Woolf.

28. Greene, *Moira: Fate, Good and Evil in Greek Thought*, p. 75.

29. Ibid., p. 137.

30. Schaefer, p. 108.

31. The story "The Ancestors" contains the information that Clarissa "had read all Shelley between the age of twelve and fifteen" (in McNichol, p. 46).

32. Frye, p. 203.

33. Ames (p. 373) observes that the mock-heroic tone of the novel is distancing and complements Clarissa's characterization. As the sylphs in *Rape of the Lock* protected the heroine against Fate, so decorum protects Clarissa from intensity. Cf. Clarissa's notion that "the Gods . . . were seriously put out if, all the same, you behaved like a lady" (117).

34. Ames believes that Clarissa's encounter with Peter Walsh is matched in Pope's *Rape of the Lock* by Belinda's encounter with Baron Petre, "a curious resemblance of names" (p. 367). One might also compare Woolf's encounter scene (Clarissa with scissors) to these lines: "Just then, Clarissa drew with tempting grace / A two-edg'd weapon from her shining case: / So Ladies in Romance assist their Knight, / Present the spear, and arm him for the fight" (*Rape of the Lock*, 3.127–30).

35. Ames, who sees in this scene an ironic contrast to The *Rape of the Lock* description of "Belinda at her toilette" (p. 367), calls this curious bramble image "a happy blending of the erotic and the protective" (p. 366). It is also a very precise evocation of the Sleeping Beauty analogue.

36. In the fable the Prince and Sleeping Beauty marry and have a daughter called Dawn and a son named Day. Thus the tale is a rebirth myth, blending personal regeneration through love with the cycles of time and nature. The same rebirth theme echoes and reechoes throughout *Mrs. Dalloway*, but its sexual aspects remain largely unrealized; that is to say, they are ironically presented, as unattainable or frustrated ideals.

37. For a discussion of this and other psychoanalytic aspects of the novel, see my article, "A Freudian Look at *Mrs. Dalloway*," in *Literature and Psychology* 23, no. 2 (1973): 49–58.

38. A description of Elizabeth's difficulties can be read as a parallel to Clarissa's; for example, Elizabeth misapprehends Wickham (the very name Clarissa mistakenly calls Richard) "because *she wants to avoid entanglement* with Darcy . . . she is essentially indifferent to him" (Andrew H. Wright, *Jane Austen's Novels: A Study in Structure* [London: Chatto and Windus, 1961], p. 123, italics mine). Avoiding the dreaded entanglement with Peter Walsh, Clarissa marries her Wickham/Richard, a man to whom she is essentially indifferent.

39. Tindall, *The Literary Symbol*, p. 230.

40. Frye reminds us that "the most common settings" for moments of epiphany are "the tower, the lighthouse, and the ladder or staircase" (p. 203). Woolf employed all of them in her novels; in *Mrs. Dalloway*, Clarissa climbs a staircase to reach an attic room, which is likened to "a tower" (45, 70).

41. Because it deals with war and the masculine life-style, the Marbot allusion also relates Clarissa to her male double, Septimus Smith.

42. "Money and Love," *Collected Essays*, 3:175.

43. Marbot's *Memoires*, 2:283–84 and 323–24.

44. Guiguet mentions the *Othello* quotation with no comment at all (p. 419), and Richter calls it "a suggestive leitmotif" with "ambiguities" (p. 217) left unex-

plored. Nora C. Groves ("The Case of Mrs. Dalloway," *Virginia Woolf Quarterly* 1, no. 3, Spring 1973) cites only the repetition of the quotation; her omission of its first appearance leads her into a less defensible interpretation of Clarissa's "so-called Lesbian tendencies" (p. 55). The allusion indicates that skepticism about Clarissa's powerful attraction to Sally is unwarranted.

45. Several critics who note the quotation show evidence of not knowing how many times it is repeated, or even in whose consciousness the line occurs. Brower says the quotation "occurs some six or seven times" (p. 52); Schaefer (p. 105) says three; Hafley says four (p. 66). Hafley appears to have left out the line's recurrence in Septimus' mind, while Keith Hollingsworth ("Freud and the Riddle of *Mrs. Dalloway*," in *Studies in Honor of John Wilcox*, ed. A. Dayle Wallace and Woodburn O. Ross [Detroit: Wayne State University Press, 1958]) declares (p. 240) that it occurs in Peter Walsh's reveries. William Troy objects to its use altogether, calling it "an insidious infiltration of [the literary] tradition into the sensibility" (in Sprague, p. 37).

46. Cf. "Mrs. Dalloway in Bond Street," in which Clarissa sees in Hatchard's window "the frontispiece of some book of memoirs spread wide in the bow window. . . . And there was that absurd book, *Soapy Sponge*, . . . and Shakespeare's sonnets" (in McNichol, p. 23).

47. Irene Simon, "Some Aspects of Virginia Woolf's Imagery," *English Studies* 41, no. 3 (June 1960): 183.

48. Stephen, *Swift*, p. 26.

49. Cf. this telling passage: "It would be intolerable if dowdy women came to her party! Would one have liked Keats if he had worn red socks?" ("Mrs. Dalloway in Bond Street," in McNichol, p. 26).

50. Moody, "The Unmasking of Clarissa Dalloway," p. 71.

51. This very early introduction of the theme of death, rendered allusively, seems to have been Woolf's persistent purpose. In the "Bond Street" story, the "fear no more" line is juxtaposed to lines from Shelley's *Adonais*, and Clarissa concludes that "the moderns had never written anything one wanted to read about death" (in McNichol, p. 23).

52. Cf. the "Bond Street" story, in which Clarissa waits in the glove shop and thinks: "Fear no more, she repeated. . . . Thou thy wordly [sic] task hast done. Thousands of young men had died that things might go on" (in McNichol, p. 28).

53. Marilyn Schauer Samuels ("The Symbolic Functions of the Sun in *Mrs. Dalloway*") notes that the "fear no more" line follows the placing of Clarissa's umbrella in the stand, and reminds us that an umbrella is a "shield from *the sun's heat*, the troubles of life" (p. 391, italics mine).

54. Edwin Muir, *Transition: Essays on Contemporary Literature* (New York: Viking Press, 1926), p. 79.

55. Brower, p. 56.

56. Harrison, p. 267.

57. See, for instance, Septimus' hallucination that "red flowers grew through his flesh" (103). Wyatt (p. 443) suggests an analogue to Adonis, from whose blood there sprang up the red anemone. Indeed Septimus' preoccupation with trees finds an echo in the worship of Adonis as a tree-spirit.

58. Richter likens Septimus' madness to "the visions in De Quincey's opium dreams" (p. 91). Thakur (p. 63) compares Septimus' suicide to that of De Quincey's young man in *On Suicide*, which argues that self-homicide is to be preferred to ignominy and dishonor.

Notes

59. "Notes on an Elizabethan Play," *Collected Essays*, 1:54. Daiches (*Virginia Woolf*, p. 34) quotes this without linking it to the character of Septimus Smith.

60. *Mrs. Dalloway* was first called *The Hours*, to stress time's passing.

61. Alex Page ("A Dangerous Day: Mrs. Dalloway Discovers Her Double," *Modern Fiction Studies* 7, no. 2, Summer 1961) calls Septimus "a neurasthenic Keats" (p. 121).

62. *A Room of One's Own*, p. 107.

63. Ibid. The Berg Collection TS of the undated story, "The Prime Minister," has Septimus fancying that "now he understood all that he had read. . . . Shakespeare's sonnets for example written of course by a woman. Only that has been concealed. It must be made known."

64. Woolf called Shakespeare's mind while writing *Antony and Cleopatra* "incandescent" (*A Room of One's Own*, p. 58).

65. Cf. Woolf's comment that Shakespeare's "grudges and spites and antipathies are hidden from us. We are not held up by some 'revelation' which reminds us of the writer" (*A Room of One's Own*, p. 58).

66. On Septimus' homosexuality, see my article, pp. 52–54 and 56–57.

67. Wyatt, p. 440. Other critics seem unwittingly to concur, by speaking of *Mrs. Dalloway* as offering "the quick succession of shadowy states of paradise and purgatory" (Page, p. 115), or by noting that a triad of fish, tree, and plane images forms a subterranean, terrestrial, and aerial structure (McLaurin, p. 151). Love (p. 157) notes that the curtains in Septimus' room have the birds of Paradise on them.

68. Canto and line numbers will be cited in the text; they are given from the Rutgers University Press (New Brunswick, 1954) translation of the *Inferno* by John Ciardi.

69. Cf. Peter Walsh's feelings of having "suffered so infernally!" (93) over Clarissa's rejection. The pain of love makes him feel "he was in Hell!" (93).

70. Mitchell Leaska, who was acquainted with my interpretation of the relevance of the *Inferno* allusion to Septimus (via his reading of my 1973 dissertation), recently devoted a long footnote to "Dante's Seventh (Septimus) Circle of the Inferno," detailing the way in which the first, second, and third Rounds join the sins of war, violence, and sodomy. (See "Virginia Woolf, the Pargeter: A Reading of *The Years*," *Bulletin of the New York Public Library* 80, no. 2, Winter 1977, p. 206n.) He repeats my findings about "the *septimus circle*" (p. 111 and p. 230n) in his *The Novels of Virginia Woolf from Beginning to End*.

71. Samuels has remarked that the image of the leaf-encumbered soul "raises questions" (p. 388). Page (p. 118) has suggested that it is a Biblical allusion. But Septimus' experience of the tree image is *terrifying*; moreover, a Biblical attribution does not begin to have the necessary comprehensiveness of explanation: it cannot account, as the *Inferno* allusion can, for the significance of Septimus' name, for the bird, dog, tree, and leaf images, or for the suggestions of falling and flames.

72. Richter, observing that Rezia thinks of her husband as "a young hawk" (222, 225), ventures the Icarus myth as an analogue for Septimus (p. 217). The repeated Shakespearean motif of the heat of the sun could then be related to the melting of Icarus' wax wings. She also notes (p. 217) that the description suggests the hawklike Stephen Dedalus in Joyce's *Portrait of the Artist*. However, these possibilities do not account for the negative, destroyer quality Rezia sees in her husband.

73. Cf. Carlyle's metaphors for Dante and Shakespeare, the two "world-

voices of literature": "Dante, deep, fierce as the central *fire* of the world; Shakespeare, wide, placid, far-seeing, as the *sun*, the upper light of the world" ("The Hero as Poet," *Heroes and Hero Worship*, italics mine).

74. Dante's revered master, Latini, punished in the *septimus* circle for sexual perversion, wrote two works: *Livre dou Treser* (*The Book of the Treasure*) and *Tesoretta* (*The Little Treasure*). He charges Dante to "remember my *Treasure*, in which I still live on" (15.118).

75. Bazin, p. 114.

76. *Abinger Harvest*, p. 111.

77. "The Pastons and Chaucer," *Collected Essays*, 3:13.

78. There are other suggestive parallels. Clarissa's experience of Sally's kiss compares to Shelley's "that word, that kiss, shall all thoughts else survive, / With food of saddest memory kept alive" (26.229–30). And Clarissa's vicarious identification with Septimus echoes the line "Who in another's fate now wept his own" (34.300).

79. For instance, Clarissa considers her party-giving "an offering; to combine, to create; but to whom?" (185). Shelley concludes his poem *The Question* with the line, "That I might there present it!—Oh! to whom?" Cf. Rhoda's use of the refrain "Oh!—to whom?" (and other lines from *The Question*) in *The Waves*, discussed below.

4. *Orlando*

1. Morris Beja, *Epiphany in the Modern Novel* (Seattle: University of Washington Press, 1971), p. 118; Guiguet, p. 425; Moody, *Virginia Woolf*, p. 43; Hafley, p. 99; Rose Macaulay, "Virginia Woolf," *The Spectator* 166, no. 5885 (11 April 1941), p. 394; John Graham, "The 'Caricature Value' of Poetry and Fantasy in *Orlando*," *University of Toronto Quarterly* 30 (July 1961), rpt. in Sprague, p. 116; Adam A. Mendilow, *Time and the Novel* (London: Peter Nevill, 1952), p. 229. Clive Bell (*Old Friends* [New York: Harcourt, Brace, 1956]) was enough impressed by the congruences between the two works to declare that a reader who finds "fault with *Orlando* . . . must find fault with *Tristram Shandy* too" (p. 110).

2. Aileen Pippett, *The Moth and the Star: A Biography of Virginia Woolf*, p. 256; Brewster, p. 121; Leon Edel, *Literary Biography* (Toronto: University of Toronto Press, 1957), p. 93.

3. A year after *Orlando*, Woolf wrote, naming Sterne as one of her examples, "It is useless to go to the great men writers for help. . . . [They] never helped a woman yet, though she may have learnt a few tricks of them and adapted them to her use. The weight, the pace, the stride of a man's mind are too unlike her own for her to lift anything substantial from him successfully" (*A Room of One's Own*, p. 79).

4. The London edition (William Heinemann, 1931) of the 1922 *Knole* volume will hereafter be cited in the text as *Knole*.

5. Paul West, *The Modern Novel* (London: Hutchinson, 1963), p. 36.

6. Actual employees of Richard Sackville, third Earl during the seventeenth century—Mr. Dupper, Mrs. Field, Mrs. Grimsditch, Grace Robinson, and Mrs. Stewkley—are named in *Orlando*. (See Elizabeth Steele, Karen

Reynders, and Judith Lange's recent "Glossary Index to Virginia Woolf's *Orlando*," *Virginia Woolf Quarterly* 3, nos. 1–2 [Winter and Spring 1977].) The way in which Woolf "mixes" these facts with the fiction of other allusive names can be seen in the *Orlando* list of allusions above.

7. Holtby, p. 161.

8. Gindin, p. 180.

9. Conrad Aiken, "*Orlando*," pp. 147–48. Aiken offers no examples of "too esoteric" allusions. Guiguet also finds *Orlando* "an esoteric work which can only yield its secret to a handful of initiates" (p. 279). Cf. Woolf: "I am writing *Orlando* half in a mock style very clear and plain, so that people will understand every word" (*A Writer's Diary*, p. 117).

10. In an essay entitled "Robinson Crusoe," Woolf ridiculed the biographical approach to criticism, demanding: "If we knew the very moment of Defoe's birth and whom he loved and why, . . . should we suck an ounce of additional pleasure from *Robinson Crusoe* or read it one whit more intelligently?" (*Collected Essays*, 1:69–70).

11. *A Writer's Diary*, p. 86. Woolf's reference to Emily Brontë constitutes her only allusion in *Orlando* to the quartet of women writers whom she considered "great."

12. Richter has suggested that Woolf names De Quincey in the Preface because she learned "contraction and expansion" of time from his works (p. 156). In "De Quincey's Autobiography," Woolf noted his ability to reveal himself and to analyze hidden states of mind, adding that the art of biography could be "transformed" by such powers (*Collected Essays*, 4:6).

13. *A Writer's Diary*, p. 70.

14. "The Historian and 'The Gibbon,' " *Collected Essays*, 1:115.

15. Guiguet, p. 268.

16. In *A Groats-Worth of Witte, Bought with a million of Repentance*, Robert Greene produced his famous attack on Shakespeare: "There is an upstart Crow, beautified with our feathers, that with his *Tygers hart wrapt in a Players hyde* [Greene here parodies *3 Henry VI*'s "O tiger's heart wrapt in a woman's hide!"— 1.4.137] supposes he is as well able to bombast out a blanke verse as the best of you: and . . . is in his own conceit the onely Shakes-scene in a countrey."

17. Discussing Orlando's multiple selves, Guiguet declares that "Orlando is either, or both, as you like. As you like it, not merely because Orlando was born in Shakespeare's day, but because the complexity of a personality is an elusive and incommunicable mystery" (p. 271). Nevertheless Shakespeare's play has its Italian-French progenitors, and Shakespeare implicitly acknowledges *Orlando Furioso* in his line "love is merely a madness" (*As You Like It*, 3.2.420). Hafley scorns the *As You Like It* comparison (p. 99) for the "much more interesting similarity of *Orlando* to Gautier's *Mademoiselle De Maupin*" (p. 178), but the latter—with its bisexual loves and sex changes through clothing changes— uses the plot idea of Shakespeare's comedy, even alludes to *As You Like It* at length.

18. Guiguet, p. 263.

19. *A Writer's Diary*, p. 146, italics mine.

20. Aiken has observed that this is a sly pun: Knole is at *Seven*oaks (p. 147).

21. Milton, *Paradise Lost*, 2.921–22.

22. Moody (*Virginia Woolf*, p. 43) and Hafley (p. 92) put the opening date at 1586. Charles Hoffmann ("Fact and Fantasy in *Orlando*: Virginia Woolf's Manuscript Revisions," *Texas Studies in Literature and Language* 10, no. 3, Fall

1968) suggests 1553 (p. 443), citing the Knole MS. Woolf speaks of writing "a biography beginning in the year 1500" in *A Writer's Diary* (p. 116).

23. In "The Strange Elizabethans," Woolf declared: "There are few greater delights than to go back three or four hundred years and become in fancy at least an Elizabethan" (*Collected Essays*, 3:32). In her *Writer's Diary* she confessed, "It was the Elizabethan prose writers I loved first and mostly wildly" (p. 146).

24. In *The Voyage Out* Woolf had likened Rachel Vinrace's mind to "an intelligent man's in the beginning of the reign of Queen Elizabeth" (34). In "Women in Fiction" she remarked that "Elizabethan literature is exclusively masculine" (*Collected Essays*, 2:142). In *A Room of One's Own* she pointed out that "no woman wrote a word of that extraordinary literature when every other man, it seemed, was capable of song or sonnet" (p. 43).

25. Richter views the incident as a thematic metaphor: the attic room is Orlando's brain, his ancestor who had decapitated the Moor is Orlando's inherited past, and the Moor's head is a symbol of time, which Orlando "kills" by living several hundred years (pp. 154–55). She suggests that Andrew Marvell's *Upon Appleton House* supplies "the parody-pattern" for this scene by synthesizing personality and history: Orlando's estate is "a surrogate for Orlando himself, as is Appleton House for its owner, Lord Fairfax" (p. 155). Like *Orlando*, Marvell's poem presents a mystic experience of personality integration, and a conflict of active and intellectual life-styles such as Orlando experiences in his Elizabethan life. There is even an oak tree used to symbolize England. But it does seem a strained analogy, somewhat less than organic, as neither the poem nor Marvell is alluded to within *Orlando*.

26. Blackstone, p. 133.

27. Woolf makes the same point in *A Room of One's Own*: "Imaginatively, she is of the highest importance; practically she is completely insignificant" (p. 45).

28. Noted in *Knole*, p. 115. The verses include "Knotting," in which "Young Chloris, innocent and gay" (l. 3) is addressed, and an eight-line "Song to Chloris" (Chalmers, *The Works of the English Poets*, 8:343–44).

29. Chalmers, 8:345. Interestingly, the "Summer" section of Vita Sackville-West's *The Land* also mocks the name-labeling proclivities of Elizabethan sonneteers, noting the welter of Julias, Lucastas, Corinnas, and Perillas.

30. Cf. *Furioso*, 24.4: "In love's extreme, extreme of madness dwells." This, with canto and line numbers, is given from the John Hoole translation of the *Furioso* in Chalmers, vol. 21.

31. Vita Sackville-West remarks that *Gorboduc* "is sometimes noble, and always dull" (*Knole*, p. 43).

32. Cf. Orlando's "Vice, Crime, Misery" (9) to Thomas Sackville's allegorical figures, Remorse of Conscience, Dread, Misery and Old Age in *Mirror for Magistrates* (*Knole*, p. 44).

33. This association of Shakespeare and Elizabeth helps strengthen the theme of androgyny, for the Queen "combined masculine vigor and ruthlessness with feminine wiles and trickery. . . . She was a man in petticoats" (Pippett, p. 277). Lytton Strachey described Elizabeth's temperament as a "mixture of the masculine and the feminine" in *Elizabeth and Essex: A Tragic History* (New York: Harcourt, Brace, 1928), p. 12.

34. Shakespeare at work is a recurring image in Woolf. In the story, "The Mark on the Wall," there is a passage that anticipates *Orlando* by a decade: people look in through an open door to spy Shakespeare writing.

Notes

35. *A Room of One's Own* stresses Shakespeare's "creative, incandescent, and *undivided*" mind (p. 102, italics mine). "If ever a human being got his work expressed completely," Woolf believed, "it was Shakespeare" (ibid., p. 59).

36. Richter finds the seventeenth-century setting a parody of Sir Thomas Browne and of "Bacon's essay on gardens" (p. 155), without indicating what in Bacon's "Of Gardens" she finds especially relevant.

37. "Induction to the Mirror for Magistrates," in *The Works of Thomas Sackville, Lord Buckhurst*, ed. Reginald Sackville-West (London: John Russell Smith, 1859).

38. *Religio Medici*, part 2, section 12. In *Urn-Burial* Browne calls Sleep "the brother of Death."

39. Guiguet, p. 265.

40. Cf. Lytton Strachey: "Everyone knows that Browne was a physician who lived at Norwich in the seventeenth century" (*Books and Characters: French and English*, p. 33).

41. "Notes on an Elizabethan Play," *Collected Essays*, 1:61.

42. In "Reading" Woolf spoke of Browne's "crabbed sentences. . . . Dilatory, [and] capricious" (*Collected Essays*, 2:32).

43. Woolf's vaguely inaccurate sense of chronology regarding Browne has provoked Bennett (p. 79) to complain that Orlando is reading Browne in the Elizabethan reign. But the atmosphere of chapter 2 is early seventeenth-century Jacobean. While it is a shade too early for Browne—who would have been a mere child at the time—his allusive value is great enough for Woolf to have risked mild anachronism.

44. This is Woolf's own phraseology, from a 1926 letter to Vita Sackville-West (quoted in Pippett, p. 224). Cf. "It is from the middle class that writers spring. . . . Thus it must have been harder for Byron to be a poet than Keats" (*Collected Essays*, 1:222). Woolf's father had written: "Our aristocracy as such has been normally illiterate" (*English Literature and Society in the Eighteenth Century*, p. 149). Hereafter abbreviated as *EL&S*.

45. Robert Greene imitated the euphuistic mode of Lyly, and pastoral romances like Sidney's *Arcadia*. His play *Alphonsus* was an attempt to match Marlowe's *Tamburlaine*; his *Friar Bacon* and *Friar Bungay* (1591) used Marlowe's *Faustus* theme of necromancy (Daiches, *PCEL*, p. 225). Greene's own "History of Orlando Furioso" is yet another instance of his following established literary patterns to popularity.

46. "Donne After Three Centuries," *Collected Essays*, 1:39–40.

47. Ibid., p. 36.

48. See Rowse, *Christopher Marlowe: His Life and Work*, for comments on Greene's jealousy of Marlowe's triumphs and his "would-be superior fashion" (p. 76) of denouncing Marlowe in print.

49. Rowse, p. 143.

50. The irony of this allusive characterizing stroke resides in the reader's knowledge that Ben Jonson generously spoke *well* of *his* friends, especially Shakespeare and Marlowe. For example, "He was not of an age, but for all time," and the reference to "Marlowe's mighty line" in Jonson's "To the Memory of My Beloved Master William Shakespeare."

51. Thakur has suggested a source in Vita Sackville-West's life for Greene's treacherous nature toward Orlando: Vita once offered her hospitality to a poet who afterward wrote against her (p. 96).

52. Rowse, p. 143.

53. Nick Greene reappears in *A Room of One's Own*, where his treachery has a sexist quality: Shakespeare's imaginary sister, Judith, with her "poet's heart caught and tangled in a woman's body," kills herself after discovering she is "with child" by Nick Greene (p. 50).

54. Cf. Ann Radcliffe, who wrote of a tree that had "grandeur and . . . suggested an idea at once of the strength and fire of a hero . . . the hero of the forest, as the oak was called the king" (*Knole*, p. 24). Nick Greene, by comparison, "did not know . . . an oak from a birch tree" (59).

55. Cf. *Knole*'s "long monotonous list of Sir Jordans, Sir Andrews, Sir Edwards, Sir Richards" (p. 30).

56. Edward Sackville mentions a "Bergen-op-Zoom" in a letter (*Knole*, p. 86).

57. Thakur likens the three Ladies to "De Quincey's Ladies of Sorrow" (p. 101): the Ladies of Tears, of Sighs, and of Darkness, from his 1845 sketch, "Levana and Our Ladies of Sorrow." Ruth Gruber (*Virginia Woolf: A Study*) thinks the Ladies are "echoes of De Quincey's vision in his 'Dream Fugue' " (p. 33). Gruber believes Woolf "literally copied" (p. 33) De Quincey's prose rhythms, allegory, and symbolism, and that the "fantastic vision" of a sex change duplicates De Quincey's fantastic imagination. In his *Confessions* De Quincey describes a dream in which a group of long-dead Ladies "from the unhappy times of Charles I" ("The Pains of Opium," 4) dance about in a pageant. If Woolf is echoing De Quincey, it would give added point to her allusion to him in the Preface. There is, however, precedent in Woolf's own works for this scene: the allegorical figures of Proportion and Conversion in *Mrs. Dalloway*. And there are other writers besides De Quincey (for example, Plato in the *Symposium*) from whom Woolf could plausibly have drawn inspiration.

58. In *A Room of One's Own*, Woolf speaks of "the relic" of chastity (p. 52).

59. Plato, *Symposium*, p. 25.

60. Leslie Stephen wrote: "The watchword of every literary school may be brought under the formula 'Return to nature,' though 'Nature' receives different interpretations" (*EL&S*, p. 218).

61. As Vita Sackville-West's husband was named Harold, so Lord Lascelles, an unsuccessful suitor for Vita's hand, signed himself Harry (Nicolson, p. 94).

62. *Orlando*'s vivid evocation of this century is undoubtedly the result of Virginia Woolf's knowledge of the period. In *Jacob's Room* we were repeatedly told that "the eighteenth century has its distinction," and Woolf's many essays on the period's writers bear witness to her belief that the century was "a haven of bright calm and serene civilization" ("Two Antiquaries: Walpole and Cole," *Collected Essays*, 3:112). Clive Bell's *Civilization*, published in the same year as *Orlando* and dedicated to Virginia Woolf, praises the eighteenth century for having combined reason and a sense of values, to produce charm, "high civility," and "exquisite urbanity" (p. 144).

63. While Addison and Pope are quoted, Dryden appears only as a name in *Orlando*; he died in the first year of the eighteenth century and does not quite suit the Augustan setting. But his influence on Woolf reaches back to her sixteenth year, when she wrote "a long picturesque essay, . . . called *Religio Laici*" (*A Writer's Diary*, p. 146).

64. *Books and Characters*, p. 95.

65. Ibid., p. 98. One of the Marquise's guests was describing the martyrdom of Saint Denis the Areopagite: how he walked, with his own decapitated

head tucked under his arm, six miles to reach a church. " 'Ah, Monseigneur!' said Madame du Deffand, 'dans une telle situation, il n'y a que le premier pas qui coute' " (p. 98).

66. *Books and Characters*, p. 95.

67. Cf. Strachey, who while admitting that the circle was "never profound," also called it "never dull" (ibid., p. 97).

68. This is perhaps an allusion to Calderón's *La Vida Es Sueño*, but more plausibly traced to Shelley (who speaks of "the dream of life" in *Adonais* (39.344) and was himself familiar with Calderón's dramatic works).

69. Woolf's father wrote in his *History of English Thought* that Pope was "the typical representative" of his time (2:297) who "reflects the thoughts of his day with a curious completeness" (p. 298). In *EL&S* Stephen again declared: "No writer, that is, reflects so clearly and completely the spirit of his own day" (p. 109).

70. Not surprisingly, Woolf's father listed—in addition to Pope—Addison and Swift as the best representatives of their day (*History of English Thought*, 2:297).

71. Dryden was in fact saved from debt by Charles Sackville (*Knole*, p. 145), who paid his pension even after he was ousted as Laureate. Indeed Dryden so depended on Sackville's aid that the situation was satirized in a poem, *Prince Arthur*, by Sir Richard Blackmore (*Knole*, p. 148).

72. In fulsome gratitude for Charles's patronage, Dryden dedicated both his *Essay on Dramatic Poesy* and his *Essay on Satire* to Sackville (*Knole*, p. 148). As a final tribute, Pope wrote Charles's epitaph for the chapel monument at Withyham (*Knole*, p. 151).

73. In her 1919 essay "Addison," Woolf had quoted the same lines, remarking: "As for women—or 'the fair sex,' as Addison liked to call them—their follies were past counting. He did his best to count them, with a loving particularity" (*Collected Essays*, 1:90). Woolf's father had observed that under Addison's urbane kindliness there was "a tone of superiority to women which is sometimes offensive. It is taken for granted that a woman is a fool" (Stephen, *Pope*, p. 41).

74. Cf. Woolf's father: "If Addison's manner sometimes suggests the blandness of a don who classes women with the inferior beings unworthy of Latin grammar, Pope suggests the brilliant wit whose contempt has a keener edge. . ." (*Pope*, p. 41).

75. Like the other writers-as-characters who grace this chapter, Swift had Sackville connections. He was "an intimate friend of the Dorsets" (*Knole*, p. 141).

76. Stephen, *EL&S*, p. 119.

77. Swift exerted a powerful attraction on Virginia Woolf, as on her father before her. Stephen's essay *Swift* contains a chapter entitled "Stella and Vanessa"; his daughters carry those names. In "Swift's *Journal to Stella*," Virginia Woolf deals with Swift's "baby language" and his final "violent outbursts of mad rage" (*Collected Essays*, 3:71, 79).

78. Woolf's father, observing that the general moral tone of the age could be "gathered from Chesterfield's *Letters*" (*EL&S*, p. 110), quoted the same passage. Stephen observes that women, to Chesterfield, "are invaluable as tools, though contemptible in themselves" (*EL&S*, p. 113). Cf. Woolf's own essay, "Lord Chesterfield's Letters to His Son," *Collected Essays*, 3:80–85.

79. Her father before her had found the same. Stephen observed Addison's "air of gentle condescension, especially when addressing ladies who cannot even translate his mottoes" (*EL&S*, p. 74). He noted that Pope sneered at their fickle-

ness, out of resentment over the deformity which rendered him unattractive (*Pope*, p. 41); that Swift was a "self-appointed sultan" (*Swift*, p. 121) with women; that Chesterfield spoke of women "with the true aristocratic contempt" (*EL&S*, p. 113).

80. In "Dr. Burney's Evening Party," Woolf wrote that Dr. Johnson "was the force that sent an impudent and arrogant young man like Boswell slinking back to his chair like a beaten boy when Johnson bade him" (*Collected Essays*, 3.141). Johnson included the Earl of Dorset (that is, Charles Sackville) in his *Lives of the Poets*.

81. Cf. "Horace Walpole," in which Woolf spoke of "the first solemn chimes of the nineteenth century" (*Collected Essays*, 3:105).

82. Cf. "Even in the nineteenth century a woman was not encouraged to be an artist. On the contrary, she was snubbed, slapped, lectured and exhorted" (*A Room of One's Own*, 56).

83. Elsewhere Woolf recognized how extraordinarily productive those first decades of the nineteenth century were, declaring: "*Waverley*, *The Excursion*, *Kubla Khan*, *Don Juan*, Hazlitt's *Essays*, *Pride and Prejudice*, *Hyperion*, and *Prometheus Unbound* were all published between 1800 and 1821" ("How It Strikes A Contemporary," *Collected Essays*, 2:156).

84. There is a TS fragment of the exact MS transcription of *Orlando* (undated, Berg Collection) in which Woolf mentions "lectures upon Byron's place in English poetry, and Shelley, Wordworth [sic], Byron, or the Romantic Revival . . . all very nice and interesting." This brief passage did not survive in the published text, except as a fleeting remark upon lectures devoted to "the Classical revival; the Romantic survival" (190).

85. Shelmerdine *is* "lame in the left foot" (165), but Woolf's opinion of Rochester would seem to rule him out as a paradigm: she called him a portrait "drawn in the dark," born of fear, oppression, and "buried suffering" (*A Room of One's Own*, p. 76). Perhaps the limp indicates Byron.

86. Nearly a decade later, in *The Years*, Woolf would refer to "October, the birth of the year" (p. 91).

87. *The Land* is prefaced by a Latin quotation from Virgil's *Georgics*, 3.

88. *Encyclopaedia Britannica*, 1910 edition, 4:811.

89. Woolf did not care for the spectacle of "good" women writers upon whom "some shiny prize" might be bestowed, if they were properly decorous (see *A Room of One's Own*, p. 78). She recorded her reactions to "Vita given the Hawthornden [Prize]" as "a horrid show-up . . . chattering writers. My word! how insignificant we all looked! . . . the mildness, the conventionality of them all struck me" (*A Writer's Diary*, p. 109).

90. Cf. Vita Sackville-West's reference, in the "Summer" section of *The Land*, to oak trees lasting "three hundred English years." Two other authors with whom Woolf was familiar have used oak tree metaphors. In the "Hero as Poet" (Lecture 3, *Heroes and Hero Worship*) Carlyle declares that a great writer's works "grow up withal *un*consciously, from the unknown deeps in him . . . as the oak-tree grows from the Earth's bosom." And in *Howards End*, E.M. Forster described a "ruined oak" as "an English Tree . . . bending over the house, strength and adventure in its roots" (chapter 24).

91. "An Essay in Criticism," *Collected Essays*, 2:256.

92. As Professor of Literature, Sir Nicholas receives the same sort of witty maltreatment Woolf accorded Sir Walter Raleigh, "one of the best Professors of Literature of our time; he did brilliantly whatever it is that Professors are supposed to do" ("Walter Raleigh," *Collected Essays*, 1:315).

93. Rowse, p. 112.

94. Browning is not mentioned again, but Carlyle's "soundproof room at Chelsea" (190) is referred to later on, and Tennyson had earlier been called "the last person to suffer from" the "disease" of genius in England (135). The Berg Collection TS fragment details a visit to Carlyle and his shrewish wife, a journey to "Tennyson's address," where *his* wife frustrates the meeting, and proposals to visit "Browning in Florence, Swinburne at Putney, or Meredith at Box Hill." The point is made that, compared to Dryden's time, great writers are now sequestered away, guarded by zealous wives.

95. Pope wrote a "Prologue to Mr. Addison's Tragedy of *Cato*," and Dr. Johnson praised *Cato* highly, calling it "the noblest production of Addison's genius" (Stephen, *EL&S*, p. 84). Woolf later quoted this very same judgment of her father's in her own essay "Addison" (*Collected Essays*, 1:88). Nevertheless *Cato*'s good taste did not raise it above a certain antique insignificance. Woolf's father declared it "contrived, not inspired" (*EL&S*, p. 86). Compare Woolf's "occasionally in *Cato* one may pick up a few lines that are not obsolete" ("Addison," *Collected Essays*, 1:88).

96. This Berg TS fragment, omitted from the final text, shows how blunt Woolf's point originally was: "She was forced to consort with the ~~riff raff~~ . . . writers who managed to write without a trace of ~~the~~ it [greatness]: the Smiles, the Tuppers, the Smiths, the Hemans, the Prossers, their names are legion and all forgotten now, . . . it is only ~~the~~ when the shelf creaks a little that we remember their names."

97. In "I Am Christina Rossetti," Woolf speaks of "how absolute and unaccommodating" this poet was (*Collected Essays*, 4:57). Rossetti figures prominently in *A Room of One's Own*, where she is quoted and called one of the great poets of the Victorian age, along with Tennyson. The Berg TS fragment of *Orlando* begins: "Here the footman brought in a note from Miss Christina Rossetti to say that she was sorry to find she had a previous engagement."

98. This is but one small, telling example of how persistently Woolf added allusions to her materials. There is a description in *Knole* of "portentously important chairs," which are "for ever holding out their arms and for ever disappointed" (p. 13). Woolf imagines them waiting specifically to receive England's great Bard.

99. *A Room of One's Own*, p. 108.

100. *Symposium*, p. 22.

101. Rebecca West, *The Court and the Castle: Some Treatments of a Recurrent Theme* (New Haven: Yale University Press, 1957), p. 220.

102. Fleishman, "Tradition and Modernity," p. 157.

103. Pippett, p. 257.

104. This judgment is from William Troy, one of the critics who faults Woolf's antirealistic approach to the novel. In *Orlando* he finds her allusive technique—which he branded "facile traditionalism" (p. 38) in most of her other novels—pertinent and convincing.

5. The Waves

1. *A Writer's Diary*, p. 109. Cf. "Aurora Leigh," in which Woolf discussed Elizabeth Barrett Browning's use of the term "novel-poem" (*Collected Essays*, 1:214).

Notes

2. That is, "the gathering of waves to a head, at death they break into a million fragments, each one of which, however, is absorbed at once into the sea of life and helps to form a later generation which comes rolling on till it too breaks" (from Butler's *Notebooks*, quoted in McLaurin, p. 5).

3. That is, "The sea appeared paved with innumerable faces, upturned to the heavens; . . . my mind tossed, as it seemed, upon the billowy ocean, and weltered upon the weltering waves" (from *Confessions of an English Opium Eater*, quoted in Bennett, 106). In the Berg MS of *The Waves*, Woolf develops images of the mother-sea and her children-waves, for example, "Every wave . . . cast a child from it; before it sank into the objective body of the sea" (vol. 1, July 2, 1929), and again, in this cancelled passage: "Many mothers and many mothers, and each . . . forced onto the beach a child" (vol. 1, September 4, 1929).

4. That is, "In tragic hints here see what evermore / Moves dark as yonder midnight ocean's force, / Thundering like ramping hosts of warrior horse, / To throw that faint thin line upon the shore!" (50, 13–16), suggested by John William Cunliffe (*English Literature in the Twentieth Century* [New York: Macmillan, 1933], p. 250).

5. Margaret Church (*Time and Reality: Studies in Contemporary Fiction* [Chapel Hill: University of North Carolina Press, 1963]) has noted that Joyce's *Portrait* capitalizes upon the permanency of the sea as a "perspective" on human life (p. 92), a larger reality of which the individual is a part, just as waves are part of the sea. Thus a sense of "unity beneath change" (p. 97) is common to the *Portrait* and to *The Waves*.

6. Hafley, p. 70. In *Creative Evolution* Bergson wrote: "All the living hold together, and all yield to the same tremendous push. The . . . whole of humanity, in space and in time, is one immense army galloping before and beside down every resistance and clear the most formidable obstacles, perhaps even death" (quoted in Hafley, p. 120).

7. For example, noting that Proust's characters originate in what she called a deep "reservoir of perception," Woolf declared that they "rise, like waves forming, then break and sink again into the moving sea of thought and comment and analysis which gave them birth" ("Phases of Fiction," *Collected Essays*, 2:85).

8. Merton P. King, "*The Waves* and the Androgynous Mind," *University Review* 30, no. 2 (1963): 128.

9. Edward Wagenknecht, *Cavalcade of the English Novel: From Elizabeth to George VI* (New York: Henry Holt, 1943), p. 532.

10. Collins, *Virginia Woolf's Black Arrows of Sensation: "The Waves*," p. 45.

11. The Berg MS shows that in one of the interludes mention was made of "the figure of Buddha" (vol. 1, September 22, 1929). In the subsequent MSS (notebooks), however, the meditative figure was dropped.

12. Love, p. 197.

13. The title page of the first MS volume reveals that "The Life of Anyone, life in general" was one of the earliest considered titles for *The Waves*.

14. Arthur Robert Reade, *Main Currents in Modern Literature* (Folcroft, Pa.: Folcroft Press, 1970), p. 178.

15. The plain misreadings this difficult novel has occasioned may be illustrated by the "simple" fact of the characters' names, which are given at the outset of the monologues, in the first six sentences of the novel. Yet Gindin refers to four characters (pp. 200–201), then to five (p. 203). Lord David Cecil (*Poets and Story-Tellers: A Book of Critical Essays* [New York: Macmillan, 1949]) speaks of five characters (p. 171). Frank Swinnerton (*The Georgian Literary Scene* [New York:

Farrar, Straus, 1934]) disparages the sameness of diction in "four poetic some-things" (p. 301). Robert Humphrey (*Stream of Consciousness in the Modern Novel* [Berkeley: University of California Press, 1954]) refers to "seven groups of stylized soliloquies" (p. 103).

16. For example, Bernard was called "Johnnie" in the MS (vol. 1, July 2, 1929). See *Bernard* entry in allusion list.

17. "Modern Fiction," *Collected Essays*, 2:106.

18. Leaska offers precisely this information on Rhoda's Shelleyan diction, *The Novels of Virginia Woolf From Beginning to End*, p. 164n.

19. In the MS (vol. 1, September 1929), lines 28–30 of the fourth stanza of *The Question* are used, also the final question, "Oh! to whom?" In the second draft (vol. 4, April 29, 1930) Woolf has Rhoda talking much more generally: "I will find a book; . . . I will ~~go on~~ read a poem; I will go into the library and take out one of the ~~books that poetry~~ books."

20. Cf. Shelley on may (l. 18) and roses and ivy (l. 21) with Rhoda's "moonlight coloured may, wild roses and ivy serpentine" (213). Rhoda continues: "I will sit by the river's trembling edge and look at the water lilies, broad and bright, which lit the oak that overhung the hedge with moonlight beams of their own watery light" (213). This appropriates (from stanza 4) Shelley's lines about the river edge (l. 25), the water lilies (l. 28), and the oak, hedge, and moonlight (ll. 29–30). Then she paraphrases the last stanza; where Shelley makes "a nose-gay" of his "visionary flowers" (5.33–34), Rhoda says, "I will bind flowers in one garland" (213). Finally she reverts to the question with which Shelley's poem concludes: "Present it!—Oh! to whom?" (5.40).

21. In the Berg MS, there were only three volumes: "Horace, Tennyson, and Wordsworth" (vol. 4, April 29, 1930).

22. Neville's choice in the Berg MSS had been the words "of Caesar and Cicero" (vol. 4, April 13, 1930). Woolf even toyed with, then abandoned, the possibility of Livy and Tacitus.

23. In "Montaigne" Woolf wrote: "[Let us] relish to the full before the sun goes down the kisses of youth and the echoes of a beautiful voice singing Catullus" (*Collected Essays*, 3:24).

24. In the Berg MS, next to Neville's question, in the left-hand margin, Woolf had written "Catullus, Shakespeare" (vol. 4, April 13, 1930).

25. In the MS, Woolf shows Bernard characterizing by allusion. Spinning one of his stories, he postulates a character who "had never heard of M. de la Rochefoucauld" (vol. 4, dated Rodmell, July 30, 1930).

26. Rhoda's tiger may be an approximation of T.S. Eliot's "the tiger springs in the new year. Us he devours" (*Gerontion*, l. 47). In Draft I, Woolf had written of "the desire for action, something like the spring of a tiger, some passion released, and pouncing." See *Virginia Woolf: THE WAVES*, Two Holo-graph Drafts Transcribed and Edited by J.W. Graham (Toronto: University of Toronto Press, 1976), p. 237.

27. "The Pastons and Chaucer," *Collected Essays*, 3:13.

28. These are opinions Woolf once built into *Bernard's* allusive portrait: in volume 6 (dated Monks House, December 31, 1930) Bernard is reading Donne.

29. *A Writer's Diary*, p. 149.

30. Ibid., pp. 149–50.

31. Ibid., p. 150.

32. The situation reverses the *Don Juan* episode in which it is Julia who writes Juan a love letter (1.192.1529ff).

33. In *The Voyage Out* there was a similar literary discussion between St. John Hirst and Terence Hewet, who in many ways are fledgling portraits of Neville and Bernard. Some of the Bonamy-Jacob conversations in *Jacob's Room* are also analogous, for Jacob, like Bernard after him, combined Byron's classic and romantic qualities, and Bonamy was guilty of Neville's inconsistent self-blindness when he denigrated Romanticism even as he participated in it. (Then too, Bonamy dislikes women even as much as Hirst and Neville.)

34. On a somewhat lesser scale than Byron, Gray was also a poet of varied sensibility. Writing between the Neoclassic and Romantic movements, his best poetry, like Byron's best, mingled lucid form and romantic feeling. Gray peopled his *Elegy* with human figures, much as Bernard populates his stories. It is, in short, an apt allusion.

35. In the Berg MS, it was plainer yet. Bernard thinks of Neville, "He desires order; & architecture: . . . in the manner of Pope: he dislikes my Byronic untidiness" (vol. 5, dated Rodmell, August 5, 1930). Perhaps Woolf realized that this set up a false distinction, for the protean Byron in fact admired Pope's poetry.

36. Woolf thought the poetry of *Don Juan* flexible enough to "keep pace with the mind and . . . its various sufferings and joys" ("The Narrow Bridge of Art," *Collected Essays*, 2:224).

37. For example, both know the significance and power of words ("But words are things, and a small drop of ink, / Falling like dew upon a thought, produces / That which makes thousands, perhaps millions think," *DJ*, 3.88.793–95); the limits of words ("But words are not enough in such a matter," *DJ*, 5.143.1138); the frustration that results when verbal expression cannot do justice to the event ("Would that I were a painter! . . . Oh that my words were colours! but their tints / May serve perhaps as outlines or slight hints," *DJ*, 6.109.869, 71–72).

38. With mock-serious intent, *Don Juan* points out the "pithy phrase" (7.39.310); "the affected phrase" (8.90.714); the "diplomatic phrase" (9.49.386); "that portentous phrase" (14.50.395); "the strict sense of the phrase" (17.2); the tender phrase (8.128.1021); and even the allusive phrase: "Pope's phrase" (9.68.542), "Moore's phrase" (11.65.519), the phrase of Shakespeare (9.4.26).

39. As if to heighten the contrast, Woolf omits from the published text the Berg MS statement in which Bernard credits Neville for having introduced him to *classics* like Catullus, Lucretius, and Horace (vol. 6, December 14, 1930).

40. For example, Woolf warns the poet of the dangers of living in his hermetic universe: "But how are you going to get out, into the world of other people? That is your problem now" (*Collected Essays*, 2:191), and alludes to his self-centered vanity: "The poet is much less interested in what we have in common than in what he has apart" (ibid., 189).

41. Woolf very nearly reproduces Bernard's diction. She says: "We prose writers . . . are *masters* of language, not its *slaves*; . . . we are the *creators*, we are the *explorers*" (*Collected Essays*, 2:183, italics mine). Cf. Bernard: "We are not *slaves*. . . . We are not sheep either, following a *master*. We are *creators*" (276, italics mine).

42. In the light of extrinsic (Woolf's expressed opinions) *and* intrinsic evidence (content and structure of *The Waves*, which finally becomes Bernard's book), critical contentions that Woolf does not mean to give Bernard final title to being "her" voice are less than convincing. I shall point out further indications of the Woolf/Bernard correspondences below.

43. Just how vividly Bernard identifies with Byron is clear in a Berg MS passage in which he invents a story with "Byron in the centre; and his tongue itched to be describing Byron's house and his appearance: and his limp & . . . Lady Byron" (vol. 2, November 29, 1929).

44. Some critics have repeated Neville's error by declaring that Bernard poses as "a Tolstoyan young man" (Brewster, p. 130).

45. The Berg MSS establish Lucretius as a characterizing allusion for Louis, offering the hint that he wished he "could be without any support; like Lucretius, like Plato" (vol. 6, November 24, 1930). Lucretius was the subject of that midnight conversation in which some mysteriously important lines were being sought by Jacob Flanders.

46. Richter, p. 53.

47. In Draft I (in Graham's transcription of *The Waves* holographs, p. 251), Woolf had given Rhoda this Shakespearean reaction to Percival's death: "We are sport of They kill us for their sport" (canceled). That is, "As flies to wanton boys, are we to the gods; / They kill us for their sport," *King Lear*, 4.1.36–37.

48. Cf. "I should have been a pair of ragged claws / Scuttling across the floors of silent seas" (*Prufrock*, ll. 79–80).

49. In the last lines of that poem, Shelley speaks of being close to death and hearing "the sea / Breathe o'er my dying brain its last monotony" (4.35–36), foreshadowing Bernard's final experience.

50. The final lines of Byron's *Prometheus* anticipate Bernard's situation at the close of the novel:

> And Man in portions can foresee
> His own funereal destiny,
> His wretchedness, and his resistance
> And his sad unallied existence:
> To which his Spirit may oppose
> Itself— . . .
> Triumphant where it dares defy,
> And making Death a Victory.

51. McLaurin, p. 135.

52. In "The Narrow Bridge of Art," Woolf quotes the "Jug Jug to dirty ears" phrase, contrasting Eliot's nightingale with Keats's, making the point that Eliot's bird mocks beauty and tries to show the side that is "pitted and deformed" (*Collected Essays*, 2.223).

53. See, for instance, the much more forcefully worded version in Draft II: "Jug jug jug I cry. And I feel the blood boiling in my throat" (Graham's transcription of *The Waves* holographs, p. 599).

54. Frank D. McConnell (" 'Death Among the Apple Trees': *The Waves* and the World of Things," *Bucknell Review* 16 (December 1968), rpt. in Sprague, p. 126.

55. The Berg MS makes this point even more explicitly. Neville addresses his partner: "And then let us read Milton together, or Catullus: . . . and the page is only your voice ~~made articulate~~: . . . Alcibiades, Ajax, Hector are you" (vol. 6, November 5, 1930).

56. McLaurin observes that Jinny "sees the Underground as a sort of Hell" (p. 141). Richter notes that Jinny is "like one of Dante's sinners in the fiery desert of the sodomites, [when she] asserts the lust which gives a mechanized motion to her world" (p. 108).

57. In Draft I (in Graham's transcription of *The Waves* holographs, p. 333),

Neville speaks not only of the Shakespearean fool and villain, but of "the fine fellow . . . the pompous ass; and heres [sic] Cassandra and Ophelia," both of whom were deleted in the final version.

58. In Draft II (Graham's transcription, p. 610), Bernard says, "I shall never read the Vedas; or Don Quixote in Spanish."

59. All of the quotations are taken from *The Ten Principal Upanishads*, trans. Shree Purohit Swami and W.B. Yeats (London: Faber & Faber Limited, 1937). Italics are mine.

60. The Berg MS shows that the walking stick was first attributed to Pope (vol. 3, March 25, 1930; vol 6, November 11, 1930).

61. My own feeling that Louis's images were suspiciously similar to Eliot's poetry is at least partially substantiated by a recent article by Doris L. Eder, "Louis Unmasked: T.S. Eliot in *The Waves*" (*Virginia Woolf Quarterly* 2, nos. 1–2, 1975), in which Eder finds that "Louis was inspired by and modeled on [T.S.] Eliot" (p. 13).

62. "How Should One Read A Book?," *Collected Essays*, 2:6.

63. Cf. Virginia Woolf's own "when I wake early I say to myself, Fight, fight" (*Writer's Diary*, p. 143).

64. Cf. Woolf: "Life is always and inevitably much richer than we who try to express it" ("The Narrow Bridge of Art," *Collected Essays*, 2:229).

65. Bernard's sentiment—"we need not whip this prose into poetry. The little language is enough" (359)—is rather Byronic. Cf. "Besides, I hate all mystery, and that air of / Clap-trap which your recent poets prize" (*Don Juan*, 2.124.987–88).

66. Cf. Lear on "the pelting of this pitiless storm" (3.4.29) and his famous speech beginning, "Blow, winds, and crack your cheeks! rage! blow!" (3.2.1), which refers to *sulphurous* fires, the same word used by Bernard.

67. In the Berg MS, Woolf experimented with giving "the hero ~~of a book~~ now ~~forgotten~~ I forget his name in The Possessed" (vol. 6, dated Monks House, December 31, 1930), but opted to omit the title of the Dostoevsky novel in the final text.

68. "Phases of Fiction; The Psychologists," *Collected Essays*, 2:86.

69. The Berg MSS reveal an even larger gallery of literary role models than survive in the published text. At one time Bernard identified with characters in the works of Stendhal, Turgenev, and Henry James. He read Pepys, Donne, Montaigne, Milton, and Pope, and declared that he could not find himself in the works of Dickens or Trollope (vol. 4, April 1930, rewritten June 13, 1930). He further asserted: "I relate myself . . . to the wider . . . world: to Shakespeare, Dryden, Racine, Baudelaire, Keats & Coleridge," adding Horace Walpole and Madame du Deffand (vol. 6, dated Monks House, December 31, 1930).

70. That is, the shrivelled leaves recall the withered sedge in Keats (ll. 3, 47), and Bernard's "no bird sang" directly evokes Keats's "And no birds sing" (*La Belle Dame Sans Merci*, ll. 4, 48).

71. In the Berg MS Bernard says, "I can be heroic: I who make phrases" (vol. 3, January 19, 1930), and "we create. A phrase. That is our great achievement . . . It is victory: it is triumph: it gives one dominion" (vol. 6, dated Monks House, December 31, 1930). Woolf's unsigned Holograph Notes (June 15, 1930–January 30, 1931, Part I) contain a fragment labeled "A refrain" with the revealing line: "We only dominate when we make phrases."

72. Collins, p. 42. Art as an immortal form of truth and beauty is a familiar concept in Keats; for example, the famous "a thing of beauty is a joy

forever: / Its loveliness increases; it will never / Pass into nothingness" (*Endymion*, 1.1–3). There is an interesting omission from MS to published text: in Draft II of *The Waves*, when Bernard is in Rome, the *eternal* city, he thinks: "(Keats died in that room beside these steps)" (Graham transcription, p. 615).

73. The Berg MSS show much experimentation with snatches of poetry and nursery rhymes. In volume 4 (April 13, 1930: finished April 29, 1930, rewritten June 13, 1930), for example, three additional lines from Shakespeare were contemplated, which do not survive into the published text. The MS speaks of "fragments of half remembered songs," and offers, "Sigh no more ladies, ladies sigh no more [from *Much Ado About Nothing*, 2.3.64] . . . Let us not upon the rack of this tough world [from *King Lear*, 5.3.314]—It was a lover and his lass [from *As You Like It*, 5.3.17]." The final text is also more selective with regard to nursery rhymes, omitting several of the considered choices: for example, "Ride a cock horse to Banbury Cross," "Little Jack Horner," "Old Mother Hubbard," and "The Queen was in her parlour eating bread and honey."

74. Schaefer, p. 158.

75. *Adonais*, 52.463. Bernard remains Shelleyan in his desire to "cast and throw away this veil of being, this cloud that changes" (381). His veil metaphor echoes Shelley's "veil of life and death" (*Mont Blanc*, 3.54), as does his effort to throw off changing clouds for the timeless reality behind temporal objects.

76. Woolf spoke of "the common life which is the real life" (*A Room of One's Own*, p. 117).

77. Cf. Ernst Cassirer: "The further a Being's power extends, the more mythic potency and 'significance' he embodies, the greater is the sphere of influence of his name" (*Language and Myth*, trans. by Susanne K. Langer [New York: Harper & Brothers, 1946], p. 53).

78. See Tindall's *The Literary Symbol*, pp. 187–88. Irma Rantavaara in *Virginia Woolf's "The Waves"* equivocates, remarking that "the name may be a coincidence" (p. 29), though she concedes the presence of teasing clues throughout the novel. Leaska (*The Novels of Virginia Woolf*, p. 182) repeats my dissertation findings on the multiplicity of sources for the Percival legend. While admitting that *The Waves* "reverberates with allusive images and interlocking references related to the legendary Percival" (pp. 182–83), Leaska mysteriously concludes that the mere fact of myriad variations shows "how immune to analysis is Mrs. Woolf's choice of name for her symbolic hero" (p. 182).

79. In the Berg MS Percival is referred to as "a pagan knight" (vol. 1, September 22, 1929), and "a Crusader" (vol. 2, January 3, 1930).

80. The Berg MSS show the persistence of the name Elvedon, from the first, a singularly disembodied setting. In the first complete draft, the garden is described as "going back ~~to the~~ under earth to the beginning of time" (vol. 1, September 22, 1929). It is also asserted that "the woods of Elvedon are seen through the soul" (vol. 1, July 2, 1929).

81. Bruce, *The Evolution of Arthurian Romance from the Beginning Down to the Year 1300*, 1:33.

82. Loomis, *Arthurian Literature in the Middle Ages*, p. 66. Collins links the garden and the apple tree to Biblical sources, but since even in the Bible, banishment from the garden was equivalent to "the punishment of death" (p. 20), the apple Isle of Death in Arthurian legend does not contradict the implications of the Biblical imagery.

83. Bruce, 1:327.

84. For example, there is a shining Grail in Chrétien's *Perceval* (Bruce, 1:227).

85. See for example Tennyson on Sir Percivale's helmet in *Idylls of the King* ("The Holy Grail," l. 6).

86. Jessie Laidlay Weston, *From Ritual to Romance*, p. 66.

87. Bruce, 1:270.

88. Ibid., 224. In the MS, Bernard imagined Percival "riding: now he goes in *Court*" (vol. 3, January 19, 1930, italics mine).

89. Bulfinch, *Bulfinch's Mythology*, p. 481.

90. Cf. the absent hero theme in *Jacob's Room*, and the "lost son . . . a rider destroyed . . . killed in the battles of the world" in *Mrs. Dalloway* (87).

91. For example, in *Perlesvaus*, Perceval's visit to the Grail castle is an abortive failure (Bruce, 2:10). In the anonymous addition to Chrétien's work known as the *Second Continuation*, Perceval's mission is "only partially successful" (Loomis, p. 214).

92. Wisely, Woolf omitted from the published text a Berg MS image of Percival reading—from Johnson's *Vanity of Human Wishes* (vol. 5, October 23, 1930).

93. Chrétien's Perceval, Wolfram's Parzival, and the hero of the *Perlesvaus* all neglect to ask the proper questions (Bruce, 1:227, 337; 2:10).

94. *A Writer's Diary*, p. 156.

95. Cf. the early MS draft in which a first-person narrator stated, "I am ~~trying to tell~~ telling myself the story of the world from the beginning" (vol. 1, July 2, 1929).

96. Weston, p. 68.

97. Loomis, p. 270.

98. Bruce, 1:279.

99. Cf. Woolf's Berg MS statement: "I have dispatched my *enemy* in the moment when I have made a *phrase*" (vol. 6, dated Monks House, December 31, 1930, italics mine).

100. Jack F. Stewart, "Existence and Symbol in *The Waves*," *Modern Fiction Studies* 18, no. 3 (Autumn 1972): 443.

101. McConnell, p. 127.

102. Cyril Connolly in *Enemies of Promise*, 2d ed. (1939; rpt. New York: Macmillan, 1948), p. 49.

103. *A Writer's Diary*, p. 161.

104. "Letter to a Young Poet," *Collected Essays*, 2:184.

105. In Bernard's "we are creators" speech (276), from which the phrase about "the illumined and everlasting road" comes, there was originally this addition: "Shakespeare and Sophocles—lie behind us, luminous and hard" (Draft 2, in Graham's transcription, p. 556).

Bibliography

Aiken, Conrad. *"Orlando." Dial* 86, no. 2 (February 1929): 147–49.

Ames, Kenneth J. "Elements of Mock-Heroic in Virginia Woolf's *Mrs. Dalloway." Modern Fiction Studies* 18, no. 3 (Autumn 1972): 363–74.

Bell, Clive. *Civilization: An Essay.* London: Chatto and Windus, 1928.

Bell, Quentin. *Virginia Woolf: A Biography.* 2 vols. New York: Harcourt Brace Jovanovich, 1972.

Benjamin, Anna S. "Towards an Understanding of the Meaning of Virginia Woolf's *Mrs. Dalloway." Wisconsin Studies in Contemporary Literature* 6, no. 2 (Summer 1965): 214–27.

Bennett, Joan. *Virginia Woolf: Her Art as a Novelist.* Cambridge: Cambridge University Press, 1945.

Blackstone, Bernard. *Virginia Woolf: A Commentary.* London: Hogarth Press, 1949.

Brewster, Dorothy. *Virginia Woolf.* New York: New York University Press, 1962.

Bruce, James Douglas. *The Evolution of Arthurian Romance from the Beginning Down to the Year 1300.* 2 vols. 2d ed., 1928; rpt. Gloucester, Mass.: Peter Smith, 1958.

Bulfinch, Thomas. *Bulfinch's Mythology.* New York: Thomas Y. Crowell, 1913.

Chalmers, Alexander. *The Works of the English Poets.* 22 vols. London: J. Johnson, et al., 1810.

Collins, Robert G. *Virginia Woolf's Black Arrows of Sensation: The Waves.* Ilfracombe: Arthur H. Stockwell, 1962.

Daiches, David. *Virginia Woolf.* 2d ed. Norfolk: New Directions, 1963.

———, ed. *The Penguin Companion to English Literature.* New York: McGraw-Hill, 1971.

Dante Alighieri. *The Inferno.* Trans. John Ciardi. New Brunswick: Rutgers University Press, 1954.

Doner, Dean. "Virginia Woolf: The Service of Style." *Modern Fiction Studies* 2, no. 1 (February 1956): 1–12.

Fleishman, Avrom. *Virginia Woolf: A Critical Reading.* Baltimore: Johns Hopkins Press, 1975.

———. "Virginia Woolf: Tradition and Modernity." *Forms of Modern British Fiction.* Ed. Alan Warren Friedman. Austin: University of Texas Press, 1975, pp. 133–63.

Forster, E.M. *Abinger Harvest.* New York: Harcourt, Brace, 1936, pp. 106–15.

Frazer, Sir James George. *The New Golden Bough.* Ed. and abr. Theodor H. Gaster. New York: Criterion Books, 1959.

Frye, Northrop. *Anatomy of Criticism: Four Essays.* Princeton, N.J.: Princeton University Press, 1957.

Bibliography

Geoffrey of Monmouth. *Historia Regum Britanniae.* Trans. Sebastian Evens. London: J.M. Dent, 1912.

Gibbon, Edward. *The Decline and Fall of the Roman Empire.* 6 vols. London: J.M. Dent, 1910.

Greene, William Chase. *Moira: Fate, Good and Evil in Greek Thought.* New York: Harper and Row, 1963.

Gruber, Ruth. *Virginia Woolf: A Study.* Leipzig: Verlag von Bernhard Tauchnitz, 1935; rpt. New York, 1966.

Guiguet, Jean. *Virginia Woolf and Her Works.* Trans. Jean Stewart. New York: Harcourt, Brace and World, 1965.

Hafley, James. *The Glass Roof: Virginia Woolf as Novelist.* Berkeley: University of California Press, 1954.

Holtby, Winifred. *Virginia Woolf.* London: Wishart, 1932.

Interpreter's Dictionary of the Bible. 4 vols. New York: Abingdon Press, 1962, 2:782–87.

Jones, E.B.C. "E.M. Forster and Virginia Woolf." *The English Novelists: A Survey of the Novel by Twenty Contemporary Novelists.* Ed. Derek Verschoyle. New York: Harcourt, Brace, 1936, 281–97.

Kelley, Alice van Buren. *The Novels of Virginia Woolf: Fact and Vision.* Chicago: University of Chicago Press, 1973.

Leaska, Mitchell A. "Virginia Woolf's *The Voyage Out*: Character Deduction and the Function of Ambiguity." *Virginia Woolf Quarterly* 1, no. 2 (Winter 1973): 18–41.

———. *The Novels of Virginia Woolf from Beginning to End.* New York: John Jay Press, 1977.

Loomis, Roger Sherman. *Arthurian Literature in the Middle Ages.* Oxford: Clarendon Press, 1959.

Love, Jean O. *Worlds in Consciousness: Mythopoetic Thought in the Novels of Virginia Woolf.* Berkeley: University of California Press, 1970.

McLaurin, Allen. *Virginia Woolf: The Echoes Enslaved.* Cambridge: Cambridge University Press, 1973.

Marbot, Jean Baptiste Antoine Marcellin de. *Memoires du général Baron de Marbot.* 2 vols. Trans. Arthur John Butler. London: Longmans, Green, 1892.

Marder, Herbert. *Feminism and Art: A Study of Virginia Woolf.* Chicago: University of Chicago Press, 1963.

Mollach, Francis L. "Thematic and Structural Unity in *Mrs. Dalloway.*" *Thoth* (Spring 1964): 62–73.

Moody, A.D. "The Unmasking of Clarissa Dalloway." *Review of English Literature* 3, no. 1 (January 1962): 67–79.

———. *Virginia Woolf.* Edinburgh: Oliver and Boyd, 1963.

Newton, Deborah. *Virginia Woolf.* Melbourne: Melbourne University Press, 1963.

Noble, Joan Russell, ed. *Recollections of Virginia Woolf.* New York: William Morrow, 1972.

Opie, Iona and Peter, eds. *The Oxford Dictionary of Nursery Rhymes.* Oxford: Clarendon Press, 1952.

Peel, Robert. "Virginia Woolf." *The Criterion* 13, no. 50 (October 1933): 78–96.

Perrault, Charles. *Complete Fairy Tales.* Trans. A.E. Johnson. New York: Dodd, Mead, 1961.

Pippett, Aileen. *The Moth and the Star: A Biography of Virginia Woolf.* Boston: Little, Brown, 1955.

Bibliography

Plato. *Symposium*. Trans. Percy Bysshe Shelley. Chicago: Henry Regnery, 1949.

Rantavaara, Irma. *Virginia Woolf's "The Waves."* Port Washington, N.Y.: Kennikat Press, 1969.

Richter, Harvena C. *Virginia Woolf: The Inward Voyage*. Princeton, N.J.: Princeton University Press, 1970.

Robbins, Harry Wolcott, and Coleman, William Harold, eds. *Western World Literature*. New York: Macmillan, 1938.

Rosenberg, Stuart. "The Match in the Crocus: Obtrusive Art in Virginia Woolf's *Mrs. Dalloway*." *Modern Fiction Studies* 13, no. 2 (Summer 1967): 211–20.

Rowse, A.L. *Christopher Marlowe: His Life and Work*. New York: Harper and Row, 1964.

Sackville-West, Vita. *Knole and the Sackvilles*. 2d ed., 1922; rpt. London: William Heinemann, 1931.

Samuels, Marilyn Schauer. "The Symbolic Functions of the Sun in *Mrs. Dalloway*." *Modern Fiction Studies* 18, no. 3 (Autumn 1972): 387–99.

Schaefer, Josephine O'Brien. *The Three-Fold Nature of Reality in the Novels of Virginia Woolf*. London: Mouton, 1965.

Schlack, Beverly Ann. "A Freudian Look at *Mrs. Dalloway*." *Literature and Psychology* 23, no. 2 (1973): 49–58.

Sprague, Claire, ed. *Virginia Woolf: A Collection of Critical Essays*. Englewood Cliffs, N.J.: Prentice-Hall, 1971.

Stephen, Leslie. *English Literature and Society in the Eighteenth Century*. London: Duckworth, 1904.

———. *History of English Thought in the Eighteenth Century*. 2 vols. New York: Harcourt, Brace, 1962.

———. *Hours in a Library*. 4 vols. New York: Putnam, 1904.

———. *Pope*. 2d ed., 1880; rpt. London: Macmillan, 1900.

———. *Studies of a Biographer*. 4 vols. 2d ed., 1902; rpt. New York: Putnam, 1907.

———. *Swift*. New York: Harper and Brothers, 1886.

Strachey, Lytton. *Books and Characters: French and English*. New York: Harcourt, Brace, 1922.

Thakur, N.C. *The Symbolism of Virginia Woolf*. London: Oxford University Press, 1965.

Tindall, William York. *The Literary Symbol*. Bloomington: Indiana University Press, 1955.

Weston, Jessie Laidlay. *From Ritual to Romance*. Garden City, N.Y.: Doubleday Anchor Books, 1957.

Woolf, Virginia. *Collected Essays*. Ed. Leonard Woolf. 4 vols. New York: Harcourt, Brace and World, 1966.

———. *Contemporary Writers: Essays on Twentieth Century Books and Authors*. New York: Harcourt Brace Jovanovich, 1976.

———. *Jacob's Room and The Waves*. New York: Harcourt, Brace and World, 1959.

———. *Jacob's Room*. Holograph MSS. 3 Parts, April 15, 1920–March 12, 1922. Berg Collection, New York Public Library.

———. *Mrs. Dalloway*. New York: Harcourt, Brace and World, 1925.

———. *Mrs. Dalloway's Party: A Short Story Sequence*. Ed. Stella McNichol. New York: Harcourt Brace Jovanovich. 1975.

———. *Orlando: A Biography*. New York: New American Library, 1960.

———. *Orlando*. TS fragment, undated. Berg Collection, New York Public Library.

Bibliography

————. *A Room of One's Own.* New York: Harcourt, Brace and World, 1929.

————. *Three Guineas.* New York: Harcourt, Brace and World, 1938.

————. *Virginia Woolf and Lytton Strachey: Letters.* Ed. Leonard Woolf and James Strachey. New York: Harcourt, Brace and World, 1956.

————. *The Voyage Out.* New York: Harcourt, Brace and World, 1948.

————. *The Voyage Out.* Earlier TS, Later TS, and Final TS, undated. Berg Collection, New York Public Library.

————. *The Voyage Out.* Holograph draft. 2 vols. March 29, 1912–December 21, 1912. Berg Collection, New York Public Library.

————. *The Waves.* MS fragment. "Articles, essays, fiction, and reviews," 4, June 1930. Berg Collection, New York Public Library.

————. *The Waves.* MS notes. June 15, 1930–January 30, 1931. Berg Collection, New York Public Library.

————. *Virginia Woolf: THE WAVES.* Two Holograph Drafts Transcribed and Edited by J.W. Graham. Toronto: University of Toronto Press, 1976.

————. *A Writer's Diary, Being Extracts of the Diary of Virginia Woolf.* Ed. Leonard Woolf. New York: New American Library, 1959.

Wyatt, Jean M. "*Mrs. Dalloway*: Literary Allusion as Structural Metaphor." *PMLA* 80, no. 3 (May 1973): 440–51.

Index

Considerations of space and redundancy dictate that this be an index of material in the text and its footnotes, exclusive of the information indexed in Allusions in the Novels.

189

Index

Browne, Sir Thomas, 78, 84–86, 97, 172
Browning, Robert, 3, 97, 176
Bruton, Lady (*Mrs. Dalloway*), 54, 56–57, 65
Buckle, Henry Thomas, 98
Buddha, 177
Bulteel, Professor (*Jacob's Room*), 43, 163
Burdett-Coutts, Baroness, 95
Butler, Samuel, 101, 177
Byron, George Gordon, Lord, x, 36, 39–40, 47, 49, 94, 96, 97, 108, 111–14, 116, 119, 122–24, 162, 172, 175, 179, 180, 181
Byzantine Empire (Finlay), 46

Caesar, 178
Carlyle, Thomas, 41–43, 47, 97, 162, 163, 168–69, 176
Cassandra, 181
Cato (Addison), 98, 176
Catullus, 10, 108, 178, 179, 180
Ceres/Demeter, 52–53, 66, 68, 74, 165
Chailey, Mrs. (*The Voyage Out*), 9
Charge of the Light Brigade, The (Tennyson), 8
Charles, Lady (*Jacob's Room*), 32, 110, 160
Chaucer, 3
Chekhov, Anton, 29–30, 34, 46
Chesterfield, Lord, 92, 175
Childe Harold's Pilgrimage (Byron), 112
Chloe, 35, 161
Cicero, 86–87, 98, 178
Civilization (Bell), 173
Clytemnestra, 5, 155
Coleridge, Samuel Taylor, 9, 94, 181
Commedia (Dante), 69
Comus (Milton), x, 20–28, 60, 158, 159
Cowan, Professor (*Jacob's Room*), 32, 38, 44
Cowper, William, 6, 16, 17–18, 36, 157
Crane, Dr. (*The Waves*), 106, 109
Crane, Mrs. (*The Waves*), 109
Cruttendon (*Jacob's Room*), 46
Cymbeline (Shakespeare), x, 62; "Fear no more," 64–66, 72–75, 167; "Hang there like fruit my soul," 46, 163–64

Dalloway, Clarissa (*Mrs. Dalloway*), 51, 52, 54–56, 59–66, 68–70, 72–75, 77, 110, 161, 165, 166, 167, 169
Dalloway, Clarissa (*The Voyage Out*), 4–7, 11, 51, 74, 155
Dalloway, Richard (*Mrs. Dalloway*), 51–54, 57, 60, 61, 63, 65, 68, 166
Dalloway, Richard (*The Voyage Out*), 4, 6–7, 17, 25, 51, 53, 54, 57, 159
Damien, Father, 32, 161
Dante, 67, 69–72, 88, 103–5, 118, 161, 164, 168, 169, 180
Daphne, 116
Darwin, Charles, 4, 67
De Quincey, Thomas, 78, 101, 167, 170, 173, 177
De Rerum Natura (Lucretius), 43
Decline and Fall of the Roman Empire (Gibbon), 11, 43
Defoe, Daniel, 15, 78, 157, 170
Dekker, Thomas, 13, 82
Devotions (Donne), 111
Diana, 36, 37, 82
Diana of the Crossways (Meredith), 18, 21, 157, 161–62
Diary (Pepys), 88
Dickens, Charles, 41, 163, 181
Dictionary of National Biography (Stephen), 99
Disraeli, Benjamin, 37, 41, 42, 47, 162
Ditchling, Lady (*The Voyage Out*), 5
Dixon, Richard Watson, 98
Don Juan (Byron), 49, 108, 112, 113, 122, 124, 175, 178, 179, 181
Don Quixote (Cervantes), 181
Donne, John, 12, 13, 46, 85, 86, 97, 111, 113, 117, 178, 181
Dostoevsky, Fyodor, 123, 124, 181
"Dover Beach" (Arnold), 36
Drayton, Michael, 87
Dryden, John, 3, 79, 90, 92, 97, 99, 108, 173, 174, 176, 181
du Deffand, Madame (*Orlando*), 90, 91, 173–74, 181
Dudden, F. Holmes, 155
Duggan, Mrs. Sally (*Jacob's Room*), 32
Dumas, 33, 34

190

Index

Index

Index

Index